SAYING YES

IN DEFENSE
OF **DRUG** USE

JEREMY P. TARCHER/PENGUIN
a member of Penguin Group (USA) Inc.
New York

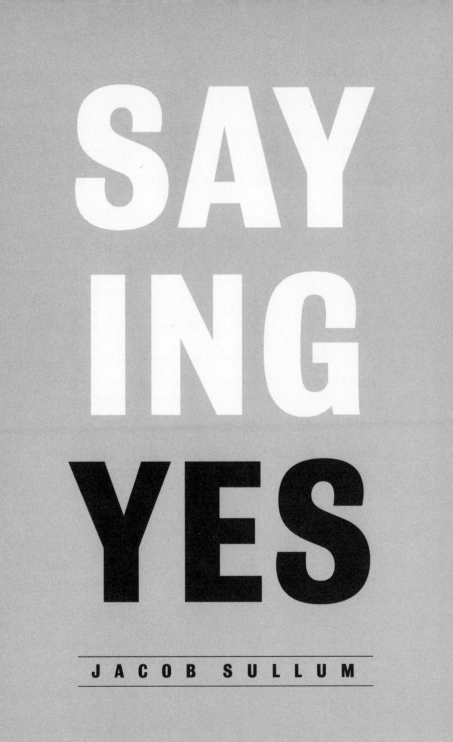

SAY
ING
YES

JACOB SULLUM

Most Tarcher/Penguin books are available at special quantity discounts for bulk purchase for sales promotions, premiums, fund-raising, and educational needs. Special books or book excerpts also can be created to fit specific needs. For details, write Penguin Group (USA) Inc. Special Markets, 375 Hudson Street, New York, NY 10014.

Jeremy P. Tarcher/Penguin
a member of
Penguin Group (USA) Inc.
375 Hudson Street
New York, NY 10014
www.penguin.com

First trade paperback edition 2004

The Library of Congress catalogued the hardcover edition as follows:

Sullum, Jacob.
Saying yes : in defense of drug use / Jacob Sullum.
p.   cm.
Includes bibliographical references and index.
ISBN 1-58542-227-4
1. Drug abuse—United States—Public opinion.   2. Drug abuse surveys—United States.
3. Drug utilization—United States.   4. Drug legalization—United States.   I. Title.
HV5825.S845   2003   2002040919
362.29'0973—dc21

ISBN 1-58542-318-1 (paperback edition)

Printed in the United States of America
1   2   3   4   5   6   7   8   9   10

Book design by Michelle McMillian

To my parents, Arnold and Helen Sullum,
models of temperance

You don't have to be part of the crowd.
Be who you are, and stand up proud.
Say no. Just say no.

—1983 ANTI-DRUG AD

CONTENTS

ACKNOWLEDGMENTS

I'd like to thank my agents, Lynn Chu and Glen Hartley, who encouraged me to tackle a subject close to my heart. My thinking about drugs has been shaped by many scholars, but Thomas Szasz and Stanton Peele stand out among contemporary writers for the clarity of their analysis and the depth of their concern about the implications of reductionist approaches to human behavior that give short shrift to moral values and individual choice. Among the books that I read early in my research, Douglas N. Husak's *Drugs and Rights* and James Bakalar and Lester Grinspoon's *Drug Control in a Free Society* were particularly illuminating. The Drug Policy Alliance (www. drugpolicyalliance.org), the Alchemind Society (www.alchemind. org), the DRCNet Online Library (www.druglibrary.org), the National Organization for the Reform of Marijuana Laws (www.norml.org), and the Multidisciplinary Association for Psychedelic Studies (www.maps.org) were invaluable sources of documents and analysis. Many people suggested sources, answered questions, or brought interesting points to my attention, including Manja Abraham, Peter Cohen, Brian Doherty, Lisa Gordis, Mark Kleiman, Ellen Komp, Michael Lynch, Ethan Nadelmann, Virginia Postrel, Josh Shenk, Harvey Silverglate, Eric Sterling, John Swann, Whitney Taylor, Peter Webster, and Kevin Zeese. The NORML Foundation's Allen St. Pierre was especially generous with his time, always quick to answer my questions and supply me with articles. *Reason* interns Jessica Cater and Rhys Southan promptly tracked down articles and book excerpts for me, saving me trips to the library. Paul M. Bischke and Thomas Nicholson provided papers that pointed me to useful references. My brother Daniel, a psychiatrist and antique dealer, has kept me in mind when going through his auction purchases, turning up several books and documents that have been relevant to my work. My wife, Michele, was patient as always, assisting me with Jewish sources and giving me immediate feedback on the manuscript. Bruce Alexander, Drew Clark, Rick Doblin, Paul Fishbein, Dale Gieringer, Nick Gillespie, Lester Grinspoon, Stanton Peele, Allen St. Pierre, Rob Stewart, and Neguin Yavari read some or all of the manuscript and offered valuable guidance. Jeremy Tarcher and my editor, Mitch Horowitz, were both genuinely interested in the topic of the book, and their advice showed it. Mitch's careful readings and astute suggestions helped me sharpen my argument and organize the book more logically. Finally, I want to express my gratitude to everyone who volunteered to discuss their drug use. Even when I did not quote them directly, their comments informed my discussion and reinforced my determination to talk about drugs from the perspective of the temperate user.

AUTHOR'S NOTE

Along with its many other unfortunate side effects, prohibition makes life harder for researchers trying to study drug use. In particular, it casts doubt on the accuracy of drug-use surveys, on which I rely heavily in this book. People may be reluctant to admit illegal behavior even when they're assured of confidentiality, especially if the survey is sponsored by the government. The results of studies such as the National Household Survey on Drug Abuse (which uses electronic questionnaires administered at home) and the Monitoring the Future Study (which uses questionnaires distributed in schools) therefore hinge not only on drug use but on people's willingness to report it. It seems likely that the household survey understates the percentage of Americans who have used various drugs, although it's unclear by how much.[1]

On the other hand, some people—adolescents in particular—may be reluctant to admit that they *haven't* used drugs if they consider the lack of such experience a sign of immaturity or timidity. The way questions are framed may also boost reported drug consumption. Questions that ask about frequency of use (such as, "During the past thirty days, on how many days did you use marijuana or hashish?") seem to encourage overestimation.[2] And there's always the danger— again, especially with teenagers—that respondents will not take the survey seriously. One teacher who witnessed the administration of the Monitoring the Future questionnaire at his school told me the kids seemed to be goofing around, filling in answers that had little connection to reality.

It's tempting to brush aside these complications by noting that politicians and bureaucrats routinely rely on the government's survey data. When reported drug use goes down, they argue that it proves current policies are working and demonstrates the need for more spending to make sure the gains are not lost. When reported drug use goes up, they argue that it proves current policies are not backed by sufficient resources and demonstrates the need for more spending to prevent the problem from getting worse. Since the government commissions these surveys and cites them with confidence, it seems unfair to put the burden of defending them on the government's critics.

Still, anyone who is interested in getting at the truth has to admit that self-reports are apt to be less than 100 percent accurate. The question is how much this matters. For my purposes, the most important number is not the percentage of respondents who have tried a given drug but the percentage of users whose consumption is excessive. The reported survey data are usually not specific enough to answer this question directly, but they do suggest ceilings: The number of daily cocaine users, for example, has to be lower than the number who use cocaine every week. The upper limit indicated by a survey may be misleading if there are many daily users who claim to use the drug only once a month or once a year. That seems unlikely, however. While problem users might be inclined to say they use cocaine less often than they really do, such misreporting would tend to occur when they were asked if they used the drug every day and, if so, how many times. They could easily report weekly use, which might be no more than a Saturday night snort, without admitting to a drug problem. Likewise, some respondents who use cocaine every day may deny that they have ever even tried the drug, but this group is probably not very large.

Another drawback of the surveys, discussed in Chapter 7, is that they exclude some groups (e.g., people living on the street) in which drug abuse is especially common. The omission of these groups may mean that the overall frequency of heavy use is somewhat higher than the surveys suggest. On the other hand, members of the armed forces, where illegal drug use is less common than in the general population, are also excluded from the surveys, so the net effect is unclear. In any case, given the sizes of the excluded groups (which together represent about 2 percent of the total population), the difference would not be great enough to change the general picture, in which experimenters and occasional users far outnumber addicts.[3] This pattern is found consistently in broadly representative surveys taken by different people at different times with different methods, and it jibes with data on "drug-related" emergencies and deaths, which involve only a small percentage of users.[4]

In addition to the survey data, I draw on detailed interviews with thirty-two drug users. Most were conducted on the telephone or in person; the rest were carried out by e-mail. I use material from the interviews purely for illustrative purposes. The sample was self-selected in response to my request for "controlled drug users," so it is not necessarily representative. Among other things, my questions were designed to test the respondents' candor and to verify that they were in fact controlled users. Since the subjects volunteered to talk about their drug use, they had little motive for lying.

Another source of information about drug use has been my own experience with illicit intoxicants, which is modest but instructive. In addition to marijuana, I've sampled psychedelics, cocaine, opioids, and tranquilizers. I see the appeal of each, but I did not find any of them overwhelmingly attractive, and I've never had any difficulty keeping them in their proper place. This experience was the seed of my conviction that it's reasonable to expect drug users to exercise self-control, and in my research I've seen nothing to contradict that belief.

THE SILENT MAJORITY

The picture they try to paint of drug users makes me mad. It's kind of insulting.
—A POT-SMOKING MBA IN HIS THIRTIES

The Seen and the Unseen

Peter B. Lewis, who stepped down in 2001 after thirty-six years as CEO of Progressive Insurance, is widely admired as a hard-driving, innovative executive who transformed his company from a tiny player into the nation's fifth-largest auto insurer—"a prodigiously growing, solidly successful stock market standout," as *Fortune* put it. Originally specializing in coverage for high-risk drivers, an area where it quickly became a leader, Progressive later moved into other types of auto insurance, making a name for itself through direct sales, candid price comparisons, and fast claims service. Between 1990 and 1999, the company had compounded growth of more than 23 percent, compared to an industry average of less than 5 percent. Progressive was the first insurer with a website and the first to sell policies online, pioneering forays that paid off dramatically: Its revenues jumped from $3.4 billion in 1996 to $6.1 billion three years later.[1]

Lewis, the man who accomplished all this, still serves as Progressive's chairman and owns about 13 percent of the company, making him a billionaire. Observers call him a perfectionist, "an extraordinary businessman," and "an absolutist about untiring effort." They also call him "a functioning pothead."[2]

Although he declined to comment on the question while he was CEO, friends said Lewis was a regular marijuana smoker. In 2000 these reports were confirmed in a very public way: Lewis was arrested for marijuana and hashish possession at the Auckland, New Zealand, airport. The authorities released him after he made a donation to a local drug rehabilitation center. The next year, when he was interviewed by the *Wall Street Journal* about his financial support for drug policy reform, he observed, "My personal experience lets me understand and have a view of the relative effects of some of these substances."[3]

With his remarkable record of achievement, Lewis does not quite fit the pothead stereotype promoted in taxpayer-funded public service announcements: the lazy, stupid loser who can't get it together. A knowledge engineer in his early thirties who smokes marijuana about once a week summed up the official message this way: "Pot will destroy your life, and you'll end up sitting in a room, not caring about anything, watching TV, unemployed, and broke."[4] Most marijuana users do not become billionaires, of course, but neither do most of them lead empty, unproductive lives. As misleading as it may be to hold Peter Lewis's career up as an example of what marijuana can do, it is equally misleading to cite users who never amount to anything as evidence of the drug's effects. The typical pot smoker lies somewhere between these two extremes.

Yet the failures spring to mind when people think about marijuana, mainly because they're conspicuous. They call attention to themselves through excessive, ostentatious indulgence that gets them into trouble at school and work. Responsible users, by contrast, have something to lose and therefore tend to be circumspect. If they acknowledge their drug use, they risk being tarred by stereotypes that manifestly do not apply to them. In 2001 Nick Gillespie, editor of *Reason* magazine (where I work), wrote an editorial in which he mentioned his own recreational use of drugs and observed: "Far from our drugs controlling us, by and large we control our drugs; as with alcohol, the primary motivation in taking drugs is to enjoy ourselves, not to destroy ourselves. . . . There is such a thing as responsible drug use, and it is the rule, not the exception."[5] He and his colleagues were later mocked by the editors of the *Wall Street Journal's* opinion pages, who wrote, "We imagine the editorial meetings at *Reason* consisting of a bunch of earnest, well-scrubbed young wonks in bow ties sitting around a table debating the fine points of Social Security reform amid a haze of marijuana smoke."[6] The humor here (such as it is) hinges on the idea that pot smokers are the sort of people who think nothing of getting stoned at work. If Gillespie had admitted a fondness for single-malt Scotch whiskey, the *Journal's* editors presumably would not have imagined the *Reason* staff conducting their business in a drunken stupor.

Given this kind of prejudice, it's easy to understand why the average marijuana user prefers to remain silent. As a pot-smoking MBA in his mid thirties put it, "If I had to staple it to my résumé, I wouldn't get any jobs."[7] Others worry about losing professional licenses or about negative reactions from relatives or acquaintances. The upshot is that the most noticeable pot smokers, who tend to be the most dysfunctional, are the ones who come to represent the whole class in the public mind. Well-adjusted, high-achieving pot smokers tend to keep their drug use private, so they're not even recognized as marijuana users—unless, like Peter Lewis, they happen to get arrested.

More generally, people who use illegal drugs in a controlled, inconspicuous way are not inclined to stand up and announce the fact. Prohibition renders them invisible, because they fear the legal, social, and economic consequences of speaking up. The illegal drug users who register with the general public are the ones who get into trouble or make a nuisance of themselves. We see the drug users who get hauled away by the police, who nod off in doorways and on park benches, who beg on the street or break into cars. We do not see the drug users who hold down a job, pay the rent or the mortgage, and support a family. In the absence of evidence to the contrary, people naturally assume that most illegal drug users are like the ones they notice, who are apt to be the least discreet and the most antisocial. This is like assuming that the wino passed out in the gutter is a typical drinker.

Voodoo Pharmacology

The main purpose of this book is to contrast drug use as it is described by politicians and propagandists with drug use as it is experienced by the silent majority of users: the decent, respectable people who, despite their politically incorrect choice of intoxicants, earn a living and meet their responsibilities. The lives they lead challenge a central premise of the war on drugs: the idea that certain substances have the power to compel immoral behavior. During his 2000 presidential campaign, Steve Forbes neatly summed up this understanding of drugs as forces of evil. "Drugs are wrong," he said, "because they destroy the body, enslave the soul, and take away people's freedom to think and choose for themselves."[8] According to this view, a drug user is not an independent moral agent because his will has been hijacked by a chemical.

If some drugs really do turn people into zombies, it makes no sense to expect self-control. But if voodoo pharmacology is a myth, it's reasonable to talk about illegal drugs the way we talk about alcohol. Anyone who is familiar with alcohol understands that there is nothing inevitable about the damage that drinkers can do to themselves and others. Reactions to alcohol depend upon individual characteristics and social context. Some people find that alcohol stimulates their thinking, while others find that it makes them stupid. There are happy drunks and sad drunks, outgoing drunks and shy drunks, loud drunks and quiet drunks, mean drunks and maudlin drunks, violent drunks and affectionate drunks, amorous drunks and impotent drunks. Not only do reactions vary from one person to another, but the same individual may display dramatically different reactions on different occasions.

"With alcohol inside us," the psychologist Craig MacAndrew and the anthropologist Robert B. Edgerton observed, "our comportment may change in any of a wondrously profuse variety of ways. . . . How can the conventional understanding of alcohol *qua* disinhibitor possibly accommodate the fact that even within our own culture people who have made their bodies alcoholled differ so drastically both within and among themselves in their subsequent doings? . . . How is it . . . that the same man, in the same bar, drinking approximately the same amount of alcohol may, on three nights running, be, say, surly and belligerent on the first evening, the spirit of amiability on the second, and morose and withdrawn on the third?"[9]

In their 1969 book *Drunken Comportment,* MacAndrew and Edgerton pointed out that the behavior of drinkers varies between individuals in the same culture, across situations in the same individual, over time in the same individual, across cultures, across situations in the same culture, and over time in the same society. Their most interesting evidence came from cross-cultural comparisons, including societies in North America, South America, Africa, and Asia. They cited examples of societies where people would get falling-down drunk without any dramatic changes in demeanor and others where people routinely got into bloody fights after drinking. Within the same society, people drinking in a ceremonial context would be peaceful and friendly, while people drinking in a less structured situation would be raucous and violent, even though the amounts consumed were comparable. MacAndrew and Edgerton concluded that "drunken comportment is essentially a *learned* affair. . . . The way people comport themselves when drunk is determined not by alcohol's toxic assault upon the seat of moral judgment, conscience, or the like, but by what their society makes of and imparts to them concerning the state of drunkenness."[10]

The psychiatrist Norman Zinberg made a similar point when he talked about the three factors that shape a drug's perceived effects. In addition to the drug itself, Zinberg said, the user's experience is influenced by his personality, expectations, and emotional state—the "set"—and by the physical, social, and cultural environment—the "setting."[11] As another keen observer of human behavior once noted, "A drug is neither moral nor immoral—it's a chemical compound.

The compound itself is not a menace to society until a human being treats it as if consumption bestowed a temporary license to act like an asshole."[12] In other words, drugs do not cause behavior. How a person acts after taking a drug is determined by a complex interaction of variables, a process in which the user's beliefs and choices play crucial roles.

These observations suggest the importance of developing and inculcating a culture of controlled use that delineates the boundaries of acceptable behavior. When it comes to alcohol, a widely accepted drug with a long history in Western countries, most people readily distinguish between responsible and irresponsible use, between moderate drinkers and alcoholics, between drunks who harm no one and drunks who beat their wives or run over children. The same sorts of distinctions can and should be applied to other drugs, whatever their current legal status. The failure to do so—the insistence that all use of illegal drugs is, by definition, abuse—is a way of avoiding serious moral discourse.

Several years ago I participated in a panel discussion with Bob Barr, then a Republican congressman from Georgia, who prided himself on being "a long-time leader in America's war on drugs."[13] When the topic of drug legalization came up, Barr declared: "Mind-altering drugs are called mind-altering drugs for a reason. They alter your mind." He seemed to think that disposed of the matter. After the discussion, I pointed out that all psychoactive substances, including legal ones such as alcohol, nicotine, and caffeine, are "mind-altering." He asked me if I'd like a surgeon to operate on me after smoking a joint. I said no, but I wouldn't want a surgeon to operate on me after drinking a few beers either. If the surgeon wanted to drink beer or smoke pot when he wasn't on duty, I said, I would have no objection.

"So what you're saying," Barr responded sarcastically, "is that it depends on the situation." Exactly, I said. Moral judgments often do.

As that encounter suggests, it is difficult to distinguish between different kinds of drug use in a culture dominated by a simpleminded "Just Say No" ethos. Brian Paddick, a London police commander, found that out when he tried to explain why he was not eager to nab weekend drug users. "There [is] a whole range of people who buy drugs—not just cannabis, but even cocaine and Ecstasy—who buy those drugs with money they have earned legitimately," he told a parliamentary committee in 2001. "They use a small amount of these drugs, a lot of them just at weekends. It has no adverse effect on the rest of the people they're with, either in terms of people they socialize with or within the wider community, and they go back to work on Monday morning and are unaffected for the rest of the week. In terms of my priorities as an operational police officer, they are low down." For daring to speak the truth about recreational drug users, Paddick was reprimanded by the police commissioner.[14]

A decade earlier, Jonathan Shedler and Jack Block encountered a similar problem when they published an article in *American Psychologist* about their study of adolescent drug use. Tracking a group of children from preschool until age eighteen, the two University of California at Berkeley researchers found that "adolescents who had engaged in some drug experimentation (primarily marijuana) were the best-adjusted in the sample. Adolescents who used drugs frequently were maladjusted, showing a distinct personality syndrome marked by interpersonal alienation, poor impulse control, and manifest emotional distress. Adolescents who, by age eighteen, had never experimented with any drug were relatively anxious, emotionally constricted, and lacking in social skills."[15]

Shedler and Block did not conclude that a little pot is just the thing to help children grow up right. Rather, they found that "psychological differences between frequent users, experimenters, and abstainers could be traced to the earliest years of childhood and related to the quality of parenting received." They observed that "problem drug use is a symptom, not a cause, of personal and social maladjustment" and that "the meaning of drug use can be understood only in the context of an individual's personality structure and developmental history."[16]

These might seem like uncontroversial points, but the study caused an uproar among "drug treatment" and "drug education" specialists. One said it was irresponsible to portray "dabbling with drugs" as "part of normal adolescent experimentation." Another worried that kids who had decided not to use drugs would now be seen as "a bunch of geeks and dorks."[17] Yet Shedler and Block's major finding—that "maladjustment" leads to drug abuse, rather than the other way around—was confirmed a few years later in a study funded by the National Institute on Drug Abuse, the federal government's own research center. "Conduct disorder is in large part the common forerunner of both drug abuse and criminality," the researchers wrote, "challenging the assumption that drug use causes crime."[18]

Although such heretical notions do appear from time to time even in government-supported studies, the focus of research on drug use is almost always negative. Scientists who are interested in looking at drug use as something other than a problem are not likely to get funding from the government, which has no interest in raising questions about its war on drugs, or from academic institutions that rely on government money. In a 1999 letter to *Harper's,* a researcher at Northern Illinois University reported that he and a colleague had been unable to obtain funding for a study of why people use drugs. He suggested that "no one in the anti-drug complex wants to learn that the choice to do drugs is for most people a rational one, that users see themselves, rightly or wrongly, as benefitting from doing so."[19]

Skewed Samples

Some scientists nevertheless manage to study drug users who do not fit popular preconceptions. In the late 1990s, for example, three public health researchers from Western Kentucky and Brown universities developed Drugnet, an on-line method for surveying "the hidden population of occasional, recreational drug users." They ultimately collected responses from more than 900 people. "The typical Drugnet respondent," they reported, "was well educated, employed full-time, a regular voter, participated in recreational/community activities not involving drugs, and described their physical health status as good. Their mental well-being was similar to [that of] the general adult population." Only about one in ten of the respondents said drug use had resulted in a failure related to school, work, or family life. "This group of drug users appears to be dramatically different from the clinically observed population of drug abusers," the researchers wrote. "This sample also appears to be notably different [from the] popular image of drug consumers as personally and socially deviant individuals."[20]

The Drugnet sample was self-selected and limited to web users. But as we'll see, the thrust of its findings—that problem users represent a small minority of drug consumers—has been confirmed by surveys with nationally representative samples. The Drugnet researchers noted that the public's view of drug users has been grossly distorted by research that focuses on people who end up in treatment or jail. "These two populations are so well described," they wrote, "that many Americans incorrectly believe they adequately represent all drug abusers and users."[21]

I once debated drug policy on the radio with a minister from South-Central Los Angeles. It quickly became apparent that he and I had entirely different ideas of what it meant to be a drug user. Growing up in Pennsylvania with middle-class kids and going to college in upstate New York, I didn't know anyone with an obvious drug problem. For the most part, the drug users I knew had other important things going on in their lives, and they had little trouble keeping drugs under control. The minister, by contrast, lived in a neighborhood where drug abuse was more common, and his job brought him into frequent contact with people whose drug use had seriously disrupted their lives. The same is true of psychiatrists, psychologists, social workers, police officers, prosecutors, and judges. All are perceived as experts on drugs, but all see skewed samples of users.

Los Angeles police officer Jack Dunphy says he makes it a practice to ask the people he arrests on drug charges whether they support legalization. Almost all of them, he reports, say no. "The most common answer," he writes, "was something along the lines of, 'Drugs have ruined my life. I wish I had never started up with them.'" A heroin user with a long criminal record told Dunphy, "If they legalize that [stuff], pretty soon everyone will be like me."[22] Assuming the people Dunphy arrests are not simply telling him what they think he wants to hear, and leaving aside their strong motive to offer excuses for crimes against people and property, it is not safe to treat drug users in custody as spokesmen for drug users in general. Heavy users and users who commit predatory crimes are especially likely to attract police attention.

Stereotypes about drug users are relatively easy to maintain with a drug like heroin, which has been used (according to the government's survey data) by about 1 percent of the population. By contrast, more than one in ten Americans over the age of twelve say they have used cocaine, and more than one in three admit to having tried marijuana.[23] You will have a hard time convincing these people and those who know them well that marijuana and cocaine users are criminals and parasites. In their experience, people generally emerge unscathed from their encounters with illegal drugs.

Some of them even go on to successful careers in politics. Indeed, confessing youthful experimentation with illicit substances has become a rite of passage for middle-aged politicians. Bill Clinton did it clumsily, at first saying he had never broken the laws of *this* country, then owning up to having tried pot at Oxford but insisting that he "didn't inhale." Later on, he laughed about his widely ridiculed attempt at mitigation on MTV. Al Gore performed the ritual more gracefully, admitting that he had smoked pot on more than one occasion as a young man and adding that he regretted it.

But judging from a friend's account, Gore misled the public about the extent of his marijuana use by calling it "infrequent and rare."[24] According to John Warnecke, an old buddy of Gore with whom he worked at the *Nashville Tennessean,* "We smoked more than once, more than a few times. We smoked a lot. We smoked in his car, in his house, we smoked in his parents' house, in my house. . . . We smoked on weekends. We smoked a lot." Warnecke said he and Gore continued smoking pot together until just before Gore announced he was running for Congress in 1976.[25] As Hendrik Hertzberg observed in *The New Yorker,* "For some years, [Gore] was an occasional (by his account) or regular (by Warnecke's) marijuana user. During those years, he served in the Army in Vietnam, studied divinity and law, worked as a newspaper reporter, and prepared to run for Congress. Whatever the effect marijuana had on him . . . his ability to function as a productive citizen does not appear to have been impaired."[26]

Former Speaker of the House Newt Gingrich was breezier about his own marijuana use, telling *The Economist* in 1995, "That was a sign we were alive and in graduate school in that era."[27] Gingrich also agreed with Gore that Douglas Ginsburg, whose nomination to the Supreme Court had been scuttled after he admitted to smoking pot as a law professor, should not have been rejected simply because of his marijuana use.[28] A little pot in your past is no big deal, apparently.

Or is it? In 1994 Gingrich appeared on NBC's *Meet the Press,* where he was asked to elaborate on a connection he had drawn between the Clinton administration and the 1960s counterculture. "You've got scattered throughout this administration counterculture people," he said. "I had a senior law-enforcement official tell me that, in his judgment, up to a quarter of the White House staff, when they first came in, had used drugs in the last four or five years."[29]

Leading Democrats were outraged by this remark. "He's lost it," said Massachusetts Representative Barney Frank. "It smacks of McCarthyism," said New York Representative Charles Schumer. White House Chief of Staff Leon Panetta called the charge "absolutely false." He said Gingrich had "no evidence, no facts, no foundation, just basically smear and innuendo."[30]

Yet Gingrich's claim was actually quite plausible. According to his law-enforcement source, "up to a quarter" of Clinton staffers had used an illegal drug within the previous five years when they started work in early 1993. To assess this claim, we can take a look at the government's survey data for 1988, when 32 percent of eighteen- to twenty-five-year-olds and 23 percent of twenty-six- to thirty-four-year-olds reported illegal drug use during the previous year.[31] Given the relative youth of the people working for Clinton and the likelihood that self-reports understate drug use, "up to a quarter" is a pretty good stab at the share of White House staffers who used illegal drugs (mostly marijuana) in the five years before they were hired.

Why did Gingrich think it worth noting that members of the Clinton administration had the sort of drug-use histories you'd expect for people their age? And why did the Democrats react so hysterically to such a bland observation? Because politicians have to pretend, regardless of their own experience to the contrary, that drug users are different from you and me. This is a fundamental tenet of the prohibitionist faith. The Drug Enforcement Administration says "one of the basic contentions of legalization is that drug users are essentially normal people." Not so, says the DEA: "Drugs undo the bounds that keep many seemingly normal people on an even keel."[32]

Like the pod people in *Invasion of the Body Snatchers,* drug users may *seem* normal, but they are not to be trusted. Indeed, William J. Bennett, drug czar in the first Bush administration, argued that drug users who seem normal are especially dangerous, because they encourage others to imitate their behavior, thereby spreading the "epidemic" of substance abuse.[33] Former Los Angeles Police Chief Daryl Gates went even further, saying casual drug users "ought to be taken out and shot" for committing "treason" in the war on drugs.[34]

Inconvenient Truths

Lest they be identified as traitors, former pot smokers and coke sniffers who become politicians are especially anxious to seem tough on drugs, a position that must create a certain amount of cognitive dissonance. During the Clinton administration the government continued to arrest people, at a rate of about 700,000 a year, for doing what the president had joked about on MTV (or for enabling other people to do it). If it was a trifling matter in the sixties, why was it such a big deal in the nineties?

During his campaign for the 2000 Republican nomination, George W. Bush seemed to be troubled by this contradiction. Bush had told audiences that "drugs will destroy you," and it would have been inconvenient to admit that he was a living refutation of that claim.[35] He repeatedly declined to confirm or deny rumors that he had used cocaine in the seventies, and in a 1998 interview with *Newsweek* he suggested why. "If I were you," he said, "I wouldn't tell your kids that you smoked pot unless you want 'em to smoke pot. I think it's important for leaders, and parents, not to send mixed signals. I don't want some kid saying, 'Well, Governor Bush tried it.'"[36] In other words, we should hide the truth about drug use so as not to set a bad example for the kids.

Bush later reiterated this stance. Asked what baby boomer parents should say to kids who want to know if they have used drugs, he replied: "I think the baby boomer parent ought to say, 'I've learned from mistakes I may or may not have made, and I'd like to share some wisdom with you, and that is don't do drugs.'"[37] It's a mystery how anyone can learn from mistakes he hasn't made. But the beginning of wisdom in dealing with drug use, as in dealing with other kinds of potentially risky behavior, is understanding the importance of context. What is appropriate for an adult may not be appropriate for a child, and what is OK at home on the weekend may not be OK at work during a lunch break. A parent who refuses to talk about his "mistakes," or even to admit that he made any, is not imparting wisdom; he is reciting an incantation aimed at warding off charges of hypocrisy. In Bush's case, his refusal to talk about his own drug use, which implied that it wasn't important enough for voters to consider, was especially troubling because as governor of Texas he had signed legislation allowing jail time for first-time offenders caught with less than a gram of an illegal drug.[38]

Unlike Bush, some people are willing to discuss their use of illicit intoxicants, usually because they are protected by celebrity or anonymity. The first category includes accomplished intellectuals such as Nobel Prize–winning chemist Kary Mullis and the late astronomer Carl Sagan, a Pulitzer Prize winner (who wrote about his marijuana use under a pseudonym), as well as entertainers who, while successful, may seem to confirm stereotypes more than they challenge them (Woody Harrelson, Keanu Reeves, Willie Nelson). Most of the drug users I interviewed for this book fall into the second category, willing to talk but keen to conceal their identities. These people include physicians, scientists, academics, a social worker, a truck driver, journalists, public relations specialists, software engineers, entrepreneurs, and clerical workers. Typically they have dabbled in various drugs and now smoke marijuana from time to time. Some have occasionally used amphetamines or other stimulants to stay awake or boost their concentration. Some have sampled a bewildering variety of psychoactive substances and continue to experiment. Some are regular opiate users. What they all have in common is that they manage to lead decent, productive lives.

Putting it that way may imply more of a struggle than they typically report. These people are often puzzled by stories about individuals who lose control of their drug use. "I'm always surprised when someone ends up in rehab, when people don't know their limits or can't set boundaries with drugs," the novelist Bret Easton Ellis once remarked. "It's like eating or drinking—you sort of know when you've had enough, and you have some kind of self-control to say, 'OK, I'm not going to do enough drugs so I get to never do them again in my life.' There is a point where you *can* say no and wait a week or whatever. It doesn't seem that difficult to incorporate it into the fabric of your life."[39]

Emphasizing controlled use may strike some as insensitive, if not irresponsible. After all, many people do have serious problems with drugs, problems that disrupt their lives and cause anguish to their families and friends. These problems are real, but they are not the focus of this book. Just as writing about moderate drinking does not mean denying the harm caused by alcoholism, writing about controlled drug use does not mean denying the damage done by destructive relationships with illegal intoxicants. Rather, my intent is to add some balance to the public debate by pointing out that excess is the exception. The people quoted in this book are far more typical of illegal drug users than is the pothead dropout, the crackhead mugger, or the junkie burglar. As mainstream drug policy experts, such as UCLA's Mark Kleiman, have long conceded, the vast majority of illegal drug users do not become addicts, and the vast majority do not harm themselves or others.[40] There's no denying that drug use carries risks, but those risks do not preclude a discussion of moderate use. To the contrary, they show the need for such a discussion.

True Temperance

This book argues that the black-and-white, all-or-nothing thinking that has long dominated discussions of illegal drug use should give way to a wiser, subtler approach with deep roots in Western culture. That approach, exemplified by the tradition of moderate drinking, rejects the idea that there is something inherently wrong with using chemicals to alter one's mood or mind. Instead it emphasizes the context in which drug use occurs: how, why, when, and where intoxicants are consumed. These factors determine how likely drug use is to cause harm, the crucial consideration in making moral judgments about it.

Chapter 1 considers a contrary view, which holds that psychoactive substances are so dangerous that they should be avoided altogether. This is the general thrust of Mormon and Muslim teaching regarding drugs, although there is disagreement in both communities about how far the divine prohibition of intoxicants extends. Because the lines drawn by Mormons and Muslims are different from the distinctions embodied in the laws of most countries, their traditions represent a challenge to the conventional wisdom about drugs. In particular, Mormons and Muslims agree on the need to abstain from alcohol. But that position is not endorsed by the secular anti-drug establishment, which maintains that alcohol is different from illegal drugs because it can be used responsibly. Mormons and Muslims are right to reject this distinction, which has no basis in fact. Defenders of the drug laws have never satisfactorily explained why using the currently illegal drugs is morally problematic in a way that drinking is not. To be consistent, we must either abandon the idea of responsible drinking or extend it, apply the abstinence model to alcohol or, as I am suggesting, apply the temperance model to other drugs.

Chapter 2 explores the conflict between abstinence and moderation as responses to the dangers posed by alcohol. The biblical view of alcohol recognizes the drug's hazards yet endorses its appropriate use. This approach, a species of the virtue that Aristotle called temperance (*sōphrosunē*), was preached by Jewish and Christian thinkers for centuries. The so-called temperance movement perverted the concept, demanding abstinence rather than moderation because its leaders became convinced that people could not be trusted to drink responsibly. Prohibitionists twisted the biblical message about alcohol, emphasizing the warnings while ignoring the positive references. They could thus imply that God was on their side, when in fact their opponents had a stronger claim to be following the Judeo-Christian tradition. The repeal of Prohibition represented a repudiation of dry distortions and a return to true temperance. Although suspicion of alcohol persists, influencing attitudes and policy in various ways, mainstream opinion acknowledges that responsible drinking is not only possible but typical. While recognizing the potential for abuse, the vast majority of Americans reject the view of alcohol as a demonic force that takes possession of people and compels them to do evil. At the same time, they accept a similar portrayal of the drugs that remain illegal, which they believe are too powerful to be used responsibly.

The evidence indicates that voodoo pharmacology is wrong, that it's a mistake to think of drugs as magical potions that transform people or force them to sin. Chapters 3 through 7 deal with variations on this theme, discussing five drug-related fears—sloth, madness, lust, wrath, and gluttony—and the drugs to which they have been linked. The fact that all of these dangers have been cited by opponents of drinking does not mean they are entirely imaginary. But it does suggest that they represent extreme, exceptional cases rather than predictable drug effects.

Chapter 3 explores the idea that drugs make people slothful. A familiar theme in warnings about marijuana, this charge also has been leveled against alcohol and, more surprisingly, tobacco. It reveals more about the concerns that each generation has regarding the next than it does about the pharmacology of these substances.

Chapter 4 examines the fear of drug-induced madness, associated with LSD and other psychedelics since the 1960s but tied to alcohol and marijuana in earlier eras. Although a psychedelic trip, like any strong emotional experience, can contribute to psychological problems, such cases are far less common than anti-drug propaganda suggests. As with alcohol, the subjective effects of psychedelics vary with the context in which they are taken, which is largely determined by factors under the user's control.

Chapter 5 considers MDMA, a.k.a. Ecstasy, as the latest in a long line of drugs said to incite lust. Some reputed aphrodisiacs, such as Viagra and alcohol, have gained mainstream acceptance, while others, such as marijuana, cocaine, and opium, have been associated with outsiders accused of promiscuity, rape, and sexual slavery. The element of truth in these lurid tales is that almost any drug can play a role in sex. But the issues raised by that connection are the same for illegal drugs as they are for legal ones.

More troubling to many people than the sex supposedly fostered by MDMA is the violence blamed on drugs such as crack, PCP, and methamphetamine, which are said to inspire murderous wrath.

Chapter 6 shows that such fears exaggerate the power of these substances. Alcohol is more strongly associated with violence than any illegal drug, but that does not mean it turns peaceful, law-abiding people into brutal criminals. The link between alcohol and violence depends upon the drinker's personality, values, expectations, and circumstances. The same is true of crimes committed by other drug users, with the added complication that black-market violence fostered by prohibition is often confused with violence caused by drugs.

The terrible effects attributed to drugs raise the question of why anyone would continue taking them. The traditional answer is that addiction prevents them from stopping. Chapter 7 shows that the conventional understanding of addiction, which portrays it as a kind of chemical slavery in which the user's values and wishes do not matter, is fundamentally misleading. Although the concept of drug-induced gluttony is nowadays associated chiefly with heroin, it was originally developed to explain the behavior of habitual drunkards. The portrait of predictable escalation from experimentation to an unbreakable habit was wrong when it was applied to drinking, and it is no less mistaken as a description of illegal drug use. Just as drinkers do not typically become alcoholics, users of illegal drugs—even such reputedly powerful substances as heroin, crack, and methamphetamine—do not typically become addicts.

Given the anxieties aroused by drug use, people often feel a need to justify it. Chapter 8 considers two of the most commonly heard excuses: medical and religious. Although it is easy to think of compelling cases—the cancer patient who uses marijuana to relieve the side effects of chemotherapy, the Catholic who uses wine in communion—the elastic boundaries of these two categories make policing drug use based on motivation a hopeless task. While the government no longer recognizes the right to self-medication, the concept of illness has been expanded to include unpleasant mental states, so that legal use of prescription drugs often resembles illegal use of street drugs. Likewise, one man's acid trip is another's spiritual awakening.

The search for excuses reflects the lingering suspicion that drug use is sinful without a special justification. Yet the desire to alter one's consciousness appears to be a fundamental aspect of human nature. Like sex, it is nothing to be ashamed of, but it needs to be constrained by moral principles, which means getting beyond the unthinking, blanket rejection of drugs. In the Conclusion, I offer some suggestions about what it would mean if we managed to do that.

Opponents of the war on drugs generally argue that it does more harm than good.[41] Some also argue that people have a right to control their own bodies, even if they make foolish, self-destructive choices.[42] I agree with both of these arguments, as my writing on drug policy reflects. But I've always been troubled by the tendency of reformers to make a point of declaring their personal opposition to drug use. New Mexico Governor Gary Johnson, who showed considerable courage by criticizing the war on drugs while he was still in office, was more candid than most politicians in discussing his own history of drug use. When he first ran for governor in 1994, Johnson readily admitted that he had smoked marijuana in college. He recalled the response from reporters: "Oh, so you experimented with drugs?" He corrected them: "No, I smoked marijuana. This is something that I did . . . along with a lot of other people. . . . We enjoyed what we were doing." Johnson, a successful entrepreneur who had never held public office before, wanted to make it clear that his experience with drugs did not involve test tubes and Bunsen burners. At the same time, he emphasized that he eventually decided to avoid all drugs, including alcohol, tobacco, Coca-Cola, and chocolate as well as illegal intoxicants. A fitness enthusiast who had competed in the Iron Man Triathlon and planned to climb Mount Everest after he left office, Johnson called drugs "a handicap" and "a bad choice." During a 1999 talk at the libertarian Cato Institute (where the hosts were also keen to disclaim any tacit approval of drug use), he sounded a bit like Mr. Mackey, the guidance counselor on *South Park*. "Drugs are bad," he said. "Don't do drugs." On other occasions, however, Johnson conceded that abstinence was not the only morally acceptable choice. "I hate to say it," he told a group of college students, "but the majority of people who use drugs use them responsibly." The question is, why should he hate to say it? This is a crucial point that is too often neglected by critics of the drug laws.[43]

It's understandable that someone faced with the burden of fighting a policy that has been in place for ninety years would be reluctant to simultaneously challenge strongly held prejudices about the morality of drug use. And it's certainly correct to argue that the government should not try to stamp out all immoral behavior, which would be a recipe for totalitarianism. But reformers will not make much progress as long as they agree with defenders of the status quo that drug use is always wrong. The assumption that some drugs cannot be used responsibly is one of the biggest obstacles to serious reform. For people who do not believe in the possibility of temperance, the prospect of a world without prohibition will always be too terrifying to consider.

CHAPTER ONE

CHEMICAL REACTIONS

The simple fact is that drug use is wrong.
—WILLIAM J. BENNETT, 1990

Our Bodies, His Temple

On Chillicothe Road in Kirtland, Ohio, under a big white sign that says "N.K. Whitney & Co.," is a restored nineteenth-century general store. Inside are antiques and reproductions aimed at simulating what the store looked like when it was in operation: barrels, shelves, bottles, period china, a spinning wheel, a reflector oven, old furniture. Admission is free. It's the sort of place passers-by might visit if they happened to be in Kirtland with half an hour to kill. To Mormons, however, Newell K. Whitney's store is of more than casual interest. For several years it was the home of Mormon prophet Joseph Smith and the site of the school where he instructed his disciples. Today the upper room where Smith trained his followers for missionary work is kept clean and tidy. But at one time the air was so filled with pipe and cigar smoke, the floor so befouled by tobacco spit, that Smith sought divine guidance for dealing with these filthy habits. On February 27, 1833, according to Mormon tradition, the answer came: "Tobacco is not for the body." The revelation, known as the Word of Wisdom, also proscribed alcoholic beverages and "hot drinks," later interpreted to mean coffee and tea.[1]

The Word of Wisdom neither mentions nor alludes to any other drug. But the Church of Jesus Christ of Latter-day Saints teaches that "the message of the Word of Wisdom is to avoid all substances that are harmful to our bodies," and "drugs are harmful when used outside of specific medicinal purposes."[2] According to a statement issued in 1974, "The Church has consistently opposed the improper and harmful use of drugs or similar substances under circumstances which would result in addiction, physical or mental impairment, or in lowering moral standards."[3] As applied by the church, this standard prohibits all use of illegal drugs, along with nonmedicinal use of legal ones.

The Mormon position on psychoactive substances is far more sweeping than the policies advocated by most people who claim to favor a drug-free society. The Mormons do not recognize a moral difference between alcohol, tobacco, and coffee, on the one hand, and marijuana, cocaine, and heroin, on the other. In their view, all these substances are unhealthy, addictive, and spiritually disruptive, and all are therefore condemned by God. "Frightening and vicious though [illegal] drug use is," a church leader wrote in 1976, "equally destructive in the long run is the use of alcohol and tobacco. They constitute our major drug problems today."[4]

Because of their apparent consistency, the Mormons offer a rare opportunity to clarify our thinking about drugs. They are right to question the distinction between alcohol and illegal intoxicants that is often asserted by supporters of the war on drugs. But they are too quick to reject the idea of temperance. Their refusal to admit the possibility of ethical drug use outside of a medical context is unsupportable except as a matter of faith. Muslims are less strict on this question, but they share with Mormons a zero-tolerance approach to alcohol that highlights the arbitrariness of the lines drawn by our drug laws. By refusing to make an exception for alcohol, Mormons and Muslims challenge drug warriors to explain why it is fundamentally different from other intoxicants, something they have been unable to do.

The Mormon view begins with the premise that our bodies are entrusted to us by God, who expects us to keep them in good condition. That idea is famously expressed in 1 Corinthians, where Paul says: "Know ye not that ye are the temple of God, and that the Spirit of God dwelleth in you? If any man defile the temple of God, him shall God destroy; for the temple of God is holy, which temple ye are."[5] Citing these verses, the Mormon Sunday school curriculum explains that "our bodies are temples and are holy to the Lord. We should keep them pure because they are the dwelling places for our spirits, which are the offspring of God. Respecting our bodies as temples of God manifests our testimony that we are children of God. It also keeps our bodies pure so they can be dwelling places for the Holy Ghost."[6] In other words, failure to respect our bodies not only violates our responsibility as custodians; it cuts us off from God.

The Mormons give three main reasons why nonmedicinal drug use defiles the temple. First, it causes physical harm. "Jesus Christ as the God of this world has told us that alcoholic beverages, tobacco, tea, and coffee are all destructive of our health," writes Elder Theodore M. Burton, a member of the church's main body of leaders.

"The continued use of these substances will cause us misery and sorrow. They are not only injurious to our health, but actually destructive of our minds and bodies."[7] These assertions, of course, are open to empirical challenge. If it turns out that some uses of these or other drugs pose little or no health risk, the objection based on physical harm loses its force.

Second, the Mormons object to intoxication itself. "If someone 'under the influence' can hardly listen to plain talk," writes Elder Boyd K. Packer, "how can they respond to spiritual promptings that touch their most delicate feelings?"[8] According to church president Gordon B. Hinckley, "It is stupid . . . to use cocaine, marijuana, or any other drugs that can rob you of control of your mind."[9] Although the idea that intoxicants take control of people's minds—the essence of voodoo pharmacology—exaggerates their power, some drugs may well be incompatible with prayer or spiritual reflection. Even religions that accept alcohol, for example, frown upon praying or performing certain rites in a drunken state. But such concerns do not require complete abstinence—only abstinence in particular circumstances. And it is by no means clear that all forms of intoxication interfere with spirituality. Most religions do not condemn believers for drinking a cup of coffee or tea before praying. More controversially, as Chapter 4 discusses, some cultures endorse the use of psychoactive substances to *promote* spirituality.

Third, the Mormons warn that drug use leads to addiction. "Narcotic addiction serves the design of the prince of darkness, for it disrupts the channel to the Holy Spirit of Truth," Packer writes. "Addiction has the capacity to disconnect the human will and nullify moral agency. It can rob one of the power to decide."[10] This claim, too, can be questioned. Chapter 7 addresses it in detail, showing that addiction does not "nullify moral agency" and that drugs such as heroin, crack, and methamphetamine are neither irresistible nor inescapable.

Cold Drinks

The Mormons seem to believe that addiction itself—the very difficulty of giving up a habit—is a problem, regardless of how it affects the user's life. "The harmful substances that are prohibited in the Word of Wisdom cause addiction," the church teaches. "We should not use any substance that is habit forming."[11] And while Mormon leaders indirectly acknowledge that not all drug users become addicts, they argue that it's wrong to take the chance. "So many people say, 'One cigarette, one cup of tea or coffee, one puff of marijuana won't hurt you, and one drink of alcohol surely cannot hurt anybody,'" writes church leader N. Eldon Tanner. "I want to emphasize that if you never take the first you will never take the second. You will never become an alcoholic or an addict."[12] The Mormons take a similar stance with regard to the physical hazards of drugs: "The only wise decision regarding any harmful drugs is simply never to consume any of them, even in small amounts."[13]

This position of extreme caution ignores the principle that the dose makes the poison. Many things that are benign in small amounts—aspirin, vitamin A, water—are harmful, even deadly, in large amounts. Furthermore, just about everything we do carries some level of risk; drug use is hardly unique in that respect. The task for the prudent person is to assess the risks and decide whether they're justified. The Mormons simply assume that the benefits of drugs never outweigh the risks, except when they're used to treat disease. They discuss the hazards of drugs as if they were random, rather than factors that can be controlled by the user. Therefore, although Mormons recognize temperance as a virtue in other contexts, they leave no room for it in connection with drugs.

In addition to the implications of defiling God's temple, the Mormons worry about the effects of drug use on others. "The consumption of harmful drugs is not a private or personal matter," declares a Mormon teacher's manual. "It inevitably affects deeply the lives of others who are often innocent, and it results in needless grief."[14] Again, such a sweeping assertion invites skepticism. Does drug use *inevitably* hurt other people, or only sometimes? Can people take precautions to prevent injury to others?

It is not hard to think of examples that contradict Mormon assumptions about drug use. The typical drinker is not harming his health, is not addicted to alcohol, and is not hurting other people. By ignoring this reality, the Mormons persist in the error that drove the temperance movement toward abstinence and prohibition.

Caffeine offers an even clearer example of a drug that does not fit the Mormon template for psychoactive substances. Although the church tries mightily to indict coffee and tea on health grounds, caffeine's verified risks are either minor or associated with very high levels of consumption.[15] While caffeine addiction, including cravings, tolerance, and withdrawal symptoms, is common, most people who experience symptoms do not consider it a serious problem. They feel neither enslaved by the drug nor debilitated by its effects. And not even the Mormons have made the case that caffeine use leads to antisocial behavior.

The broader culture's nonchalance regarding caffeine—a stimulant that is easily available to children as well as adults—is reflected in the church's evolving, ambiguous position concerning products other than coffee or tea that contain the drug. "With reference to cola drinks," Mormon leaders declared in 1972, "the Church has never officially taken a position on this matter, but the leaders of the Church have advised, and we do now specifically advise, against the use of any drink containing harmful habit-forming drugs under circumstances that would result in acquiring the habit. Any beverage that contains ingredients harmful to the body should be avoided."[16] Three years later, in a magazine published by the church, Bishop H. Burke Peterson addressed the issue again: "We know that cola drinks contain the drug caffeine. We know that caffeine is not wholesome or prudent for the use of our bodies. It is only sound judgment to conclude that cola drinks and any others that contain caffeine or other harmful ingredients should not be used."[17]

Notwithstanding this advice, according to a 1988 article in another Mormon magazine, "The Church has taken no stand against any substances containing caffeine other than coffee and tea."[18] That includes chocolate, which contains both caffeine and a similar stimulant, theobromine, but is nevertheless featured in recipes published by church magazines.[19] In a 1990 article, a church leader recalled sharing chocolate with Masai children while doing missionary work in Kenya; he likened the taste of a chocolate bar to "the taste of the gospel of Jesus Christ."[20] In light of the general injunction against addictive drugs and the doctrine that any amount of a potentially harmful substance should be avoided, this tolerance of chocolate is difficult to understand. If it is based on the judgment that chocolate does not pose a serious threat when used in moderation, the same sort of analysis should be possible with other psychoactive substances. A similar question is raised by the Mormons' historical use of the stimulant plant ephedra (a.k.a. "Mormon tea"). If nonmedical drug use is sometimes permissible, what is the basis for deciding when it's OK? The answer cannot be found in the Word of Wisdom.

Satan's Handiwork

Like Joseph Smith, Muhammad was troubled by drug use among his followers. Although the Qur'an includes positive references to wine, Muhammad delivered a series of admonitions concerning drunkenness, culminating in a call for abstinence in 632.[21] (According to Muslim tradition, the Qur'an was revealed by God in pieces over a period of twenty years.) In the first admonition about alcohol, God tells Muhammad to instruct the people concerning "strong drink and games of chance": "In both is great sin, and (some) utility for men; but the sin of them is greater than their usefulness."[22] This warning was not interpreted as a ban. Neither was the second admonition, which dealt with drinking in a specific context: "Draw not near unto prayer when ye are drunken, till ye know that which ye utter."[23] But the third admonition was clear and emphatic: "Strong drink and games of chance and idols and divining arrows are only an infamy of Satan's handiwork. Leave it aside in order that ye may succeed. Satan seeketh only to cast among you enmity and hatred by means of strong drinks and games of chance, and to turn you from remembrance of Allah and from (His) worship. Will ye then have done?"[24] Upon hearing this injunction, according to Muslim tradition, Muhammad's followers poured out their wine in the street.

These verses deal with *khamr*, translated here as "strong drink." The term, which originally referred to date or grape wine, was extended to all fermented beverages and, later, to distilled spirits. More controversial was the question of whether *khamr* encompassed psychoactive substances other than alcohol. One interpretation, relying on *khamr*'s resemblance to the verb *khamara,* which means to seize or overwhelm, holds that the term "is properly applied to anything that seizes or overwhelms the mind."[25] In a similar vein, a widely accepted saying attributed to Muhammad holds that "every intoxicant is *khamr,* and every intoxicant is forbidden."[26] But even if this saying is accepted as authoritative, there remains the question of what counts as intoxicating, *muskir,* under Islamic law.

The Hanafi school of jurisprudence essentially limits *khamr* to alcoholic beverages made from grapes. It permits the use of other psychoactive substances, as long as the user does not become drunk. The Hanafi definition of drunkenness is likewise narrow: "The drunk who is to be punished is one who comprehends absolutely nothing at all, and who does not know a man from a woman, or the earth from the heavens." The three other Sunni Muslim schools of jurisprudence take a broader view of *khamr,* including any amount of a substance that can make one drunk. Their definitions of drunkenness are also less permissive. The Maliki school, for instance, says a drunk is "one who becomes absent-minded and confused."[27]

Whether a particular drug is forbidden by Islam, then, is a matter of interpretation, both of the law and of the facts. Some medieval opponents of hashish argued that the drug was intoxicating (*muskir*) in the same sense as wine. But others who condemned the use of hashish were not so sure. One scholar maintained that *muskir* referred to a substance the effect of which is "primarily *nashwah,* joy, and a certain feeling of strength and confidence in oneself." He believed hashish was more accurately described as *mufsid* ("corruptive"), which applies to a substance that "befuddles the intellect, without primarily generating joy."[28]

Instead of relying exclusively on an argument that required such abstruse distinctions, hashish's detractors also claimed that its users violated the Islamic injunction against self-harm. "The jurists who attempted to stem the use of hashish had powerful weapons in these two arguments," notes historian Franz Rosenthal. "However, it ought to be realized that theirs was not a completely impregnable position. It depended neither upon firm authority and upon precedent of the kind generally admitted nor upon the intrinsic character of hashish, which was a plant and therefore basically permitted for use, but it had to rely exclusively upon the drug's presumed effects, and they were hard to prove objectively."[29]

The Islamic case against coffee, condemned by a 1511 conference of scholars in Mecca, was even weaker. The drink's opponents likened it to wine and hashish, but its effects were so clearly different that such comparisons were readily dismissed. Trying a different tack, the anti-coffee activists suggested that "coffee euphoria"—the pleasant buzz that one aficionado described as "a sprightliness of spirit and a sense of mental well-being"—was itself suspect.[30] This argument, which suggested that Islam condemns any chemically induced change in consciousness, also failed, and nowadays coffee is ubiquitous in the Muslim world.

The use of qat, a stimulant shrub that is especially popular in Yemen and Somalia, is less widespread, but its acceptance is instructive. Qat, which originated in Ethiopia, has been used as an intoxicant in the Middle East for 600 years or more. Like coffee, it generated some controversy early on, including a sixteenth-century ban by the Yemeni imam, who repealed the decree after he was persuaded that qat's psychoactive effects were not similar to alcohol's. In 2000 the Yemeni government estimated that 90 percent of the country's men chewed qat and that the habit was almost as common among women.[31]

In the late 1990s, Yemeni President Ali Abdullah Saleh began a halfhearted effort to discourage use of the plant, announcing that he planned to give it up himself. Qat's opponents argued that growing it wastes water and that chewing it impairs productivity—not because of the drug's psychoactive effects but because Yemenis traditionally take afternoon qat breaks that can last several hours. Religious arguments were conspicuously absent from the anti-qat campaign. "The debate over qat continues," notes Hofstra University anthropologist Daniel M. Varisco. But "this debate no longer hinges on [qat's] legitimacy for Muslims—certainly not within Yemen—but rather on the alleged economic and social drain."[32]

Tobacco likewise was initially condemned as a forbidden intoxicant, but today the religious controversy hinges mainly on the health effects of smoking. A group of nine Islamic scholars consulted by the World Health Organization in the 1980s agreed that smoking was either forbidden or censurable, primarily because of "serious health hazards which can lead to destruction." (They also criticized smoking as a wasteful extravagance and an annoyance to others.) "The jurists who ruled that smoking was permissible did so prior to the recent discovery by modern medical research of the many health hazards posed by smoking," writes Sheikh Mahdi Abdul-Hamid Mustafa, director of information at Cairo's Al-Azhar Mosque. "As the harm caused by smoking has been firmly established through evidence and experience, the ruling must be anything but permissibility." In this respect, the debate over smoking among Muslims mirrors the secular world's disenchantment with tobacco during the twentieth century:

The drug's psychoactive effects and habit-forming potential, like caffeine's, did not cause much concern until it became clear how hazardous cigarettes were.[33]

As the debates over hashish and tobacco illustrate, there are two basic ways to argue that a particular drug is forbidden by Islam: You can claim that it is similar enough to wine that it falls under the ban on *khamr*, or you can claim that it causes impermissible harm to the body and mind. Either argument requires an inquiry into the drug's actual effects; it's not enough simply to ask whether the substance is legal in a given time and place.

Writing in the early 1970s, Walter H. Dixon, a political scientist at the American University in Cairo, argued that "Islamic principles are antithetical to the misuse of narcotics"—by which he apparently meant any use of illegal drugs.[34] This is a dubious claim on its face, since secular authorities determine which drugs are illegal, often in conformity with international agreements. As illustrated by the omission of alcohol from the list of proscribed intoxicants in most countries (including Egypt), these choices do not necessarily coincide with the dictates of Islam.

Still, Dixon was troubled by the fact that many Muslims did not share American attitudes toward certain drugs. He cited a survey of Egyptian hashish users in which 80 percent said the drug was not forbidden by Islam. "The same research made it clear that many drug users regularly perform their religious duties without perceiving any contradiction between the illegal consumption of narcotics and devotion to their faith," Dixon wrote. Such drug users were misinformed, he argued, because "all orthodox Muslim religious authorities agree that a condition of stupor or exhilaration induced by consumption of any substance which affects the mind is prohibited by Islam."[35]

If "stupor" is equivalent to the obliviousness that the Hanafi school equates with drunkenness, Dixon is correct that all the authorities agree it is prohibited. But it is possible to use hashish, opium, and other soporific drugs without reaching that state. As for "exhilaration," the Hanafi standard says nothing about it, and there is no mention of it in the Qur'an, which condemns *khamr* for causing enmity and forgetfulness. Even the definitions of drunkenness favored by the stricter schools do not, on their face, apply to stimulants such as caffeine, qat, nicotine, cocaine, and amphetamines. These drugs tend to focus the mind rather than cloud it; they help maintain alertness and can improve performance on mental tasks. While "exhilaration" may be a welcome side effect or even the main object for a given user, it's debatable whether that feeling is analogous to the drunkenness decried by Muhammad.

High Anxiety

While Mormons and Muslims share a general suspicion of intoxicants, Muslims are more inclined to distinguish between different psychoactive substances—in particular, between stupor-inducing drugs similar to alcohol and stimulants such as qat and coffee. But the Church of Jesus Christ of Latter-day Saints and most Muslim scholars are united in rejecting the very idea of moderate alcohol use. By contrast, the prevailing view in the United States and other Western countries is that temperance is possible for alcohol but not for illegal drugs such as marijuana, LSD, cocaine, and heroin. That distinction is not based on divine revelation, but it might as well be, given how rarely anyone bothers to justify it. When supporters of the current drug laws do attempt to offer a rationale, the results are often puzzling.

Attorney General John Ashcroft, a Pentecostal Christian, abstains from alcohol and tobacco on religious and, presumably, moral grounds. Introducing a piece of anti-drug legislation in 1999, when he was a senator from Missouri, Ashcroft complained that "too few people are willing to stand up these days and call drugs wrong."[36] Yet when he was challenged by *Mother Jones* over his support for the beer industry (Anheuser-Busch is based in St. Louis), his reply was notably lacking in moral reflection. "It's a product that is in demand," he said. "And when it's used responsibly, it's like other products."[37]

Illegal intoxicants are indisputably "in demand," of course, so drug warriors like Ashcroft have to question whether they can be "used responsibly." Thomas Constantine, then head of the U.S. Drug Enforcement Administration, tried this approach in a 1998 interview with ABC's John Stossel. "There's a difference between alcohol and cocaine," he said. "There's a difference between alcohol and marijuana. Everyone who tries that substance—marijuana, heroin, cocaine, methamphetamines, hashish—does it for a single purpose. They do it for the purpose of becoming high. I think that's wrong, and I think it's dangerous." Stossel confessed that "when I have a glass of gin or vodka, I'm doing it to get a little buzz on. That buzz is bad? [It] should be illegal?" Constantine's response made viewers wonder if he'd ever been to a cocktail party or a wedding reception: "Well, I think if you drink for that purpose, that's not too smart." He then added, perhaps briefly forgetting that he was charged with enforcing the nation's drug laws, "I can't tell you what to do with your own life."[38]

Let's give Constantine the benefit of the doubt by assuming he was not really denying that people like alcohol because of its psychoactive effects. In that case, he must have been drawing a distinction between "getting high" and "unwinding," "loosening up," or one of the other socially acceptable descriptions of what alcohol helps people do. Constantine's exchange with Stossel, then, is reminiscent of the dispute among Islamic scholars about the meaning of intoxication. Unfortunately, we can only guess at the difference between the drug-induced states of consciousness that Constantine thinks are OK and the ones he condemns. Since he acknowledged that it's possible (though not "smart") to "get a buzz" from alcohol, perhaps he was suggesting a difference in degree: moderate drinking versus drunkenness. Or perhaps, since Stossel was talking about the effect of just one drink, Constantine was asserting that it's the drinker's intent, as opposed to the quantity he consumes, that is crucial. Either way, it's not clear why the distinction he had in mind cannot be applied to other drugs as well as alcohol.

Although it raises more questions than it answers, Constantine's argument is enduringly popular among defenders of drug prohibition. "A person may drink to have a good time," Richard Nixon told domestic affairs adviser John Ehrlichman in 1971, "but a person does not drink simply for the purpose of getting high. You take drugs for the purpose of getting high."[39] Two decades later, former Attorney General Edwin Meese III drew the same contrast in a speech at the Hoover Institution. "It should be noted that alcohol can be used responsibly and that only a small percentage of those who drink liquor become intoxicated," Meese said. "By contrast, the only purpose of using illicit drugs is to 'get high,' and the inevitable intoxicating effect of such drugs provides the essential difference from alcohol."[40]

Since people who drink generally want to be affected by alcohol, Meese must have meant something more by "intoxicated"—visibly drunk, perhaps. So when he said that other drugs have "an inevitable intoxicating effect," he did not mean simply that, like alcohol, they are psychoactive. He apparently meant that, unlike alcohol, they do not produce different degrees of intoxication in different amounts. When it comes to illegal drugs, Meese was suggesting, you're either sober or totally wasted. For that reason, presumably, "alcohol can be used responsibly," but illegal drugs cannot. If this is what Meese was getting at, his argument is based on a belief that contradicts basic pharmacology, which tells us that the effects of a drug—even an illegal drug—vary with the dose.

The journalist Jill Jonnes offers a slightly more sophisticated version of this argument in her history of drug use in America. "An important distinction between alcohol and the illegal drugs," she writes, "is that while it is possible to abuse all of them, anyone who is using drugs is seeking strictly to get high. This is not true with alcohol. On any given evening in America, tens of millions come home and unwind with a glass of wine or beer or a martini. Are they seeking to get high? Not if they're having one or two glasses. This commonsense distinction between how alcohol is used widely (to relax, for the pleasure of the taste of the stuff) and how illegal drugs are used (to get high) makes alcohol much more socially acceptable."[41]

As with Constantine, Nixon, and Meese, it is not exactly clear what Jonnes has in mind when she talks about getting "high," or why it's so bad. If "high" connotes exhilaration, it's not true that people can't get high from "one or two glasses" of beer, wine, or liquor; indeed, mood elevation is more commonly reported after a drink or two than after a night of boozing. People can also get a noticeable buzz from a cigarette or a strong cup of coffee, especially if they're not used to these drugs. Does that fact make nicotine and caffeine less "socially acceptable"?

If, on the other hand, "high" means extreme inebriation, something like the stupor condemned by Islam, Jonnes seems to be asserting that people never use illegal drugs in low doses, that they never try to achieve a mental state short of oblivion. As I show in subsequent chapters, there is no basis for this claim either. Like drinkers, illegal drug users adjust their consumption according to circumstances and the effect they're seeking. (In addition to dosage, expectation and environment shape the user's experience, just as they do in the case of alcohol.) It's a mystery where Jonnes got the idea that people never smoke marijuana, say, "to relax" (probably its most common use) or never enjoy "the taste of the stuff" (whole cookbooks are devoted to recipes featuring cannabis). People use marijuana for other reasons as well: to promote camaraderie and communication, to make boring situations more tolerable, to foster introspection and creativity, to enhance the enjoyment of music, movies, food, and nature. It's not clear why a drug's versatility should be considered so important in determining its legal or moral status, but the notion that alcohol has many uses while illegal drugs have only one cannot survive even a cursory investigation.

Soul Men

If anyone can explain the moral distinction between alcohol and other drugs, William J. Bennett should be up to the task. The former "drug czar," who directed the Office of National Drug Control Policy under George H.W. Bush, holds a law degree from Harvard and a Ph.D. in political philosophy from the University of Texas. During the last decade or so, he has made a career out of pontificating about morality on TV, in op-ed pieces, and in best-selling books. Not surprisingly, Bennett often discusses drugs in moral terms. "The simple fact is that drug use is wrong," he says, writing in defense of prohibition. "And the moral argument, in the end, is the most compelling argument."[42]

Bennett's convictions are clear, but his reasoning is not. The main problem with his arguments is that he routinely obscures the distinction between use and abuse. "In the end drug use is wrong because of what it does to human character," he writes. "It degrades. It makes people less than they should be by burning away a sense of responsibility, subverting productivity, and making a mockery of virtue. Using drugs is wrong not simply because drugs create medical problems; it is wrong because drugs destroy one's moral sense. People addicted to drugs neglect their duties. The lure can become so strong that soon people will do nothing else but take drugs. They will neglect God, family, children, friends, and jobs—everything in life that is important, noble, and worthwhile—for the sake of drugs."[43] Notice that Bennett begins by referring to "drug use" in general, but eventually it becomes clear that he is actually talking about "people addicted to drugs." He thus presents the dysfunctional addict as the typical drug user, rather like portraying the broken-down alcoholic as the typical drinker.

A similar bait-and-switch occurs in the next paragraph: "Drugs undermine the necessary virtues of a free society—autonomy, self-reliance, and individual responsibility. The inherent purpose of using drugs is secession from reality, from society, and from the moral obligations individuals owe their family, their friends, and their fellow citizens. Drugs destroy the natural sentiments and duties that constitute our human nature and make our social life possible. As our founders would surely recognize, for a citizenry to be perpetually in a drug-induced haze doesn't bode well for the future of self-government."[44] At first Bennett, who elsewhere refers to "the intrinsically destructive nature of drugs,"[45] seems to be suggesting that any use of psychoactive substances is inherently immoral, perhaps because it always results in "secession from reality," which is always wrong, no matter how brief or limited. Rather than defend that view—which probably would strike most people as extreme and implausible if it were applied consistently—he shifts his focus to drug users who are "perpetually in a drug-induced haze."

One might conclude that Bennett believes all drug users are addicts who constantly walk around in a stupor. Yet as drug czar he acknowledged that most drug users are neither addicted nor dysfunctional. "Non-addicted users still comprise the vast bulk of our drug-involved population," he wrote in 1989. "The non-addicted casual or regular user . . . is likely to have a still-intact family, social, and work life. He is likely still to 'enjoy' his drug for the pleasure it offers." For Bennett, in fact, it is the temperate user's well-adjustedness that makes him such a threat. Since he enjoys drugs without suffering any serious harm, he is "much more willing and able to proselytize his drug use—by action or example—among his remaining non-user peers, friends, and acquaintances. A non-addict's drug use, in other words, is *highly* contagious."[46] This is how Bennett justifies arresting and punishing people whose drug use is not hurting anyone, not even themselves: Their success might encourage others to use drugs, and some of *those* people might develop problems. By the same logic, moderate drinkers should be held responsible for alcoholism.

Tellingly, Bennett does not assert a moral distinction between alcohol and illegal drugs. "Alcohol has a long, complicated history in this country," he says, "and, unlike drugs, the American people accept alcohol. They have no interest in going back to Prohibition."

He also argues that it would be foolish to compound the nation's problems with alcohol by making other intoxicants legally available. Paraphrasing the columnist Charles Krauthammer, he writes, "the question is not which is worse, alcohol or drugs. The question is, should we accept both legalized alcohol *and* legalized drugs?"[47] Thus, despite his passionate rhetoric about the evils of drug use, Bennett declines to defend the claim that smoking a joint is morally worse than drinking a beer.

There is a similar gap in the writings of criminologist James Q. Wilson, who, like Bennett, stresses the moral consequences of drug use. "Drug use is wrong because it is immoral and it is immoral because it enslaves the mind and destroys the soul," Wilson writes.[48] "Tobacco shortens one's life; cocaine debases it. Nicotine alters one's habits; cocaine alters one's soul. The heavy use of crack, unlike the heavy use of tobacco, corrodes those natural sentiments of sympathy and duty that make possible our social life."[49] Here Wilson seems to be drawing a distinction between legal and illegal drugs, but elsewhere he includes alcoholism in the category of addictions that make people "less than human."[50]

Both Bennett and Wilson, then, concede that legal as well as illegal drugs can be abused. Both also concede that illegal as well as legal drugs can be used in moderation. Bennett admits that "there may be a small number of people who use drugs regularly—even frequently—but whose lives nevertheless go on for the most part unimpeded."[51] Wilson notes that "some people can consume drugs and still manage to lead a stable life, discharging duties to family, maintaining valued friendships, and earning a decent living."[52] Bennett and Wilson imply that such temperate users are rare. Even without looking closely at the evidence, there is reason to be skeptical about this claim, which seems inconsistent with Bennett's assertion that "non-addicted users . . . comprise the vast bulk of our drug-involved population."[53] But if it's true that illegal drug users run a substantially higher risk of addiction than drinkers do, they might be faulted for taking that chance—assuming that addiction is essentially a random occurrence that can be confidently avoided only by abstinence. That issue is examined in subsequent chapters.

Confusing the Kids

Defenders of prohibition are not the only ones who are anxious to avoid comparisons between illegal drugs and alcohol. Manufacturers of beer, wine, and liquor indignantly object to phrases like "alcohol and other drugs," which they see as part of an attempt to delegitimize their industry. A magazine ad sponsored by the Beer Institute shows a man opening a can of beer and looking puzzled as his child asks, "Daddy! Are you using drugs?" The text reads: "What are kids to think when they are taught that the beer dad drinks with dinner is the moral equivalent of illicit narcotics use? . . . A child needs to understand why it's normal and okay for his father, mother or other adults to drink responsibly, as 100 million American adults do. Telling him the beer dad pulls from the refrigerator is the same as crack, cocaine or heroin is a damaging distortion." The closing line urges, "Let's not make the war on drugs a war on common sense."

The ad never actually explains why comparing alcohol and illegal drugs is "a damaging distortion." The closest it comes is this: "Our industry is part of the fabric of our nation's life and the lives of many honest, upright citizens. Crack, cocaine and heroin are not." The illicitness of these drugs, of course, goes a long way toward explaining the status of the people who make and sell them. The Beer Institute seems to have forgotten that the alcohol trade had a rather unsavory reputation during Prohibition. The argument that alcohol is different from illegal drugs because the alcohol business is respectable amounts to saying, "We're legal; they're not."

Significantly, the Beer Institute omits any mention of marijuana, by far the most popular illegal intoxicant. Instead the ad twice refers to heroin and two different forms of cocaine—drugs that together were consumed by around 2 percent of the U.S. population in 2001, compared to about 9 percent for marijuana.[54] Presumably the Beer Institute left out pot because too many people would find the comparison between a beer and a joint plausible. In a 2000 poll by Rasmussen Research, 56 percent of respondents said that, morally speaking, smoking marijuana is no worse than having a drink.[55]

The Beer Institute was reacting to activists and public health officials who emphasize that alcohol is a dangerous intoxicant. Typical of their efforts is a 1995 ad sponsored by the Washington State Department of Social and Health Services showing a boy standing in front of an open refrigerator, reaching for a bottle of beer. "When some parents crave their favorite drug," the headline says, "they'll even use their own kids to get it."

That sort of message drives Gene Ford crazy. A former wine salesman from Seattle, Ford describes himself as "an irate grandfather who is aggrieved by government agencies which associate moderate drinking (as taught to me by my parents) with illicit street drugging."[56] He is the author of *The Benefits of Moderate Drinking* and the publisher of *Healthy Drinking*, a bimonthly devoted to debunking anti-alcohol propaganda. A perceptive critic of the black-and-white thinking that too often characterizes alcohol policy in the United States, Ford seems blind to the fact that his attitude toward illegal drugs is similar. "The 'alcohol and drugs' linkage must go," he insists, but he never explains why it's inaccurate or misleading. He just knows that it makes alcohol look bad. "If beer or rum are just 'other drugs,' like angel dust and cocaine," he writes, "public health operatives are free to confuse use with abuse."[57]

Ford is correct that such is the usual practice when it comes to illegal drugs: As far as the government is concerned, all use is abuse. But logic dictates that we should try to distinguish between use and abuse regardless of which drug we're discussing or what its current legal status happens to be. After all, alcohol itself has not always been legal or socially approved. As the next chapter discusses, its defenders have long contended with critics who said the only wise course was not to drink it at all.

CHAPTER TWO

STRONG DRINK

Wine is the work of God, but drunkenness is the work of the devil.
—ST. JOHN CHRYSOSTOM (C. 347–407)

To alcohol—the cause of, and solution to, all of life's problems.
—HOMER SIMPSON

Bible Lessons

If it seems odd to talk about illegal drugs the way we talk about alcohol, it may be instructive to first talk about alcohol the way we talk about illegal drugs. Alcohol is a toxin that causes dizziness, headache, vomiting, and blackouts; impairs speech, judgment, coordination, cognition, and memory; and depresses respiration, which can lead to death after a single drinking session. Withdrawal symptoms include rapid heart rate, shortness of breath, chills, fever, chest pain, nausea with recurrent vomiting, abdominal pain, hallucinations, and seizures, sometimes resulting in death. Alcohol users suffer from peptic ulcers, liver failure, pancreatic cysts, high blood pressure, stroke, metabolic abnormalities, malnutrition, lung and urinary tract infections, brain damage, and cancers of the mouth, larynx, esophagus, pancreas, liver, stomach, colon, and breast. Alcohol use is also associated with depression, suicide, unemployment, divorce, domestic violence, assault, homicide, and vehicular accidents.

Presented this way, alcohol sounds like a drug that no one in his right mind would touch. But this daunting description leaves out some important information. It does not tell us how often these terrible outcomes occur, at what doses, or whether it is possible for a prudent alcohol user to avoid them. Because this particular drug is familiar, we know that its users do not typically suffer serious ill effects and that the worst consequences occur only as a result of recklessness or heavy, prolonged use. We also know that alcohol brings many people a great deal of pleasure, another factor ignored by a simple list of its potential hazards. When the discussion turns to illegal drugs, it is much easier to get away with warnings that present extreme cases as the norm. It is also easier to pretend that drug use has no value.

These mistakes, which lie at the heart of the war on drugs, were also characteristic of the crusade that led to national alcohol prohibition. The opponents of Prohibition favored a more balanced view of alcohol, conceding its dangers while defending its use in moderation. This perspective, although identified with the more secular side in the Prohibition debate, has strong roots in the Judeo-Christian tradition. Although the drys were more likely to use religious rhetoric, the wets could more plausibly turn to Scripture for inspiration.

The Bible's treatment of alcoholic beverages is worth considering in detail, both because it has been misrepresented by religious opponents of drinking and because it offers a model for thinking about psychoactive substances in general. Wine in the Bible is a symbol of plenty, an offering to God, an accompaniment to celebrations, a source of joy. It is also a cause of humiliation, incest, dissipation, corruption, and ignominious death. On balance, it is a blessing, but one with dangers that can be avoided only by careful attention to dose and context.

The positive biblical references to wine are not hard to find. When Isaac blesses Jacob (believing him to be Esau), he says, "May God give you of the dew of heaven and the fat of the earth, abundance of new grain and wine."[1] The phrase "grain and wine" recurs throughout the Hebrew Bible as a synonym for plenty. When Jacob is an old man, he blesses his son Judah, from whom the Davidic dynasty will descend: "He tethers his ass to a vine, his ass's foal to a choice vine; he washes his garments in wine, his robe in blood of grapes. His eyes are darker than wine; his teeth are whiter than milk."[2] Before they enter Canaan, God promises the Israelites that if they obey His commandments, "I will grant the rain for your land in season. . . . You shall gather in your new grain and wine and oil."[3]

Just as ample stocks of wine appear repeatedly in the Bible's blessings, the loss of wine is a recurrent theme in its curses. Warning the Israelites about the consequences of turning away from Him, God says, "Though you plant vineyards and till them, you shall have no wine to drink or store, for the worm shall devour them."[4] Echoing this prediction, the prophet Amos warns the sinning people of Israel, "You have planted delightful vineyards, but shall not drink their wine."[5] For Isaiah, who sees the Kingdom of Israel defeated by the Assyrians, the enjoyment of alcoholic beverages represents the lost happiness of a conquered people: "The new wine fails, the vine languishes; and all the merry-hearted sigh. Stilled is the merriment of timbrels, ended the clamor of the revelers, stilled the merriment of the lyres. They drink their wine without song; liquor tastes bitter to the drinker. Towns are broken, empty; every house is shut, none enters. Even over wine, a cry goes up in the streets: The sun has set on all joy, the gladness of the earth is banished."[6]

Shechar, the "liquor" mentioned here and elsewhere (also translated as "strong drink"), was not distilled spirits, which probably were not produced until the early Middle Ages. Biblical scholars believe *shechar,* which comes from the same root as the verb meaning "to become drunk," signifies fermented beverages made from raw materials other than grapes, such as dates, pomegranates, and honey. (The drug historian Antonio Escohotada, by contrast, argues that the term refers to "wine or beers loaded with extracts from one or more other drugs."[7]) Grape wine, or *yayin* (sometimes *tirosh*), was a major part of the Hebrew diet, often drunk diluted with water, and a common offering to God, along with oil, grain, and livestock. It was also a component of the incense burned in the Tabernacle and the Temple. Hence wine was one of the Temple's essential supplies, as well as part of the support the Israelites were obligated to give the Priests and the Levites for their personal consumption.[8]

In one of the most striking biblical passages dealing with alcoholic beverages, God commands the Israelites to mark the harvest by consuming "the tithes of your new grain and wine and oil, and the firstlings of your herds and flocks" at the Temple. "Should the distance be too great for you," God says, "should you be unable to transport them, because the place where the Lord your God has chosen to establish His name is far from you and because the Lord your God has blessed you, you may convert them into money. Wrap up the money and take it with you to the place that the Lord your God has chosen, and spend the money on anything you want—cattle, sheep, wine, or other intoxicant, or anything you may desire. And you shall feast there, in the presence of the Lord your God, and rejoice with your household."[9] This ceremony has not been observed since the destruction of the Temple, but it set a precedent for a divinely or-dained combination of worship, celebration, eating, and drinking in which the whole family joins—a familiar aspect of Jewish tradition to this day.

The Hebrew Bible specifically praises the mood-altering effects of alcohol. A parable in Judges has the trees asking the grape vine to be their king. The vine is not interested in the job, saying, "Have I stopped yielding my new wine, which gladdens God and men, that I should go and wave above the trees?"[10] Psalm 104 cites "wine that cheers the hearts of men" as a blessing from God.[11] Proverbs speaks approvingly of alcohol as a comfort to the downtrodden: "Give strong drink to the hapless and wine to the embittered. Let them drink and forget their poverty, and put their troubles out of mind."[12] Wine fig-ures prominently in the poetry of the Bible, perhaps most tellingly in the Song of Songs, where the lovers repeatedly declare that their mu-tual affection is better even than wine.[13]

Muddled and Inflamed

The Hebrew Bible's generally positive attitude toward wine and other intoxicating drinks is by no means unqualified. Indeed, the first reference to wine in the Bible occurs in a story about a drinker who makes a fool of himself. Noah, identified as the first man to plant a vineyard, "drank of the wine and became drunk, and he uncovered himself within his tent." Witnessing this spectacle, his son Ham tells his brothers, Shem and Japheth, who cover their father without looking at him. When he sobers up, Noah blesses them for their discreet assistance and curses Ham for his disrespect.[14] After the destruction of Sodom, Lot's daughters use wine to seduce him: "Thus the two daughters of Lot came to be with child by their father."[15] Another case of alcohol-induced vulnerability involves King David's son Amnon, who is killed by his half-brother Absalom's henchmen when he is "merry with wine."[16]

"Wine is a scoffer, strong drink a roisterer," Proverbs famously warns. "He who is muddled by them will not grow wise." The book, attributed to the wise King Solomon, offers a memorable description of habitual drunkenness that resembles modern portrayals of alcoholism: "Who cries 'Woe!,' who 'Alas!'; who has quarrels, who complaints; who has wounds without cause; who has bleary eyes? Those whom wine keeps till the small hours, those who gather to drain the cups. Do not ogle that red wine as it lends its color to the cup, as it flows on smoothly; in the end it bites like a snake; it spits like a basilisk. Your eyes will see strange sights; your heart will speak distorted things. You will be like one lying in bed on high seas, like one lying on top of the rigging. 'They struck me, but I felt no hurt; they beat me but I was unaware; as often as I wake, I go after it again.'"[17]

Isaiah, too, condemns "those who chase liquor from early in the morning and till late in the evening are inflamed by wine." He ties drinking to corruption and oppression: "Priest and prophet are muddled by liquor; they are confused by wine, they are dazed by liquor; they are muddled in their visions, they stumble in judgment. Yea, all tables are covered with vomit and filth, so that no space is left."[18] Hosea associates drunkenness with rebellion against God: "They did not cry out to Me sincerely as they lay wailing. They debauch over new grain and new wine, they are faithless to me." He chastises the people of Israel, who "turn to other gods and love the cups of the grape."[19]

Given the positive references to wine in Proverbs, Isaiah, and Hosea, these admonitions cannot be understood as blanket condemnations of drinking. Rather, all three books inveigh against excess while acknowledging that alcoholic beverages have a legitimate place in the lives of God-fearing people. Similarly, biblical disapproval of drinking in certain contexts—during prayer, for example, or by the priests before they enter the Tabernacle—does not mean that drinking in general is considered sinful. Quite the contrary: The specification of situations in which drinking is prohibited indicates that it usually is permitted.

This balanced approach to drinking is explicit in The Wisdom of Sirach, a book quoted respectfully by both Jews and Christians (Jews and Protestants consider it part of the Apocrypha, while Roman Catholics include it in their canon). "Wine is like life to men if you drink it in moderation," says the author. "What life has a man who is without wine? For it was created to give gladness to men. An exhilaration to the heart and a gladness to the soul is wine, drunk in the proper time and in sufficient quantity; bitterness to the soul is much drinking of wine, amidst irritation and conflict."[20]

Although the Bible describes individuals (such as Samson) who give up alcoholic beverages as part of a special vow, that option has long been controversial among Jewish scholars, precisely because it involves renouncing a pleasure sanctioned by God. "Are not the things prohibited you in the Law enough for you that you want to prohibit yourself other things?" asked Rabbi Isaac.[21] This Jewish suspicion of the asceticism associated with sects such as the Essenes is also reflected in a famous comment by the Talmudic sage Rav Abba ben

Aivu: "A man will have to give an account on the judgment day of every good permissible thing which he might have enjoyed but did not."[22]

Wine is assuredly "a good permissible thing" according to Jewish tradition. Unique among beverages, it has its own blessing, which thanks God for creating "the fruit of the vine." The Talmud declares, "One in whose house wine does not flow like water is not blessed."[23] It calls wine "the greatest of all medicines," an aid to appetite and digestion that "sustains and makes glad."[24] Rav Huna averred that it "helps open the heart to reasoning."[25] At the same time, the rabbis condemned excessive consumption. A legend they told about Noah encapsulates their attitude: Seeing Noah plant his vineyard, Satan offers to help. He slaughters a lamb, a lion, a pig, and an ape, pouring their blood into the soil. "This signifies," says the legend, "that before a man drinks wine he is simple like a lamb, who doesn't know anything . . . when a man drinks as is customary, he is bold like a lion, saying there is no one like him in the world; when a man drinks too much, he becomes like a swine, peeing on himself; and when he is drunk, he becomes like a monkey, standing and dancing and acting foolishly, and says inappropriate things in front of everyone, for he does not know what he is doing."[26]

Jewish law not only permits but prescribes wine consumption on certain occasions: at circumcisions, at the wedding ceremony and the weeklong celebration that follows it, as part of the evening and morning benedictions (*kiddush*) on the Sabbath and major holidays as well as the *havdalah* prayer marking their end. In accordance with the verse in Proverbs recommending wine for "the embittered," it was once customary to offer mourners a "cup of consolation" after a funeral. During the Passover *seder* Jews are supposed to drink four cups of wine, each containing at least 137 milliliters, or 4.6 fluid ounces.[27]

The total is almost three-quarters of a standard 750-milliliter bottle, enough to make most people tipsy. The Talmud actually recommends intoxication on Purim, a festive holiday that marks the defeat of the Jews' enemy Haman at the hands of Esther and Mordechai: "You should drink until you don't know the difference between 'Cursed is Haman, blessed is Mordechai.'"[28] Celebratory drinking is also customary on Simchat Torah, which marks the completion of the Torah reading cycle.

In modern times the strong association of Judaism with wine has sometimes made Jews uncomfortable. During Prohibition, abuse of the exemption for sacramental wine caused such consternation that the Talmudic scholar Louis Ginzberg issued a controversial interpretation of Jewish law permitting the use of grape juice for ceremonial purposes. In recent decades, heightened awareness of alcohol abuse has led some Jewish leaders to ban drinking from community events where wine and liquor were once taken for granted. A Beverly Hills congregant went so far as to turn in her own syngagogue for serving wine without posting the warnings required by California law.[29]

But Jewish drinking customs ought to be a source of pride, not embarrassment. While abstinence is relatively rare among Jews, so is alcohol abuse. A similar pattern can be observed in other ethnic groups that emphasize responsible drinking, including Greeks and Italians.[30] A culture where alcohol is familiar but respected, where children are taught from an early age that drinking has an appropriate time and place, where self-control is expected and excess is frowned upon, is a culture that tends to inculcate habits of moderation. As a commentary published by an Orthodox Jewish youth group observes, "Judaism demands not the extinction or the suppression of desire; it asks us to regulate, to purify, and to ennoble it. As Jews, we have to sanctify every aspect of our lives and incorporate each one into our service of Hashem [God]. Therefore, we recite a beracha [blessing] before the drinking of wine to bless God, 'the creator of the fruit of the vine,' whereas the others would abstain from alcohol altogether and would condemn it as sinful."[31]

Water Into Wine

These "others" include many Christians, although that attitude is hard to square not only with the Hebrew Bible but also with the New Testament. While some early Christians (like some early Jews) adopted an ascetic lifestyle, 1 Timothy points in a different direction, declaring that "every creature of God is good, and nothing to be refused, if it be received with thanksgiving."[32] And as one scholar notes, "Jesus was no ascetic; he endured, rather, the lying reproach of a glutton and a wine-bibber. . . . If Jesus, like John the Baptist, had not drunk wine, they could not have called him a wine-bibber."[33]

Personal habits aside, wine plays a central role in two miracles performed by Jesus. In the first, he and his mother attend a wedding where the host runs out of wine. Jesus tells the servants to fill six pots with water, which he transforms into wine so good that the groom is accused of holding out on his guests.[34] At the Last Supper, in a gesture imitated by the ritual of communion, Jesus takes a cup of wine, blesses it, and presents it to the apostles, saying, "Drink ye all of it, for this is my blood of the new testament, which is shed for many for the remission of sins. But I say unto you, I will not drink henceforth of this fruit of the vine, until that day when I drink it new with you in my Father's kingdom."[35] Aside from the divine approval implicit in these incidents, the New Testament's clearest endorsement of wine is Paul's advice to Timothy: "Be no longer a drinker of water, but use a little wine for thy stomach's sake and thine often infirmities."[36]

The same book, on the other hand, says deacons should not be "given to much wine," while Titus says "a bishop must be blameless, as the steward of God"—meaning, among other things, that he be "not given to wine."[37] 1 Peter recalls a sinful past, "when we walked in lasciviousness, lusts, excess of wine, revellings, banquetings, and abominable idolatries."[38] Regarding Judgment Day, Jesus warns, "Take heed to yourselves, lest your hearts be weighed down with carousing, drunkenness, and cares of this life, and that Day come on you unexpectedly."[39] And Ephesians recommends communion with God over intoxication: "Be not drunk with wine, wherein is excess, but be filled with the Spirit."[40]

The very concept of excess, of course, implies a corresponding ideal of moderation. It cannot be said that the New Testament sees wine as an unalloyed good, but neither can the plain meaning of the text be reconciled with a total rejection of alcohol.

Recognizing this problem, Christian opponents of drinking have tried to explain away the scriptural endorsement of wine. The nineteenth-century biblical scholar Moses Stuart argued that all the positive mentions of wine in the Hebrew Bible and the New Testament, including the story of the Last Supper, actually refer to grape juice. "Wherever the Scriptures speak of wine as a comfort, a blessing, or a libation to God, and ranks it with such articles as corn or oil, they mean only such wine as contained no alcohol," he wrote. "Wherever they denounce it, prohibit it, and connect it with drunkenness and reveling, they can mean only alcoholic or intoxicating wine."[41] Since unpasteurized grape juice ferments spontaneously, especially in a warm climate, the distinction urged by Stuart would have been hard to maintain. In any event, since biblical passages praising wine refer to its mood-elevating power, tie it to celebrations, pair it with "strong drink," and use the same term (*yayin*) as passages warning about wine's dangers, it is hard to take Stuart's interpretation seriously.

"The attempt to reinterpret Scripture according to the needs of the temperance movement was received with the scorn it deserved," writes Andrew Barr in *Drink: A Social History of America.* "In the opinion of many communicants, such an attack on the plain words of the Bible was tantamount to blasphemy."[42] Largely for this reason, even temperance-minded American churches initially resisted appeals to switch from wine to grape juice for communion, although by the time Prohibition was enacted the Presbyterians, Congregationalists, Methodists, and Baptists had done so. Episcopalians, Lutherans, and Roman Catholics continued to use wine.

Christian teetotalers still attempt the exegetical trick of transforming wine into grape juice. In his book *Wine in the Bible,* Seventh Day Adventist theologian Samuele Bacchiocchi takes an approach similar to Moses Stuart's.[43] A subtler way of reconciling abstinence with the Bible is to emphasize biblical warnings about alcohol while ignoring the positive references. A nineteenth-century temperance pledge, for instance, offered twelve reasons "to abstain from the use of all intoxicating drinks as a beverage," including: "The Bible pronounces no blessing upon drinking, but many upon total abstinence."[44] Likewise, a 1997 sermon circulated by the Southern Baptist Convention in connection with "Alcohol and Drug Abuse Sunday" insisted, despite all the contrary evidence, that "it is biblical to abstain from using alcohol and drugs." Neither the sermon nor a bulletin insert prepared for the same occasion dealt with any of the verses that make such a position so hard to maintain.[45]

The fourth-century archbishop St. John Chrysostom was more in tune with the biblical view when he argued that rejecting wine was a rebuke to God: "Wine is the work of God, but drunkenness is the work of the devil. . . . Do not accuse that which is the workmanship of God, but accuse the madness of a fellow-mortal. Otherwise you . . . are treating your Benefactor with contempt." Chrysostom had little patience for "the simple ones among our brethren" who would abolish drunkenness by abolishing wine. "O folly, O madness!" he said. "When other men sin, do you find fault with God's gifts? . . . If you say, 'Would there were no wine,' you will say, going on by degrees, 'Would there were no steel, because of the murderers; no nights, because of the thieves; no light, because of the informers; no women, because of the adulteries'; and, in a word, you will destroy everything." Like the Hebrew Bible, Chrysostom praised alcohol's mood-altering effects while warning against excessive intoxication: "Wine was given that we might be cheerful, not that we might behave ourselves unseemly; that we might laugh, not that we might be a laughing-stock; that we might be healthy, not that we might be diseased; that we might correct the weakness of our body, not cast down the might of our soul."[46]

St. Augustine, too, was fond of wine, especially when it was properly aged. "Who does not know that wine becomes purer and better with age?" he said. "Nor is it, as you think, more tempting to the destruction of the senses, but rather is it more useful invigorating the body—only let there be moderation, which ought to control everything."[47]

Later Christian leaders likewise viewed alcoholic beverages as a blessing. Martin Luther made his own beer and, according to one biographer, "could even call for a toast when he heard bad news, for, next to a fervent Lord's Prayer and a good heart, there was no better antidote, he used to say, to care."[48] John Calvin noted that "it is permissible to use wine not only for necessity, but also to make us merry." He added two provisos: that drinking be moderate, lest "men forget themselves, drown their senses, and destroy their strength," and that drinkers be grateful to God for His gift.[49] John Wesley, founder of Methodism, condemned the drinking of distilled spirits but spoke favorably of beer and cider as remedies for dropsy and called wine "one of the noblest cordials of nature." In an experiment with asceticism, Wesley gave up wine and meat for two years, stopping because he did not want to create the impression that such abstinence, which "Christianity does not require," was "a point of conscience."[50]

The ancient Greek view of alcohol was similar to the biblical perspective. "The norm," writes Antonio Escohotado, "was to believe that [wine] constituted a 'neutral spirit,' capable of generating good or evil depending on the individual and on the occasion."[51] In his *Laws,* Plato rejected abstinence as a response to the dangers of drinking, instead calling for regulation and supervision by those older and wiser. "Let us not then simply censure the gift of Dionysus as bad and unfit to be received into the State," he said, "for wine has many excellences." He recommended a minimum drinking age of eighteen, after which a man "may taste wine in moderation up to the age of thirty . . . when, at length, he has reached forty years, after dinner at a public mess, he may invite not only the other Gods, but Dionysus above all, to the mystery and festivity of the elder men, making use of the wine which he has given men to lighten the sourness of old age; that in age we may renew our youth, and forget our sorrows."[52]

To use wine in moderation is one species of the virtue Aristotle called *sōphrosunē,* meaning temperance or self-control (also counted by Thomas Aquinas as one of the four cardinal virtues). "The temperate man holds a mean position with regard to pleasures," Aristotle wrote in his *Ethics.* "Such pleasures as conduce to health and bodily fitness he will try to secure in moderation and in the right way; and also all other pleasures that are not incompatible with these, or dishonorable, or beyond his means." In short, "the temperate man desires the right things in the right way and at the right time." Aristotle contrasted temperance with licentiousness, an excessive response to pleasure, but he had trouble defining the other extreme. "Cases of deficiency in respect of pleasures, that is of enjoying them less than one ought, hardly occur," he wrote, "because such insensibility is sub-human."[53]

Sober Mirth

In the American context, temperance acquired a meaning very different from the one Aristotle had in mind, one closer to the vice of "insensibility," which might be better understood as abstemiousness or asceticism. Temperance came to be identified with abstinence because of the fear that alcohol could not be used prudently, that it would inevitably lead to habitual drunkenness. The belief that moderation was impossible ultimately led to the prohibition of alcohol, and the same belief underlies the ongoing prohibition of other drugs.

The American suspicion of alcohol is often described as "puritanical," but this term is somewhat misleading. Historians have long recognized that the popular perception of Puritans as dour and joyless—summed up in H.L. Mencken's often repeated definition of Puritanism as "the haunting fear that someone, somewhere, may be happy"—is oversimplified. As Bruce C. Daniels observes in *Puritans at Play*, Puritan leaders acknowledged the need for leisure and recreation, while insisting that they be contained within appropriate limits. Daniels argues that the Puritan attitude toward pleasure is more accurately characterized as ambivalence rather than hostility.[54]

This ambivalence is reflected in the Puritan concept of "sober mirth," which requires God-fearing people always to be vigilant lest fun degenerate into sin. The dividing line between the two was often fuzzy, so it would not be surprising if people imbued with such ideas felt anxious about enjoying themselves too much. "It may be reasonable to argue that a vague American uneasiness with excessive pleasure-seeking has roots in the Puritan past," Daniels concludes, "but, if so, it should be added that the unease has additional roots in most parts of Christendom and that Christians everywhere in the world are uncomfortable with immoderate social behavior."[55]

However constrained the Puritan idea of fun may have been, it did not exclude drinking. The Puritans—who, like most Englishmen, were leery of water as a beverage—brought beer with them on the *Mayflower* and started brewing their own within a few years; they also drank hard cider, wine, brandy, and rum. In colonial New England, settlers of all ages and both sexes drank alcoholic beverages throughout the day, and taverns ("ordinaries") were commonplace. At the same time, public drunkenness was not only condemned but punished by both the church and the civil authorities.

While condoning moderate drinking, Increase Mather's 1673 book *Wo to Drunkards* illustrates the Puritan fear that pleasurable activities could lead to depravity if they were not carefully controlled. "Drink is in itself a good Creature of God, & to be received with thankfulness," Mather wrote, "but the abuse of drink is from Satan: The Wine is from God, but the Drunkard is from the Devil." This formulation harks back to 1 Timothy and the writings of St. John Chrysostom. On its face, Mather's idea of temperance resembles Aristotle's: "As he that eateth more than is good for him, is guilty of the sin of Gluttony, so he that drinketh to any excess is justly charged with Drunkenness."[56] Just as starvation is not the only alternative to gluttony, abstinence is not the only alternative to drunkenness. In both cases, moderation is the key.

When it came to defining the point at which drinking becomes excessive, Mather was rather vague. He was not concerned just with "drunkenness in the sight of Man," which he said occurs "when a man is so overcome with wine, as that he can neither speak nor act like a rational Creature, when Reason is disturbed thereby, & Sense & Speech & Motion fail, when neither the Head nor Hand can do their Offices aright." He also condemned drunkenness that might not be recognized by others, or perhaps even by the drinker himself: "If there be an inordinate affection or love to strong drink, that's Drunkenness in the sight of Him that trieth the Reins and searcheth the Hearts." Under this standard, God knows when love for drink becomes inordinate, but mortals can't be sure.[57]

The puzzle is especially perplexing because Mather was not worried only about the practical consequences of drunkenness. These were troubling enough, to be sure. They included the waste of time and money, which could lead to poverty; diseases such as "Dropsies, Consumptions, Fevers, Gouts, [and] Apoplexies"; and bad habits such as lying, swearing, scoffing, indecency, blasphemy, and fighting.

But Mather also saw drunkenness as a sin in itself, apart from its consequences. "One may be Drunken, that is not a Drunkard; and one may be a Drunkard, that is seldom Drunken," he wrote. "He that abhors the Sin of Drunkenness, yet may be overtaken with it, and so Drunken; but that one Act is not enough to denominate him a Drunkard: And he that loveth to drink Wine to excess, tho' he should seldom be overcome thereby, is one of those Drunkards."[58] Someone who rarely was visibly drunk, and who suffered no obvious ill effects from drinking, could still be guilty of drunkenness, putting his immortal soul in peril. So while Puritan teaching did not require abstinence, the lack of clear guidelines to define the limits of moderation did encourage a certain anxiety about intoxication.

Colonial Americans nevertheless consumed a prodigious amount of alcohol by contemporary standards. Because it was customary to drink in the morning, afternoon, and evening, with meals and during work, on the road and at home, most people were probably at least a little buzzed for much of the day. In the late eighteenth century per capita consumption in the United States was something like six gallons of absolute alcohol a year, compared to about two gallons at the end of the twentieth century.[59] Despite the large quantities consumed, alcohol problems were relatively rare, to judge by official records and the lack of a strong public outcry. Historians Mark Edward Lender and James Kirby Martin argue that the close-knit communities of colonial America, which emphasized obedience, conformity, and mutual responsibility, kept drinking in check. In addition to fines, jail, the stocks, and the lash, habitual drunkards risked ostracism by their neighbors, condemnation by their leaders, and expulsion from church.

After the American Revolution, social and economic changes simultaneously loosened these constraints, created anxieties that encouraged people to drink more, and made drinking throughout the day (especially at work) more problematic. Per capita alcohol consumption rose from 5.8 gallons in 1790 to a peak of 7.1 gallons in 1830.[60] This trend, combined with a shift from cider and beer to distilled spirits, provoked the concerns that gave rise to the temperance movement.

In its beginnings the temperance movement, as the name implies, was neither abstinence-oriented nor prohibitionist. Its intellectual father, the Philadelphia physician Benjamin Rush, decried habitual drunkenness, which he called "an odious disease." But he distinguished between distilled spirits, which he believed led to ruin, and naturally fermented beverages, such as beer, cider, and wine, which he was confident could be consumed in moderation. "Fermented liquors contain so little spirit, and that so intimately combined with other matters, that they can seldom be drunken in sufficient quantities to produce intoxication, and its subsequent effects, without exciting a disrelish to their taste, or pain, from their distending the stomach," he wrote in his 1784 book *An Inquiry Into the Effects of Ardent Spirits Upon the Human Body and Mind*. "They are, moreover, when taken in a moderate quantity, generally innocent, and often have a friendly influence upon health and life."[61]

Not so with more concentrated alcoholic beverages. The habitual use of these, Rush said, causes rashes, bad breath, "frequent and disgusting belchings," loss of appetite, gastrointestinal ailments, "obstructions of the liver," lung diseases, diabetes, jaundice, dropsy, gout, epilepsy, and madness. He added that distilled spirits "impair the memory, debilitate the understanding, and pervert the moral faculties," leading to "not only falsehood, but fraud, theft, uncleanliness, and murder." What's more, they dissipate the drinker's property through tavern debts and idleness. In short, "poverty and misery, crimes and infamy, diseases and death, are all the natural and usual consequences of the intemperate use of ardent spirits."[62]

Rush sought to debunk three commonly held beliefs about the benefits of distilled spirits. He noted that they provide only temporary warmth in cold weather and actually increase the risk of hypothermia; that they likewise "increase, instead of lessening, the effects of heat"; and that they do not "lessen the effects of hard labour upon the body" (although they might make those effects easier for the worker to bear). He also warned against "the seducing influence of toddy and grog"—sweetened combinations of liquor and water. "No man ever became suddenly a drunkard," he wrote. "It is by gradually accustoming the taste and stomach to ardent spirits, in the forms of grog and toddy, that men have been led to love them in their more destructive mixtures and in their simple state."[63]

In response to the problems caused by alcohol abuse, Rush recommended both religious exhortation and a variety of civil measures: heavy taxes on distilled spirits, limits on the number of taverns, "a mark of disgrace, or a temporary abridgement of some civil right" for any man convicted of drunkenness, and oversight of the habitual drunkard's property by court-appointed trustees. At the same time, he urged compassion for the drunkard, despite his role in creating his own predicament, and depicted habitual intoxication more as an illness than as a sin. "It belongs to the history of drunkenness to remark, that its paroxysms occur, like the paroxysms of many diseases, at certain periods, and after longer or shorter intervals," he wrote. "They often begin with annual, and gradually increase in their frequency, until they appear in quarterly, monthly, weekly, and quotidian or daily periods. . . . It is further remarkable, that drunkenness resembles certain hereditary, family and contagious diseases."[64] Elsewhere he remarked: "The use of strong drink is at first the effect of free agency. From habit it takes place from necessity."[65]

Rush thus anticipated the modern view of alcoholism as a progressive illness, possibly inherited, in which the drinker gradually loses control of his drinking. This represented an important shift from the traditional view of drunkenness as a sinful choice, reflected in Congregationalist theologian Jonathan Edwards's 1754 book *Freedom of the Will*. "It cannot truly be said, according to the ordinary use of language," Edwards wrote, "that a drunkard, let his appetite be never so strong, cannot keep the cup from his mouth."[66] Increase Mather had likewise described intemperance not as an uncontrollable compulsion but as "an inordinate affection or love" for liquor. And whereas Mather did not rule out the possibility that the drunkard could return to moderation, Rush prescribed the same cure urged by Alcoholics Anonymous: "Persons who have been addicted to [spirits] should abstain from them *suddenly* and *entirely*," he wrote. "'Taste not, handle not, touch not,' should be inscribed upon every vessel that contains spirits in the house of a man, who wishes to be cured of habits of intemperance."[67]

Triumph of the Teetotalers

Although Rush's ideas, including the disease concept, had a powerful influence on the temperance movement, it eventually abandoned his distinction between distilled spirits and fermented beverages. During the first few decades of the nineteenth century, it was not hard to find temperance advocates who themselves drank wine or other relatively weak alcoholic beverages. They saw no inconsistency in this, since their drinking was temperate. But that posture became increasingly controversial, and in 1836 the American Temperance Society officially endorsed total abstinence as the only safe alternative to drunkenness. Temperance activists became convinced that alcohol was too powerful a drug for moderation to be possible over the long term. As the sociologist Harry G. Levine notes, "the idea that drugs are inherently addicting was first systematically worked out for alcohol and then extended to other substances. Long before opium was popularly accepted as addicting, alcohol was so regarded."[68]

The Presbyterian minister Lyman Beecher was an early advocate of the hard line against all forms of alcohol that would eventually characterize the temperance movement. In his *Six Sermons on the Nature, Occasions, Signs, Evils, and Remedy of Intemperance*, first published in 1826, Beecher combined the moral and medical views of alcohol abuse: "Intemperance is a disease as well as a crime, and were any other disease as contagious, of as marked symptoms, and as mortal, to pervade the land, it would create universal consternation; for the plague is scarcely more contagious or deadly; and yet we mingle fearlessly with the diseased, and in spite of admonition we bring into our dwellings the contagion, apply it to the lip, and receive it into the system."[69] This plague metaphor, which justifies coercive control of "carriers" without precluding sympathy for them, remains a familiar theme of public discussions about drugs.

Although Beecher's main concern was originally distilled spirits, he added an important note to subsequent editions of his *Six Sermons*: "When the following discourses were written, alcohol in the form of ardent spirits, so called at that day, was the most common intoxicating beverage in use. But as the poison in every form is the same, the argument against this form applies alike to every form."

This clarification pointed the way to complete abstinence, because Beecher had nothing but contempt for the notion of prudent liquor consumption. "We might as well speak of the prudent use of the plague—of fire handed prudently around among powder—of poison taken prudently every day—or of vipers and serpents introduced prudently into our dwellings," he wrote. "First or last, in spite of your prudence, the contagion will take—the fatal spark will fall upon the train—the deleterious poison will tell upon the system—and the fang of the serpent will inflict death." Beecher conceded that "all who receive [liquor] into the system are not destroyed by it," but he insisted that the danger was so great that "no man can use it prudently."[70]

In depicting intemperance as the norm, Beecher, like Increase Mather, broadened the category to include imbibers who would not ordinarily be accused of drunkenness. In addition to warning that apparently moderate drinking could have subtle or long-term effects on health that observers might not attribute to alcohol, he agreed with Mather that intemperance could consist of nothing more than "inordinate desire"—an elusive concept when it is divorced from measurable harms. He went further, condemning nearly every socially accepted pattern of drinking. Thus, "all such occasional exhilaration of the spirits by intoxicating liquors as produces levity and foolish jesting and the loud laugh, is intemperance." So is "a resort to ardent spirits as a means of invigorating the intellect, or of pleasurable sensation." Likewise "the daily use of ardent spirits, in any form or in any degree." (Indeed, Beecher declared that "habitual tippling is worse than periodical drunkenness.") In short, "There is no prudent use of ardent spirits, but when it is used as a medicine."[71]

This view, which resembles contemporary attitudes toward narcotics and other controlled substances, was based mainly on the danger of addiction, with its dire physical, financial, and moral consequences. "When we consider the deceitful nature of this sin, and its irresistible power when it has obtained an ascendancy, no man can use it prudently, or without mocking God can pray while he uses it, 'lead us not into temptation,'" Beecher wrote. "There is no necessity for using it at all, and it is presumptuous to do so." But he also took a dim view of using alcohol to alter one's consciousness, whatever the practical consequences. "God has made the human body to be sustained by food and sleep, and the mind to be invigorated by effort and regular healthfulness of the moral system, and the cheering influence of his moral government," he wrote. "And whoever, to sustain the body, or invigorate the mind, or cheer the heart, applies habitually the stimulus of ardent spirits, does violence to the laws of his nature, puts the whole system into disorder, and is intemperate long before the intellect falters or a muscle is unstrung."[72]

Having concluded that using alcohol for nonmedicinal purposes is both wrong and unacceptably dangerous, Beecher advocated a solution that was appropriately sweeping: "What then is [the] universal, natural, and national remedy for intemperance? IT IS THE BANISHMENT OF ARDENT SPIRITS FROM THE LIST OF LAWFUL ARTICLES OF COMMERCE, BY A CORRECT AND EFFICIENT PUBLIC SENTIMENT; SUCH AS HAS TURNED SLAVERY OUT OF HALF OUR LAND, AND WILL YET EXPEL IT FROM THE WORLD. . . . Like slavery, [the liquor trade] must be regarded as sinful, impolitic, and dishonorable. That no measures will avail short of rendering ardent spirits a contraband of trade, is nearly self-evident."[73]

Within a decade, the temperance movement had officially adopted Beecher's view of alcohol, and soon it was pushing his remedy. The first statewide ban on the sale of alcoholic beverages was adopted by Maine in 1851, and during the next four years twelve other states followed suit. But these victories, which seemed to portend a dry future for the nation, turned out to be the zenith of prohibitionist success in the antebellum period. In the face of resistance from drinkers and the liquor industry, smuggling from other states, and the distractions of the slavery issue and the impending Civil War, the prohibition laws were soon repealed or ignored, and no more would be passed until the 1880s.

Where coercion failed, however, moral suasion seemed to have a dramatic impact. Between 1830 and 1840, before any of the prohibition laws were passed, per capita alcohol consumption fell from about seven gallons a year to about three—the largest ten-year drop in U.S. history. The decline continued until the late nineteenth century, with annual per capita consumption dipping below two gallons in the 1870s. After that it went up slightly, but it has been less than three gallons ever since.[74] Industrialization, urbanization, and the accompanying shift to occupations that were less compatible with frequent drinking had much to do with this trend, but so did the exhortations of the temperance movement. While voluntary societies, such as the Washingtonians, helped drunkards straighten out their lives, millions of Americans publicly pledged to abstain either from distilled spirits or from all alcoholic beverages.

Dry Spell

Many people came to accept Beecher's argument that the only sensible way to avoid intemperance was to avoid alcohol altogether. A nineteenth-century "Family Temperance Pledge," intended for posting in the home, warned that "the idea of moderation is full of deceit, and our estimate of the power of our own will is usually mistaken. . . . Persons miscalculate their ability to drink in moderation, and become slaves to the drinking habit before they are aware of it."[75] An 1846 Nathaniel Currier print, *The Drunkard's Progress From the First Glass to the Grave,* depicted this enslavement process as steps up and down a bridge, beginning with "Step 1: A Glass with a Friend" and ending with "Step 6: Poverty and Disease," "Step 7: Forsaken by Friends," "Step 8: Desperation and Crime," and "Step 9: Death by Suicide." Under the bridge were the drunkard's abandoned wife and child.

The same basic message was elaborated upon in a genre of cautionary literature called "temperance tales." Perhaps the best-known of these is Timothy Shay Arthur's *Ten Nights in a Bar-Room,* which dramatizes the corrupting influence of a small-town tavern. After opening the Sickle and Sheaf, Simon Slade, once a friendly and popular miller, is transformed into a hard-hearted, violent drunk. During an argument with Joe Morgan, a former friend who blames the tavern keeper for turning him into a drunken ne'er-do-well, Slade hurls a tumbler at him. The glass instead strikes Morgan's angelic daughter, Mary, who has come, as usual, to guide her inebriated father home. The little girl eventually dies from the blow to her head, and on her deathbed her father promises that he will never touch a drop of liquor again.

Meanwhile, under the sway of the Sickle and Sheaf, the town's promising young men stop listening to their parents and turn to drinking, idleness, vulgar talk, and gambling. After frittering away his family's fortune, a judge's son is stabbed to death during a poker dispute, whereupon his mother drops dead from the shock. Slade, who loses an eye in a barroom brawl, is eventually killed by his own son, who hurls a liquor bottle at him during a drunken squabble. His wife, her nerves shattered by this series of alcohol-related disasters, ends up in a mental asylum, tended by her loyal daughter.

Published in 1854, *Ten Nights in a Bar-Room* is a thinly disguised polemic in favor of Maine-style prohibition laws. The female characters, who view the tavern with concern from the beginning, watch with dismay as their worst fears come true. The narrator, a strangely omniscient traveler who reports on scenes he has not witnessed, likewise knows that the opening of the tavern can mean only ruin for the town. Toward the end, Joe Morgan and other reformed drinkers unite with concerned parents to campaign for a liquor ban.

Although anti-alcohol activism crested soon after *Ten Nights in a Bar-Room* appeared, the novel's themes—in particular, the threat that taverns posed to family life and social stability, a menace to which women were especially sensitive—figured prominently in the revived temperance movement of the late nineteenth and early twentieth centuries. The Woman's Christian Temperance Union, founded in 1874, campaigned for anti-alcohol measures at the local, state, and national level under the banner of "home protection." The Anti-Saloon League, an Ohio temperance group that became a national organization in 1895, emphasized the antisocial side of the seemingly convivial places where men gathered to drink. The ASL, which described itself as "the church in action against the saloon," had strong ties to several Protestant denominations. The Methodist, Baptist, Presbyterian, and Congregationalist churches raised money for the league, selected its trustees, and urged their congregants to support anti-alcohol legislation.

Roman Catholics, whose church sanctioned moderate drinking, were much less likely to support the crackdown on alcohol. Indeed,

Prohibition has often been viewed as a cultural conflict between rural Protestants and urban Catholics, many of them recent immigrants. Support for the temperance movement certainly was reinforced by suspicion of, if not outright hostility toward, immigrants whose cultures accepted alcohol. These included Eastern European Jews and German Protestants as well as Catholics from countries such as Ireland and Italy. For their part, the immigrants were puzzled and irked by the black-and-white views of the so-called temperance movement. "For many immigrants," writes historian Thomas R. Pegram, "prohibition revealed a strain of American fanaticism that dismissed the moderating influences of tradition, family and individual self-control and insisted on the humiliating restrictions of legal compulsion. Such feelings prompted [an] Iowa German in 1887 to complain that 'a few *fanatics* who indicate that they themselves don't have the moral backbone to look at a glass of beer, or pass a saloon without getting drunk, come along and tell me that I am incapable of behaving myself or keeping sober, and so they propose to take care of me by law.'"[76]

Ultimately, the "fanatics"—who misrepresented the Judeo-Christian tradition, arguing that Scripture showed God was against drinking—prevailed over the advocates of moderation, whose views were much closer to those expressed in the Hebrew Bible and the New Testament. The Eighteenth Amendment, which prohibited "the manufacture, sale, or transportation of intoxicating liquors . . . for beverage purposes," was ratified in 1919. In a concession to wet sentiment, neither the amendment nor the legislation implementing it prohibited consumption or mere possession; those who could afford it were free to stock up on liquor and wine before Prohibition took effect (one year after ratification) and continue drinking legally until their supplies ran out. Furthermore, the Volstead Act specifically exempted the manufacture of "nonintoxicating cider and fruit juice exclusively for use in the home." Since the exemption would be unnecessary if *nonintoxicating* meant nonalcoholic, this provision was widely interpreted as allowing people to make hard cider and wine (though not beer) at home for personal consumption. The law also permitted production and sale of alcohol for religious, medicinal, and industrial purposes. And although the Volstead Act ostensibly prohibited possession "except as authorized," the courts did not apply the law to drinkers. Prohibition thus was considerably more liberal than current drug laws, which impose penalties for simple possession even in states that have "decriminalized" marijuana.

On the face of it, Prohibition appears to have reduced alcohol consumption substantially, especially in the early years. Based on four measures (cirrhosis, alcoholism deaths, arrests for drunkenness, and alcoholic psychoses), economists Jeffrey Miron and Jeffrey Zwiebel estimated that consumption dropped 60 to 80 percent immediately after Prohibition was enacted, then rebounded sharply beginning in 1921. By the end of the decade, consumption was 50 to 70 percent of the pre-Prohibition level according to three measures and slightly higher according to one. Drinking did not rise precipitously after repeal. Alcohol consumption in the late 1930s was about the same as in the final years of Prohibition; it returned to the pre-Prohibition level during the next decade.[77] There remains the question of how important a role Prohibition itself played in these trends. In a subsequent analysis that took additional factors into account, including World War I, changes in the age structure of the population, and the lag between drinking and the development of cirrhosis, Miron concluded that "Prohibition exerted a modest and possibly even a positive effect on the consumption of alcohol."[78]

That conclusion jibes with the impressions of many Prohibition critics, who complained that it was not only ineffective but actually made alcohol more attractive, especially to young people, by turning it into a forbidden fruit. More generally, advocates of repeal worried that Prohibition was undermining respect for the law by fostering widespread disobedience, official corruption, and rebellion by jurors who refused to convict defendants charged with manufacture and trafficking. They were also troubled by the invasions of privacy that accompanied searches for contraband liquor, the conspicuous violence that characterized the illicit liquor trade, and the casualties from adulterated alcohol, which one senator called "legalized murder."[79] (The government required that industrial alcohol be poisoned, typically with methanol, to discourage diversion; if bootleggers did not thoroughly remove the adulterant, it could cause blindness, paralysis, or death.) But these considerations probably would not have been decisive were it not for the widespread feeling that the government was trying to punish people for innocent behavior that harmed no one. H.L. Mencken observed that "the national government is trying to enforce a law which, in the opinion of millions of otherwise docile citizens, invades their inalienable rights, and they accordingly refuse to obey it."[80]

Supporters of Prohibition batted this argument aside. "The selfish man may feel that the prohibition law is an invasion of his personal rights," said a 1926 Methodist textbook, "but how does his personal liberty to drink affect his wife and children, not to speak of the wives and children of his neighbors? How does it affect the right of the community to be free from disorder? How does his selfishness affect your right to conditions which conduce to health and prosperity?" Just as today's prohibitionists assume that all drug use harms innocents, the prohibitionists of the 1920s implied that all drinking was accompanied by negative side effects. Irresponsible behavior was to be expected, because most people could not resist the power of this drug. "The cause of alcoholism is alcohol," the Methodists declared. "Its habitual use is likely to induce an uncontrollable desire for more in ever-increasing quantities."[81]

Such assertions flew in the face of too many people's experiences to be accepted for long as a basis for public policy. What prohibitionists took to be the norm among drinkers was in fact the exception. The repeal of Prohibition in 1933 was a decisive rejection of the idea that people cannot be trusted to drink responsibly.

Loss of Control

Prohibition's supporters implied that drink was so strong that it could corrupt any man's morals, making him unproductive, neglectful, and violent. Such thinking persists in some religious communities (among Southern Baptists and Seventh Day Adventists, for example) and even among ostensibly secular and scientific "public health" activists. By and large, however, Americans do not believe that alcohol has the transformative powers that were once attributed to it.

But if alcohol is not the cause of alcoholism, what is? In the wake of Prohibition, Alcoholics Anonymous popularized the view that *some* people are unable to drink moderately, and *for them* the only solution is abstinence. A.A. retained the idea, first suggested by Benjamin Rush, that alcoholism is a disease characterized by loss of control, but it rejected the notion that anyone who drinks can become an alcoholic. Although A.A.'s members see their condition as a disease, the organization's approach is not medical but religious, with six of its "12 Steps" referring to God.

The meaning of this new disease model, which today is widely accepted, has always been murky. What sort of disease is alcoholism? A metabolic defect? A brain disorder? Is it inherited, acquired, or both? How can the permanent disability known as alcoholism be distinguished, before the fact, from a passing phase of heavy drinking? How can a disease be treated through programs that aim primarily to change people's beliefs (in particular, by getting them to accept the disease model itself)?

To the extent that the disease model of alcoholism makes falsifiable predictions, it is not supported by the evidence. Alcoholics in experimental situations control their drinking in response to incentives, and their behavior often hinges not on whether they have consumed alcohol but on whether they think they have. In real life, too, alcoholics go through periods of heavy and light drinking; they drink moderately on some occasions and heavily on others. Follow-up studies that track alcoholics who have undergone treatment find that substantial percentages are able to drink moderately rather than abstaining. All of these findings contradict the idea that alcoholics cannot control their own behavior—as does the expectation that they can stop drinking through programs such as A.A.[82]

Whatever its conceptual and empirical flaws, the contemporary disease model shifted the focus from drinkers in general to the small minority whose drinking causes serious, ongoing problems. It thus helped rehabilitate the ideal of moderate drinking. Nowadays, researchers estimate that roughly 10 percent of drinkers are alcoholics; another 5 percent or so have experienced at least one "severe or moderately severe consequence of alcohol abuse" (such as illness, job loss, or arrest) in the last year.[83] The rest—an overwhelming majority—generally drink moderately and responsibly.

Although this basic picture is widely recognized, government policies in the United States display a lingering anti-alcohol bias. The general approach is based on a "control of availability" model, which seeks to curtail abuse by reducing overall consumption. The model hinges on the controversial premise that alcohol-related costs (including the problems created both by alcoholics and by occasionally negligent moderate drinkers) are a direct function of total drinking.[84] Advocates of this approach support higher taxes, limits on advertising, and restrictions on the place and time of sale to discourage alcohol consumption. Such measures have roots in the period immediately following the repeal of Prohibition, when the Twenty-first Amendment gave states special authority to control alcoholic beverages, even if that meant obstructing interstate commerce. The availability of alcoholic beverages varies widely across the country, from continued prohibition in some Southern counties to twenty-four-hour service in Nevada. But almost every jurisdiction imposes restrictions—such as Sunday closing laws, last calls, licensing rules, and state monopolies—aimed at making alcohol harder to obtain. Like Prohibition, such restrictions penalize and inconvenience the responsible majority in the hope of deterring a troublesome minority. The explicitly moral rhetoric of the Woman's Christian Temperance Union and the Anti-Saloon League has given way to scientific-sounding talk about "the public health," but the underlying approach is similar. Questions of fairness aside, the broad attack on drinking in general that frequently receives government support blurs the distinctions at the heart of true temperance and undermines the social forces that promote moderation.

Federal regulation of alcohol labeling illustrates the continuing influence of prohibitionist thinking. The Bureau of Alcohol, Tobacco, and Firearms has long taken a dim view of attempts by winemakers to publicize the substantial body of scientific evidence that moderate alcohol consumption reduces the risk of heart disease. The incidence of coronary artery disease is 30 percent to 50 percent lower among moderate drinkers than it is among abstainers. The difference has been found in diverse populations and among both men and women. For men, moderate drinking (under three drinks a day) is associated with a reduction in overall mortality of up to 10 percent. Alcohol's impact on high-density lipoprotein, which protects against cardiovascular disease, is considered the most plausible explanation for the health benefits of moderate drinking.[85] Although these findings have been covered in the general press, the BATF has censored references to the research on neck-hangers attached to wine bottles and even in a winery's newsletter. In 1999, after resisting industry proposals for seven years, the bureau finally approved two mild suggestions. One tells consumers to consult their doctors for information about "the health effects of wine consumption"; the other recommends that they "send for the federal government's *Dietary Guidelines for Americans.*"

Those who bother to send away for the guidelines, produced jointly by the Department of Agriculture and the Department of Health and Human Services, may be puzzled by the industry's eagerness to publicize them. "If you drink alcoholic beverages," a headline warns, "do so in moderation" (defined as no more than two drinks a day for men, one for women). The rest of the section consists almost entirely of reasons not to drink: "Alcoholic beverages supply calories but few or no nutrients." They are "harmful when consumed in excess." Too much alcohol "alters judgment and can lead to dependency and a great many other serious health problems." Heavy drinking, we are told, raises "the risk for motor vehicle crashes, other injuries, high blood pressure, stroke, violence, suicide, and certain types of cancer." It may lead indirectly to malnutrition, and it can cause "social and psychological problems, cirrhosis of the liver, inflammation of the pancreas, and damage to the brain and heart." Lest you think that moderate drinkers need not worry, "even one drink per day can slightly raise the risk of breast cancer," and "alcohol consumption during pregnancy increases the risk of birth defects." The pamphlet also lists people who "should not drink alcoholic beverages at all." These include alcoholics, children and adolescents, "women who may become pregnant or who are pregnant," people using prescription drugs, and "individuals who plan to drive, operate machinery, or take part in activities that require attention, skill, or coordination."[86]

Amid all these warnings, there is one positive statement. The pamphlet acknowledges that "drinking in moderation may lower risk for coronary heart disease, mainly among men over age 45 and women under age 55."[87] Tepid as this concession is, its inclusion in the 1995 version of the dietary guidelines (where it read, "current evidence suggests that moderate drinking is associated with a lower risk for coronary heart disease in some individuals") was highly controversial. The 1990 version had asserted that "drinking has no net health benefit." The change was partly due to additional evidence, but it also reflected a shift in attitude. "There was a significant bias in the past against drinking," said Philip Lee, then an assistant secretary at HHS. Marion Nestle, a New York University nutritionist who served on the committee that wrote the guidelines, declared that the new alcohol language represented "a triumph of science and reason over politics."[88]

Although the label statements approved by the BATF merely refer consumers to their doctors or the government for advice about drinking, critics of the industry were incensed by the bureau's decision. The National Council on Alcoholism called it "potentially disastrous," while Senator Strom Thurmond threatened to introduce legislation that would transfer the BATF's jurisdiction over alcohol to the Food and Drug Administration.[89] Since it is doubtful that the plug for the dietary guidelines will have much of an impact on alcohol consumption (a survey commissioned by HHS found that only 3 percent of wine buyers thought it would encourage them to drink more), these extreme reactions are hard to fathom. They represent the sort of absolutism that came to dominate the temperance movement when it began insisting on abstinence—an attitude that left no room for the possibility that alcohol might have a positive side.

Zero Tolerance

While the federal government still does not allow any explicit reference to health benefits on alcohol labels, since 1989 every bottle of beer, wine, and liquor sold in the United States has carried a surgeon general's warning. In addition to noting that "consumption of alcoholic beverages impairs your ability to drive a car or operate machinery" and "may cause health problems," the warning offers a more controversial piece of advice: "Women should not drink alcoholic beverages during pregnancy because of the risk of birth defects." This stricture has gained enough popularity in the United States, thanks in no small part to the government's warning label, that pregnant women who have a drink at a party or in a restaurant are apt to attract dirty looks and rude questions.

Yet the scientific basis for abstaining from alcohol during pregnancy is weak. Fetal alcohol syndrome, which results in facial deformities and mental retardation, has been observed only in the babies of women who drank heavily during pregnancy. "Recent studies reaffirm the finding that FAS is a danger only to women who are chronic excessive drinkers," writes Morris Chafetz, founding director of the federal government's National Institute on Alcohol Abuse and Alcoholism.[90] Although some researchers worry about the possibility of subtler effects at lower levels of consumption, there is little evidence that light to moderate consumption (up to two drinks a day) causes the fetus any harm.[91] Some physicians recommend that pregnant women err on the side of caution by abstaining, but many others see nothing wrong with an occasional drink. This is especially true in European countries, such as Italy and France, where it is common for women to drink moderately throughout pregnancy, with no discernible effect on the rate of birth defects.[92] Given these facts, it is hard to escape the conclusion that the no-alcohol-during-pregnancy orthodoxy is another reflection of American ambivalence regarding drinking.

The government warning about driving under the influence of alcohol has a more solid empirical basis: Drinking demonstrably affects one's ability to operate a motor vehicle, and driving while intoxicated poses a clear threat to other people's lives and property. But even here there is an element of exaggeration that encourages a policy of zero tolerance. The National Highway Traffic Safety Administation considers an accident "alcohol-related" if either a driver or a nonoccupant (a bicyclist or pedestrian) had a blood alcohol concentration of 0.01 percent or more. This is about the level a 175-pound man could expect an hour after drinking a pint of beer. Until recently, most states defined legal intoxication as a BAC of 0.10 percent or more. By this standard, 78 percent of the 15,786 "alcohol-related fatalities" counted by NHTSA in 1999 involved intoxicated drivers, pedestrians, or bicyclists, and 70 percent of the people who died were themselves intoxicated. (In other words, at least 70 percent of the fatalities did not involve innocent bystanders, which runs contrary to the popular image of alcohol-related accidents.)

The higher a driver's BAC, the more reasonable it is to assume that alcohol contributed to the accident. But this is always an assumption, since NHTSA's numbers do not rely on any evidence other than alcohol in the blood. Similarly, state laws treat a driver's BAC as definitive proof that he was intoxicated, although people's ability to perform tasks at a given BAC varies widely. This point was one of the issues in the debate over federal legislation approved in 2000 that threatens to withhold highway money from states that don't adopt a DWI standard of 0.08 percent. Laboratory studies indicate that most people are significantly impaired at that level, but some drinkers are not. In any case, it is probably a waste of law-enforcement resources to focus on drivers at the margin. NHTSA's data indicate that more than three-quarters of the drivers in fatal alcohol-related crashes have BACs of 0.10 or more, with 62 percent above 0.14. The average BAC for fatally injured drunk drivers is a whopping 0.18 percent, the sort of level a 175-pound man could expect to reach after drinking five martinis in an hour.

The lower the BAC level, the less sense it makes to rely on NHTSA's fatality statistics in deciding how to define intoxication. Arguing for a national DWI standard of 0.08 percent, Mothers Against Drunk Driving said "nearly one quarter (3,732) of the 17,126 alcohol-related traffic deaths in 1996 involved drivers with BAC levels below .10," and "MADD thinks that's a problem worth solving." Yet three-quarters of those fatalities involved drivers with BACs below

0.08. This may simply be an artifact of NHTSA's decision to define "alcohol-related" so broadly: If you happen to get into an accident after drinking a beer, the crash is "alcohol-related" by definition, even if alcohol had nothing to do with it. But by MADD's logic, it should be illegal to drive after drinking any quantity of alcohol—a position the organization officially rejects.

Whatever the legal cutoff is, it is unfair to treat drivers who are barely above it the same as those who far exceed it, which is how the law works in most states. This all-or-nothing approach seems especially unreasonable when you consider that drivers with relatively low BACs may be no more of a menace than drivers who are impaired in perfectly legal ways. One study found that drivers with mobile telephones were four times as likely to get into accidents when using the phones, a risk comparable to that faced by drivers with a 0.10 BAC.[93] (The study did not determine whether the drivers were at fault, and it could not rule out the possibility that using a phone and getting into a crash were both associated with some other factor, such as being lost or emotionally upset.) Driving while talking to a passenger, putting on makeup, eating a hamburger, or suffering from a cold may be comparably dangerous. NHTSA estimates that simple fatigue results in more than 100,000 crashes a year.[94] "Even though sleep deprivation and alcohol intoxication are largely voluntary and self-imposed conditions that can be equally impairing," notes sleep researcher William C. Dement, "the public attitude toward them is quite different."[95] The same could be said for driving under the influence of over-the-counter antihistamines such as Benadryl, which can be more dangerous than driving while legally intoxicated.[96]

Even when the law addresses other forms of impairment, the penalties are not nearly as stiff. In New York, which in 2001 became the first state to ban the use of handheld telephones while driving, the maximum penalty is a $100 fine. By contrast, first offenders convicted of "driving while intoxicated" (i.e., with a BAC of 0.08 or more) are hit with a fine of $500 to $1,000, lose their licenses for at least six months, and can go to jail for up to a year. (In New York City, they can also lose their cars through civil forfeiture.) Other factors that affect one's ability to drive clearly do not inspire anything like the moral outrage generated by driving under the influence of alcohol. The disparity suggests that people are troubled not just by impairment but also by intoxication itself. The federal government's sweeping definition of "alcohol-related fatalities" and the failure of state laws to distinguish between greater and lesser degrees of impairment also reflect an anti-alcohol bias that goes beyond concerns about traffic safety.

Preventing drunk driving deaths was the main rationale for the 1984 federal law that threatened to withhhold highway funding from any state that did not raise its legal alcohol purchase age to twenty-one. This de facto national drinking age has created a legal anomaly: The same eighteen-, nineteen-, and twenty-year-olds who are considered old enough to live independently, marry, sign contracts, vote, and enlist in the military are not allowed to order a beer. The absurdity of this situation was highlighted by Jenna and Barbara Bush's brush with the law at an Austin restaurant in the spring of 2001. Surely something is wrong when a nineteen-year-old's hankering for a margarita is the occasion for police intervention and a media stampede.

Far from showing signs of antisocial tendencies or incipient alcoholism, the president's daughters were behaving quite normally. Most Americans of college age still drink, but now they do so illegally, which makes it more likely that they will get into trouble. They drink clandestinely, without the guidance of older role models, and they are more apt to drink off campus, which often means driving home drunk. Colleges cannot try to foster responsible drinking habits through explicit instruction or faculty-supervised events. Not surprisingly, surveys taken during the 1990s indicated that "binge" drinking—defined as consuming five or more drinks on one occasion for men, four or more for women—was on the rise. Amid all the hand-wringing over this trend, little attention was given to the possibility of training students to drink moderately, because any college that tried to do so would risk losing federal funding. In the late nineties, however, a few colleges experimented with an intriguing program that, rather than trying to scare students about the consequences of drinking, simply informed them about typical drinking patterns for people their age. These schools found that students tended to drink less after learning that their peers were not drinking as heavily as the furor over alcohol on campus might have led them to believe. At Northern Illinois University, for example, the share of students who reported drinking heavily fell from 45 percent in 1989 to 25 percent in 1998.[97]

These programs implicitly acknowledge that students will continue to drink regardless of the law. Rather than demanding abstinence, they try to limit the damage that drinkers do to themselves and others. If that approach is controversial for college-age drinkers, it is considered all but unthinkable for teenagers. This taboo was apparent in a 2000 report on alcohol from Drug Strategies, a Washington, D.C.–based organization that aims to promote "more effective approaches to the nation's drug problems." The report's authors worried that in one survey "eight in ten teens said there is nothing wrong with underage drinking as long as teens are responsible about the amount they consume." They were also dismayed at the fact that one-quarter of parents in another survey said they would definitely or probably allow their teenagers to attend a New Year's Eve party "where you suspected that alcohol was going to be served, but you knew that everyone would be required to give their keys to the host and that no one would be able to drive themselves home afterward."[98]

From a less absolutist perspective, these findings could be seen as encouraging rather than alarming. Building on the concept of responsible drinking that seems to be accepted by most teenagers, adults could try to educate them about the dangers of acute poisoning and traffic accidents. They could also try to channel teenage drinking into controlled environments, such as the hypothetical New Year's Eve party, where excessive consumption would be less likely and less apt to cause permanent harm. Organizations and government agencies that deal with alcohol abuse tend to reject such possibilities out of hand, insisting on zero tolerance of underage drinking. Since more than 70 percent of teenagers are drinking by their senior year in high school, this approach seems unrealistic.[99]

Nor is the acceptance of some drinking by teenagers simply a concession of defeat. The Drug Strategies report lamented that "fewer than one-quarter of parents give their children a no-use message about alcohol."[100] The Pennsylvania Liquor Control Board urges parents to "discourage alcohol use by those under twenty-one," adding that, under state law, "it's a crime to sell or give alcoholic beverages to anyone under 21—even your own kids."[101] Leaving aside the astonishing presumption of this attempt to interfere with child rearing, it's hardly reasonable to expect people to suddenly know how to drink responsibly when they turn twenty-one if they've had no experience with alcohol until then.

True Temperance

The wisdom that parents should pass on to their children about drinking (assuming the government will let them) is not complicated. It starts by recognizing that not everyone cares for alcohol, and people should not feel pressured to drink if they don't want to. Those who do enjoy drinking should have a healthy respect for alcohol's dangers as well as its potential benefits. Since it is relatively easy to overdose on this drug, with potentially fatal consequences, inexperienced drinkers should start gradually, learning how much their bodies can comfortably tolerate. They should not engage in drinking contests that encourage rapid consumption. They should be cautious about drinking on an empty stomach. They should be aware of how alcohol affects their abilities and their behavior. They should not drink in circumstances that put themselves or others at risk. If they intend to have more than a drink or two away from home, they should have a plan for getting back that does not involve driving. They should not drink when it might interfere with their responsibilities at work, home, or school. They should be careful about combining alcohol with other drugs, especially depressants. They shouldn't use alcohol as a way of avoiding personal problems.

It is often said that the key to moderation is to drink without becoming drunk. There's a measure of truth to this, but the formulation is misleading, as are the unqualified condemnations of drunkenness that have been heard from moralists for thousands of years. Drinking alcohol for pleasure always involves some measure of intoxication, which is what "cheers the hearts of men" and helps bring them together in fellowship. The question of how much intoxication is too much cannot be answered definitively ahead of time; it depends upon the drinker and the situation. It may hinge on whether you plan to drive home or take the subway, whether you're having lunch or dinner, whether it's Saturday night or Sunday night. As Aristotle said, "the temperate man desires the right things in the right way and at the right time."[102]

If this advice—much of which could also be applied to other drugs—strikes most adults as commonsensical, it's because they have absorbed these lessons through their own hard experience, by observing other people's mistakes, or, if they're lucky, through the positive influence of parents and other role models. Adolescents ought to learn responsible drinking habits at home, instead of having to figure them out, in hit-or-miss fashion, at clandestine parties. Given the potentially high stakes involved, it's reckless to neglect such instruction because teenagers are expected to be abstinent. The need for adult guidance in this area should be understood both by liberals, who make similar arguments in favor of sex education, and by conservatives, who value the traditions and institutions that help people avoid pitfalls identified by earlier generations.

One such institition is the neighborhood bar. Although condemned by the temperance movement as a source of numerous evils, taverns can serve a positive social function, helping to channel and tame drinking. The tavern keeper has an interest in selling drinks, but he also has an interest in maintaining order, both to protect his property and to create the sort of environment that customers like. He will therefore intervene to prevent fights and contain boisterous behavior; he may even, contrary to his immediate financial interest, cut off a customer he thinks has had enough. The management's restraining influence is reinforced by the presence of other customers: The desire to avoid public embarrassment encourages drinkers to control themselves. Drinking with other people around also means that someone is on hand to help in the event of an emergency. When drinking is incorporated into other social activities—conversation, dancing, billiards, darts, watching sports—it is less likely to be seen as an end in itself and less likely to cause trouble.

It bears emphasizing that responsible drinking is something the vast majority of alcohol consumers do eventually learn. This is a remarkable fact, given the drug's hazards and easy availability. Nearly every American has the financial means to drink all day long, remaining intoxicated throughout his waking hours. Yet very few people choose to do this, and perhaps the reason is too obvious to need stating: They have more important things to do. They have responsibilities to employers, family members, friends, and neighbors. Failing to meet these responsibilities results in unpleasant consequences that people generally strive to avoid. Put in a more positive way, most people do not choose to be drunk constantly because it would interfere with activities they find more rewarding. Without too much effort, they manage to balance drinking with the other things that give them pleasure and make their lives meaningful.

The temperance movement, which achieved more success when it advocated moderation than when it began insisting on abstinence enforced by law, was too quick to abandon the ideal after which it was named. Today most Americans seem willing to give true temperance a chance. They have seen that the side effects of alcohol consumption can be controlled without prohibition. Per capita alcohol consumption has been falling since 1981, a period during which drinkers' preferences have shifted from distilled spirits toward beer and wine.[103] Between 1970 and 1998, the age-adjusted death rate for alcohol-related cirrhosis of the liver—a frequently used index of alcohol abuse—fell by 32 percent.[104] The ratio of alcohol-related deaths to vehicle miles traveled fell 52 percent between 1977 and 1999, and the share of fatal accidents involving alcohol has been falling since the mid-1980s.[105]

Most people are leery of applying the temperance model to other drugs because they continue to view these intoxicants the way dry activists viewed alcohol: as a malevolent agent with a will of its own, capable of forcing people to act against their own interests and those of society. The next five chapters consider variations on this theme, including fears that certain drugs cause laziness, insanity, promiscuity, violence, and addiction. The fact that all these charges have also been made against alcohol does not mean they have no basis in reality. But it does suggest that the idea of drug-induced behavior, what I call voodoo pharmacology, is misleading, portraying complex interactions as simple cause-and-effect relationships. If so, it should be possible to control drug use without resorting to prohibition. Drug users themselves show that it is.

CHAPTER THREE

GOING NOWHERE

Millions of young people are living as shadows of themselves, empty shells of what they could have been and would have been without pot.
—ROBERT DUPONT, FOUNDING DIRECTOR OF THE NATIONAL INSTITUTE
  ON DRUG ABUSE, 1985

Nothing Happening Here

A TV spot produced by the Partnership for a Drug-Free America shows two young men smoking marijuana, one watching television, the other ridiculing warnings about the dangers of pot. "We've been smoking for fifteen years," says the skeptic, "and nothing has ever happened to me." Then we hear the voice of his mother, asking him if he's looked for a job today. The announcer says, "Marijuana can make nothing happen to you, too."

In a similar vein, another PDFA ad shows a stoned teenager turning down invitations from friends to play baseball, go skateboarding, or listen to music. "You always thought marijuana would take you places," the announcer says. "So how come you're going nowhere?"

In the world of anti-drug commercials, pot smokers are stupid as well as lazy. One spot compares smoking marijuana to being hit in the head over and over again by a professional boxer. Another, a cartoon, shows a pot repeatedly hitting a man's head. "If you smoke pot one time," says the voice-over, "it probably won't kill you. But if you keep smoking it, you might just get dumber and dumber and dumber and dumber and dumber."

The themes of laziness and stupidity are combined in an ad featuring Alex, a bleary-eyed teenager who looks like he was stoned during the taping. "Marijuana cost me a lot of things," he says. "I used to be a straight-A student. I was liked by all the neighbors. . . . I was always a good kid." Then, "before I knew it, I was getting thrown out of my house. . . . I just became a total loser."

This familiar image of the dull, listless pothead has a scientific-sounding name: "amotivational syndrome." People afflicted by this condition don't care enough to study, go to class, get a job, show up at work, or perform their duties conscientiously. According to voodoo pharmacology, these are drug effects; instead of making people do evil things, marijuana makes them do nothing. Adding it to someone's brain creates the sin of sloth.

As a comic figure, the aimless, clueless pot smoker has proven remarkably durable, in movies ranging from the Cheech and Chong oeuvre to more recent farces, such as *Dude, Where's My Car?* and *Jay and Silent Bob Strike Back*; in the late 1990s Tommy Chong even reprised his out-of-it hippie character, decades after it was created, for the sitcom *That '70s Show*. Such clowns may be hard to take seriously as a threat to society, but they represent one of the central fears aroused by drugs: that intoxicants will strip people of the ambition and ability to succeed in school and at work, undermining the conditions essential for prosperity.

Such anxieties played an important role in the temperance movement, which emphasized the difficulty of reconciling constant drunkenness with the demands of industrialization. Themes of indolence and poverty were prominent in the "temperance tales" of the nineteenth century. A pair of popular Currier and Ives prints contrasted *The Fruits of Temperance,* a happy, well-dressed family in a parlor, with *The Fruits of Intemperance,* a shabby, apparently homeless family on the road. Another print showed a dozing, disheveled man lying against a keg on the sidewalk outside a saloon beneath a sign that read, "Specimen of the work done inside."

Although few people nowadays would see this fellow as representative of drinkers in general, the idle, good-for-nothing lush remains a staple of popular culture, so his appearance in dry propaganda seems natural. More surprisingly, the fear of impaired productivity also figured prominently in efforts to discourage tobacco use during the early decades of the twentieth century. Long before the marijuana joint came to be identified with underachievement, youthful rebellion, and juvenile delinquency, the tobacco cigarette had those connotations for its opponents.

Although tobacco has been widely used by Americans since colonial times, cigarettes did not start to catch on until production was mechanized in the 1880s. By 1910 cigarettes had become the leading tobacco product in the United States. Per capita consumption skyrocketed from eighty-five that year to nearly 1,000 in 1930.[1] The rise of the cigarette caused alarm not only among die-hard opponents of tobacco but also among pipe and cigar smokers, who perceived the new product as qualitatively different. Critics believed (correctly) that cigarettes were more dangerous to health because the smoke was typically inhaled. They also worried that boys and women would be attracted by the product's milder smoke and low price.

In contrast to contemporary anti-smoking activists, who talk almost exclusively about the habit's effect on the body, the critics of the early twentieth century were just as concerned about its impact on the mind. In the 1904 edition of *Our Bodies and How We Live,* an elementary school textbook, Albert Blaisdell warned: "The cells of the brain may become poisoned from tobacco. The ideas may lack clearness of outline. The will power may be weakened, and it may be an effort to do the routine duties of life. . . . The memory may also be impaired." Blaisdell reported that "the honors of the great schools, academies, and colleges are very largely taken by the abstainers from tobacco. . . . The reason for this is plain. The mind of the habitual user of tobacco is apt to lose its capacity for study or successful effort."[2]

Cigarette smokers were said to be bad sons as well as bad students. "The action of any narcotic is to break down the sense of moral responsibility," wrote the drug treatment entrepreneur Charles B. Towns in 1912. "If a father finds that his boy is fibbing to him, is difficult to manage, or does not wish to work, he will generally find that the boy is smoking cigarettes. . . . The action of a narcotic produces a peculiar cunning and resource in concealment." Noting the rudeness of smokers who light up despite the complaints of bystanders, Towns concluded that "callous indifference to the rights of others" was another effect of the drug.[3]

This indifference could even lead to crime. In 1904 Charles B. Hubbell recalled that during his service as president of New York City's Board of Education, "it was found that nearly all of the incorrigible truants were cigaret fiends." He added that "the Police Magistrates of this and other cities have stated again and again that the majority of juvenile delinquents appearing before them are cigaret fiends whose moral nature has been warped or destroyed through the instrumentality of this vice."[4]

The industrialist Henry Ford, who in 1914 published a collection of anti-cigarette testimonials called *The Case Against the Little White Slaver,* suggested that smokers tended to be delinquents for social rather than pharmacological reasons. "If you will study the history of almost any criminal you will find that he is an inveterate cigarette smoker," Ford averred. "Boys, through cigarettes, train with bad company. They go with other smokers to the pool rooms and saloons. The cigarette drags them down."[5]

Even if they stayed on the right side of the law, cigarette smokers were not to be trusted as employees. "The time is already at hand when smokers will be barred out of positions which demand quick thought and action," wrote Towns.[6] Thomas Edison declared, "I employ no person who smokes cigarettes."[7] With Ford and Edison leading the way, many leading businessmen adopted the same policy during the first two decades of the twentieth century. Hundreds of large companies, including Montgomery Ward and Sears Roebuck, refused to hire cigarette smokers.

While such policies may have helped make their expectations self-fulfilling, the cigarette's opponents seem to have honestly believed that smokers were destined to be losers. "Boys at the age of ten to fifteen who have continued smoking cigarettes do not as a rule amount to anything," wrote Connie Mack, manager of the Philadelphia Athletics, in 1913. "They are unfitted in every way for any kind of work where brains are needed. No boy or man can expect to succeed in this world to a high position and continue the use of cigarettes."[8] The biologist David Starr Jordan, the first president of Stanford University, concurred. "The boy who smokes cigarettes need not be anxious about his future," he said. "He has none."[9]

Today, when employers who prefer to hire nonsmokers are worried mainly about health insurance costs and secondhand smoke, the idea that cigarettes cause moral and intellectual degradation seems quaint. Far from being incompatible with "quick thought and action," nicotine can actually enhance job performance. Were it not for the noxious mode through which it is usually consumed, nicotine, like caffeine, would continue to be welcomed in the workplace, as it was for most of the twentieth century. The anti-smoking messages we see every day never warn that cigarettes will make you stupid and unambitious, because such claims would not pass the laugh test.

But the early anti-cigarette campaigners should not be dismissed as a few scattered cranks. Not only did they include prominent citizens such as Ford, Edison, and Jordan; they achieved substantial legislative success: Between 1893 and 1921, fourteen states and one territory enacted laws banning the sale of cigarettes.[10] Those victories reflect the potency of the themes employed by the anti-cigarette movement, which closely resemble the themes of today's anti-pot propaganda. In every generation, adults worry about adolescents who talk back, flunk out, run with the wrong crowd, and cannot hold a decent job. In hindsight, it's clear that such problems, although they might have been associated with cigarette smoking, were not caused by it. Rather, the cigarette became a symbol of everything that might go wrong on the way from childhood to adulthood.

The fact that cigarettes got a bum rap, of course, does not mean that marijuana is innocent of the charges against it. But given the pharmacological differences between tobacco and marijuana, the parallels suggest that responses to drug use have less to do with the inherent properties of the substance than with perennial fears that are projected onto the chemical menace of the day. That suspicion is reinforced by the fact that marijuana's reputation for making its users dumb, lethargic, and unemployable did not come to the fore until cannabis became popular among middle-class white kids in the 1960s.

Drop-Out Drug

When marijuana was banned by Congress in 1937 and for many years afterward, its users were not generally described as dimwitted layabouts. Strange as it may seem to us now, they were more likely to be perceived as homicidal maniacs. (See Chapter 6.) By the late sixties, however, that image had changed. As the sociologist Jerome L. Himmelstein puts it, "Marihuana was no longer described as a 'killer weed' that fostered aggression and violence but as a 'drop-out drug' that sapped users' wills, destroyed their motivation, and turned them into passive drop-outs from reality and society."[11]

The outlines of this new image could be seen in a 1965 report from the World Health Organization's Expert Committee on Addiction-Producing Drugs. "For the individual," the report said, "harm resulting from the abuse of cannabis may include inertia, lethargy, self-neglect, feeling of increased capability, with corresponding failure, and precipitation of psychotic episodes. . . . The harm to society derived from the abuse of cannabis rests in economic consequences of the impairment of the individual's social functions and his enhanced proneness to asocial and anti-social behavior."[12] Two years later, in a decision upholding his state's marijuana law, Massachusetts judge G. Joseph Tauro wrote: "Many succumb to the drug as a handy means of withdrawing from the inevitable stresses and legitimate demands of society. The evasion of problems and escape from reality seem to be among the desired effects of the use of marijuana."[13]

Similar descriptions of marijuana began to show up in congressional testimony. In 1968 Donald Louria of the New York State Council on Drug Addiction told a House committee that "marihuana in heavy doses can, after repeated use, produce . . . loss of ambition, rejection of previously established goals, and retreat into a solipsistic, drug-oriented cocoon." Testifying in 1970, Dana Farnsworth of Harvard University's Health Services referred to the problem by the name psychiatrists had given it: "I am very much concerned about what has come to be called the 'amotivational syndrome.' I am certain as I can be . . . that when an individual becomes dependent upon marijuana . . . he becomes preoccupied with it. His attitude changes toward endorsement of values which he had not before; he tends to become very easily satisfied with what is immediately present, in such a way that he seems to have been robbed of his ability to make appropriate choices."[14]

As arrests of middle-class college students prompted growing criticism of the marijuana laws, government officials latched onto amotivational syndrome for justification. In 1971 John Ingersoll, director of the Bureau of Narcotics and Dangerous Drugs, told *Time* that marijuana can be "psychologically habituating, often resulting in an amotivational syndrome in which the user is more apt to contemplate a flower pot than try to solve his problem."[15] Assistant Treasury Secretary Eugene Rossides warned that "if we should ever, in a wild moment, decide to legalize marijuana, I think we could sap the strength and energy of the entire nation. Any disrespect for the law could be minor compared to the lack of drive, goals and ambition that legalization could produce. I really think it could make the United States a second-rate nation."[16]

Amotivational syndrome played a conspicuous role in the 1974 hearings that Senator John Eastland called to oppose the decriminalization movement and rebut the widely heard argument that marijuana was not as bad as the government had made it out to be. According to a summary presented at the hearings, "The most notable and consistent clinical changes that have been reported in heavy marihuana smokers include apathy approaching indolence, lack of motivation . . . reduced interest in socializing, and attraction to intense sensory stimuli. Possibly the issue of greatest importance in the area of behavioral toxicity of marihuana is the question of amotivational syndrome."[17]

As Jerome Himmelstein observes, "The amotivational syndrome was not simply one important effect attributed to marihuana. It formed the core of the dominant image of both drug and user. Marihuana did not simply cause an amotivational syndrome among other things; it was in essence a 'drop-out drug.'"[18] This specter has haunted the anti-marijuana movement since the 1960s. Seeing marijuana smokers lose their motivation, anti-pot propagandists found theirs.

Gabriel Nahas, an Egyptian-born physician and longtime opponent of pot, seemed to blame hashish for his native country's decline during the last millennium. "The appearance of cannabis products in the Middle East," he wrote in his 1976 book *Keep Off the Grass,* "did coincide with a long period of decline during which Egypt fell from the status of a major power to the position of an agrarian slave state." In the same book, Nahas describes a childhood incident that shaped his attitude toward cannabis. On his way to school in Alexandria when he was about eight, Nahas would sometimes pass "a man sprawled on the sidewalk, apparently sleeping in the blazing sun." In response to Nahas's questions, his father informed him, "The man is a *hashishat,* an unfortunate individual who is addicted to a drug called hashish. He is sleeping there because the drug has dulled his mind and sapped his energy."[19]

Marijuana's opponents are quick to cite such examples, implying that the most conspicuous cannabis users are also the most representative. Peggy Mann's 1985 book *Marijuana Alert,* described by then First Lady Nancy Reagan in the foreword as "a true story about a drug that is taking America captive," is full of anecdotes about sweet, obedient, courteous, hardworking kids transformed into lazy, moody, slovenly, insolent, bored, apathetic monsters. (As Mann conceded, the symptoms of marijuana use—like the traits that were once seen as the hallmarks of cigarette smoking—are often hard to distinguish from the symptoms of adolescence.) Robert DuPont, former director of the National Institute on Drug Abuse, told Mann that "millions of young people are living as shadows of themselves, empty shells of what they could have been and would have been without pot."[20]

Sounding like the anti-cigarette campaigners of another era, Mann blamed marijuana for impairing productivity. "Inevitably," she wrote, "chronic pot-smokers are eliminating themselves from being able to handle a job that calls for precision timing and precision thinking." She quoted Carlton Turner, drug policy adviser to President Reagan, who tied marijuana to national decline in words strikingly similar to those used by Eugene Rossides fifteen years before. "We must realize that there will be no free ride for marijuana users," he said. "Unless we come to grips with this problem, they may take our nation with them on their downhill course. . . . If our country does not wake up and address the disastrous and wide-ranging effects of drug abuse in the workplace, the United States is doomed to become a second-rate power."[21]

Beyond Cheech and Chong

Such anxieties remain at the heart of anti-pot sentiment. "Young marijuana users," wrote then Secretary of Health and Human Services Donna Shalala in 1995, "are less likely to achieve their academic potential, which detracts from national productivity."[22] A 1998 pamphlet produced by the National Institute on Drug Abuse warns that "some frequent, long-term marijuana users show signs of a lack of motivation (amotivational syndrome). Their problems include not caring about what happens in their lives, no desire to work regularly, fatigue, and a lack of concern about how they look. As a result of these symptoms, some users tend to perform poorly in school or at work."[23] While NIDA's language is cautious, suggesting that amotivational syndrome afflicts a minority of pot smokers, the same cannot be said for messages like the ones described at the beginning of the chapter, produced by the Partnership for a Drug-Free America and sponsored in recent years by the White House Office of National Drug Control Policy. These ads portray the typical marijuana user as "a total loser."

The image of the indolent, unproductive pot smoker is reinforced by the drug's association with the counterculture of the 1960s and seventies. A 1971 *National Review* article complained that "the weed is an adjunct, forcing tool and instrument of initiation for a lifestyle that generally seeks to bring down 'ordered life as we know it.'"[24] Nearly three decades later, a booklet entitled *How Parents Can Help Children Live Marijuana Free,* distributed by the Salt Lake Education

Foundation, listed "excessive preoccupation with social causes, race relations, environmental issues, etc." among the "social signs of regular users."[25] Especially among baby boomers, marijuana retains its countercultural connotations, which elicit nostalgic affection from some and bitter hostility from others. For conservatives of a certain age, cannabis will forever be linked to lazy, smelly, draft-dodging, flag-burning hippies. Even for those who do not assume that marijuana use implies a particular ideology, the Cheech & Chong odor lingers.

As with most stereotypes, there is an element of truth to popular perceptions of marijuana users. Under the influence of marijuana, for example, short-term memory often seems to be impaired. One way of understanding this phenomenon is that marijuana focuses concentration on the immediate present. Users may welcome this effect, which makes them less likely to dwell on fleeting anxieties. To observers, however, pot smokers may seem stupid, especially if they have difficulty carrying on a conversation. Like drinkers, marijuana users may have an exaggerated sense of their own profundity, prattling on about trivia or reciting clichés as if they were novel insights. Because marijuana affects sense perceptions in interesting ways, pot smokers may become absorbed in stimuli that ordinarily would not draw their attention, reinforcing the impression of vacuity by staring at reflected light or listening intently to background noises. And since marijuana often acts as a sedative and is commonly used to relax, it's hardly surprising that it would come to be associated with inactivity.

Then, too, most Americans under fifty probably have known people who seemed to confirm the pothead stereotype: the guy in your college dorm who never cracked a book and flunked out after freshman year, the co-worker in the cubicle next to yours who was always goofing off, staring into space, and talking in non sequiturs.

Some of these slackers may actually be stoned most of the time, which is not exactly conducive to academic or professional excellence. They may also be unambitious by nature, and therefore attracted to a lifestyle in which pot smoking plays a major role. But the existence of lazy potheads hardly proves that marijuana saps people of their drive to achieve, any more than the existence of lazy drunks proves the same thing about alcohol.

Adults are rightly concerned about marijuana use by minors. Smoking pot during school, getting high to ward off negative emotions, or using marijuana to avoid dealing with family conflicts will tend to exacerbate the usual problems of adolescence. But these concerns are not fundamentally different from those raised by alcohol.

To justify viewing pot in a different light than alcohol, marijuana's detractors insist that its impact extends beyond the immediate effects of intoxication. Peggy Mann and Gabriel Nahas argued that because tetrahydrocannabinol (THC), marijuana's main psychoactive ingredient, is stored in fatty tissue for days, anyone who smokes the equivalent of three or more joints a week is essentially stoned all the time without realizing it. In Mann's view, this subtle, ongoing intoxication was what accounted for the personality changes she attributed to marijuana.

While it's true that THC can be detected in a user's body days after he smokes marijuana, the level is too low to be psychoactive. "A few researchers have reported subtle marijuana effects persisting up to twenty-four hours," write sociologist Lynn Zimmer and pharmacologist John P. Morgan in *Marijuana Myths, Marijuana Facts*. "However, in dozens of other studies measuring psychomotor ability and intellectual performance, researchers have found that all marijuana effects disappear within a few hours of smoking."[26]

Another potential explanation for amotivational syndrome, the claim that marijuana causes brain damage, is rarely heard nowadays because it has never been substantiated. (Indeed, it is inconsistent with claims by Mann and other anti-pot crusaders that users return to normal after they stop smoking marijuana.) As a National Academy of Sciences panel noted in a 1999 report, "Earlier studies purporting to show structural changes in the brains of heavy marijuana users have not been replicated using more sophisticated techniques." A few researchers have reported modest differences in cognitive performance between heavy users and nonusers, but it's not clear that the subjects were similar enough to the controls to rule out alternative explanations.[27] A 2001 study found "virtually no significant differences" in performance on ten neuropsychological tests between long-term daily pot smokers who had abstained for a week and controls who had used marijuana fewer than fifty times in their lives.[28] (The researchers did report that heavy users performed worse than controls on one test, measuring memory of word lists, for up to a week after the last time they smoked.) A 2002 report from the Canadian Senate's Special Committee on Illegal Drugs concluded that "long-term effects on cognitive functions have not been established in research."[29]

Speculating about possible causes of amotivational syndrome is premature, of course, until the condition has been shown to exist. "This syndrome is not a medical diagnosis," noted the National Academy of Sciences report, "but it has been used to describe young people who drop out of social activities and show little interest in school, work, or other goal-directed activity. When heavy marijuana use accompanies these symptoms, the drug is often cited as the cause, but there are no convincing data to demonstrate a causal relationship between marijuana smoking and these behavioral characteristics."[30]

In fact, there is substantial evidence against such a relationship. Two surveys of college seniors, done in 1969 and 1978, found that marijuana users were indistinguishable from nonusers on measures of grades, athletic activity, career plans, and feelings of alienation. Regarding academic performance, the researchers wrote: "No differences even approaching significance were found between regular users of marijuana (once a week or more) and nonusers. This is consistent with the findings both of the 1969 study and other studies, and would seem inconsistent with suggestions that marijuana may produce an 'amotivational syndrome,' at least in the dosages used by the population in this study."[31]

As for job performance, one study conducted in the 1970s looked at farm workers in Jamaica, who often smoked marijuana while they worked. The researchers found that cane cutters who smoked marijuana were just as productive as those who did not.[32] This study's relevance to jobs that impose greater intellectual demands can fairly be questioned. As we have seen, colonial Americans got away with drinking throughout the day during a period when the economy was mainly agricultural, but theirs is not an example that modern-day office workers or telecommuters (let alone surgeons or pilots) can safely imitate. The real question is not whether smoking pot on the job is a good idea; it's whether employees who smoke pot on their own time are any less efficient or reliable than employees who drink away from work.

More relevant to the U.S. workplace are laboratory studies in which subjects performed cognitive tasks in exchange for tokens they could trade in for marijuana or cash. In all of these studies, the heavier marijuana smokers were at least as accurate and productive as the lighter smokers. In a 1990 laboratory study, subjects did boring tasks to earn the right to do slightly more interesting work. Contrary to the researchers' expectations, the subjects worked harder during the periods when they were smoking marijuana. Researchers have also used survey data to compare the work patterns and wages of marijuana users to those of nonusers. "There is nothing in these data to suggest that marijuana reduces people's motivation to work, their employability, or their capacity to earn wages," write Zimmer and Morgan. "Studies have consistently found that marijuana users earn wages similar to or higher than nonusers."[33]

According to the National Household Survey on Drug Abuse, about 8 percent of full-time workers are "current" (past-month) users of illegal drugs, mostly marijuana. Illegal drug use is twice as common among the unemployed, a disparity that may in part reflect the consequences of drug abuse. But it may also be that people with characteristics that make them less employable—for example, poorly educated, impulsive, and rebellious individuals—are more apt to use illicit drugs. Then, too, drug use could be a response to, rather than a cause of, unemployment. In any case, it's clear that drug users typically are productive members of society: 70 percent have full-time jobs. Illegal drug use is more common among people earning less than $9,000 a year, but it's also more common among people earning $75,000 a year or more.[34] A 2001 study, based on data from the household survey, found that casual drug users (those who used illicit drugs less often than once a week) were just as likely to be employed as respondents who reported no drug use.[35]

Urine Trouble

Regardless of what the data show, many employers seem convinced that pot smokers make bad workers. Since the 1980s, when President Reagan issued an executive order declaring that "drugs will not be tolerated in the federal workplace" and Congress passed a law requiring businesses that receive federal money to adopt anti-drug programs, the degrading ritual of peeing into a cup on demand has become increasingly familiar to American employees. In 2000, 66 percent of the large companies surveyed by the American Management Association had drug testing programs—down from 81 percent in 1996 but still more than three times the figure in 1987.[36] In the 1997 National Household Survey on Drug Abuse (the source of the most recent nationwide data), 49 percent of respondents said their employers required some kind of drug testing.[37]

Drug testing was pioneered in the military, on the assumption that a soldier who uses illegal intoxicants is not fit to serve. Soldiers are still permitted to drink, however, even though alcohol can have a more serious effect on preparedness than marijuana. Joseph P. Franklin, a retired general and former commandant of West Point, served as a battalion commander in Vietnam, where marijuana use was so common that enforcing the Army's ban on it would have been impossible. In theory, Franklin said, a soldier could be court-martialed for marijuana possession, but "as the troops used to say, 'What are you going to do, send me to Vietnam?'" His policy was to "turn a blind eye," which "made it a very difficult command environment because you're tolerating something that by our regulations was illegal." At the same time, Franklin found that soldiers who smoked pot were generally more reliable than the ones who drank. "If we got into any kind of trouble—say, an evening attack on a perimeter—the marijuana smokers were much more alert than the drinkers," he recalled. "You didn't have them lying around in the bunkers, totally incapable of performing."[38]

Thus, to the extent that drug testing encourages servicemen to drink rather than smoke pot, it may actually impair effectiveness. A former Navy psychiatrist reported another perverse effect of the military's "zero tolerance" policy: He said a member of an aircraft carrier's crew told him LSD was more popular at sea than marijuana because it was much easier to conceal. "Instead of occasionally smoking a joint on a carrier," the psychiatrist said, "guys were tripping! Oh, my God. That scared me."[39]

Whatever the merits of the military's approach to illegal drug use, private employers have followed suit, although pre-employment screening is more common than random testing. Just as Thomas Edison and other businessmen who worried about tobacco's impact on productivity once refused to hire cigarette smokers, businesses nowadays proudly proclaim themselves "drug-free." In practice, this does not mean that they never hire drug users, or even that they prevent people from working while intoxicated. It typically means that they refuse to hire applicants who test positive for marijuana, cocaine, amphetamines, opiates, or phencyclidine (PCP).

A positive urinalysis result does not show that an applicant or employee is under the influence—only that he has ingested the drug at some time in the recent past. Marijuana metabolites can be detected for three days or more after a single dose, so someone who smoked a joint on Friday night could test positive on Monday morning. Regular marijuana smokers can test positive for weeks after their last dose. Because traces of marijuana persist for so long, and because marijuana is much more popular than the other drugs for which employers test, pre-employment drug tests serve mainly to screen out pot smokers.

But not all pot smokers. Since people looking for a job know they may have to undergo a drug test, and since the tests themselves are announced in advance, marijuana users can simply abstain until after they've passed. (They can also use a variety of techniques—ranging from drinking a lot of water to putting additives in their sample or substituting someone else's urine—to defeat the test.) I once asked a spokesman for a drug test company to explain the rationale for pre-employment screening, given how easily drug users can avoid a positive result. "It's an IQ test," he said. More seriously, one could argue that it's a way of identifying pot smokers who are so attached to marijuana that they are willing to risk getting passed over for a job rather than give the drug up for a few weeks.

Pre-employment tests, then, mainly catch pot smokers who lack the foresight or the willpower to abstain, along with those who are suddenly thrust into the job market—possibly a bad sign in itself. Another important factor to consider in judging the effectiveness of pre-employment screening is that, for some job categories, applicants who are prone to lateness, absences, insubordination, slacking off, or accidents may also be more likely to smoke marijuana. Illegal drug users are disproportionately young men, and it seems plausible that they would be, on average, less risk-averse and less respectful of authority than people who don't use illegal drugs. As a National Academy of Sciences panel observed in a 1994 report, "drug use may be just one among many characteristics of a more deviant lifestyle, and associations between use and degraded performance may be due not to drug-related impairment but to general deviance or other factors."[40]

The upshot of all this is something that neither supporters nor opponents of drug testing like to admit: Even if drug use itself has little or no impact on job performance (perhaps because it generally occurs outside the workplace), pre-employment testing might help improve the quality of new hires. Drug testing is a crude tool, however, and whether it's worth the investment will depend upon the job, the applicant pool, and the economics of the industry. It's certainly not safe to assume that drug tests are cost-effective, since correlations between drug use and job performance are generally modest.[41]

In a study of postal workers conducted in the late 1980s, for example, those who tested positive for marijuana when they were hired were more prone to accidents, injuries, absences, disciplinary action, and turnover. The differences were relatively small, however, ranging from 55 percent to 85 percent. By contrast, previous estimates had ranged from 200 percent for accidents to 1,500 percent for sick leave. "The findings of this study suggest that many of the claims cited to justify pre-employment drug screening have been exaggerated," the researchers concluded.[42] Even these comparatively modest results may be misleading. The study's methodology was criticized on several grounds, including an accident measure that gave extra weight to mishaps that occurred soon after hiring.[43] A larger study of postal workers confirmed the finding regarding absenteeism but found no association between a positive pre-employment drug test and accidents or injuries. On the other hand, workers who had tested positive were more likely to be fired, although their overall turnover rate was not significantly higher.[44]

While allowing for the possibility that drug testing might be a good investment for a particular employer, the National Academy of Sciences report found that "the preventive effects of drug-testing programs have never been adequately demonstrated."[45] The Drug-Free America Foundation, which supports drug testing, concedes that "only limited information is available about the actual effects of illicit drug use in the workplace. . . . We do not have reliable data on the relative cost-effectiveness of various types of interventions within specific industries, much less across industries. Indeed, only a relatively few studies have attempted true cost/benefit evaluations of actual interventions, and these studies reflect that we are in only the very early stages of learning how to apply econometrics to these evaluations."[46]

For some employers, drug testing may actually be counterproductive. A 1998 study of sixty-three high-tech companies found that pre-employment and random drug testing were both associated with *lower* productivity. The researchers speculated that drug testing programs may create a "negative work environment" that repels qualified applicants and damages employee morale.[47] Companies looking for highly skilled employees such as software engineers may find they can't afford to insist on drug tests. But when Home Depot and Wal-Mart hire cashiers, they have a bigger pool of suitable prospects, so they needn't worry too much about turning off potential employees by demanding their urine. And if it turns out that the people discouraged by this requirement are, on average, less competent (whether or not that has anything to do with drug use), the policy might even do these companies some good, although perhaps not enough to outweigh the cost of carrying out the drug tests.

Instead of focusing on the value of urinalysis as a predictive tool or a safety measure in particular industries, the case for drug testing is usually made in global terms. In 1989, for example, President George H.W. Bush claimed that "drug abuse among American workers costs businesses anywhere from $60 billion to $100 billion a year in lost productivity, absenteeism, drug-related accidents, medical claims, and theft." This estimate, adjusted upward over time, has been cited repeatedly by advocates of drug testing. It is based mainly on a 1984 calculation of "lost productivity" using data from the National Household Survey on Drug Abuse. The researchers found that the average income for households of people who had been daily marijuana smokers at some point in their lives was somewhat lower than the average income for other households. They attributed the difference to drug use, and this became the basis for the "lost productivity" estimate. In addition to ignoring other possible explanations for the income gap, this calculation glosses over the fact that other comparisons did not fit so well with the assumption of drug-impaired productivity: For example, households with *current* pot smokers had incomes just as high as households where no one was using marijuana.[48]

Although couched in the language of sound business management, the eagerness to stigmatize marijuana smokers as bad employees has more to do with politics than with economics. Through mandates and exhortation, the government has conscripted and enlisted employers to enforce the drug laws, just as it has compelled them to enforce the immigration laws. Government policies requiring or encouraging drug testing by private employers include transportation regulations, conditions attached to Defense Department contracts, and propaganda aimed at convincing companies that good corporate citizens (especially those that want to do business with the government) need to take an interest in their workers' urine. From the government's perspective, it does not matter whether this urological obsession is good for a company's bottom line. In fact, it has never been shown that routine drug testing makes economic sense.

Even in safety-sensitive industries such as trucking and aviation, tests that measure current impairment—whether the cause is illegal drugs, alcohol, medication, illness, personal problems, or a bad night's sleep—are more appropriate than tests that detect traces of a joint someone smoked over the weekend. Drug testing probably would be much less popular with employers if it were purely a business practice rather than a weapon of prohibition. If it weren't for the war on drugs, it seems likely that employers would treat marijuana and other currently illegal intoxicants the way they treat alcohol, which they view as a problem only when it affects job performance.

Marijuana in Moderation

As with alcohol, of course, it is possible to use marijuana so much that it interferes with one's work, studies, or relationships. But excessive use is far from typical. In 1972 the National Commission on Marihuana and Drug Abuse reported that "the largest number of marihuana users in the United States today are experimenters or intermittent users, and 2 percent of those who have ever used it are presently heavy users."[49] The pattern has not changed much since then, although many more Americans have tried marijuana—some 83 million, more than a third of the population over the age of twelve, according to government survey data. About one quarter of these people (21 million) report using marijuana in the previous year, and about 15 percent (12 million) say they've used it in the previous month. Around 12 percent of the people who use marijuana in a given year, and about 3 percent of those who have ever tried it, report smoking it on 300 or more days in the previous year.[50] Even this level of use does not necessarily signify a problem. Daily users include people who smoke marijuana in the evening, in much the same way as others might enjoy a beer or a cocktail, as well as people who are stoned all the time.

Other indicators come closer to suggesting what share of marijuana smokers could reasonably be considered problem users. About 4 percent of the people who use marijuana in a given year report undergoing treatment for drug abuse.[51] (Since treatment often occurs as a result of arrest or a positive drug test at work, it is not safe to assume that all of these people actually had drug problems. Most men and about half of all teenagers treated for "marijuana abuse" are referred by the criminal justice system.[52]) A 1994 study based on data from the National Comorbidity Survey estimated that 9 percent of marijuana users have ever met the American Psychiatric Association's criteria for "substance dependence." The comparable figure for alcohol was 15 percent.[53] These numbers indicate that the vast majority of marijuana smokers, like the vast majority of drinkers, do not get into serious trouble with the drug.

Even moderate users, of course, may act irresponsibly on occasion. The most familiar example in the case of alcohol is driving while intoxicated. With marijuana, there is less cause for concern on this score, although it may contribute to accidents in certain situations. Both laboratory and road tests find that typical doses of marijuana impair some abilities related to driving, but not to the same extent as alcohol. Furthermore, pot smokers seem to be more aware of their own impairment than drinkers are, compensating by taking fewer risks and driving more slowly. In its 2002 report on marijuana, the Canadian Senate's Special Committee on Illegal Drugs concluded that "cannabis alone, particularly in low doses, has little effect on the skills involved in automobile driving."[54]

A Dutch driving study found that the only significant effect from three different doses of THC was on the subjects' ability to stay in the middle of the lane. The researchers likened the subjects' performance to that of drivers with a 0.04 BAC, well below the legal limit.[55] A British study also found modest effects from typical doses of marijuana. "In terms of road safety," the researchers wrote, "it cannot be concluded that driving under the influence of cannabis is not a hazard, as the effects on various aspects of driver performance are unpredictable. However . . . the severe effects of alcohol on the higher cognitive processes of driving are likely to make this more of a hazard, particularly at higher blood alcohol levels."[56]

Marijuana does not appear to play an important role in traffic accidents. In a 1992 analysis of accidents in which the drivers were killed, the National Highway Traffic Safety Administration reported: "The THC-only drivers had a responsibility rate below that of the drug-free drivers. . . . While the difference was not statistically significant, there was no indication that cannabis by itself was a cause of fatal crashes."[57] Like drinkers, however, marijuana users need to exercise caution, especially if they are inexperienced or have consumed an unusually high dose. The safest course is simply to avoid driving after smoking pot.

Psychological and behavioral issues aside, marijuana users might be faulted for endangering their own health, especially if some of the more disturbing warnings about pot—including the possibility of brain shrinkage, heart disease, immune system impairment, genetic abnormalities, reduction in testosterone levels, and sterility—had been borne out by research. Yet the evidence of serious hazards is so weak that a 1995 editorial in *The Lancet*, the prestigious British medical journal, could assert that "the smoking of cannabis, even long term, is not harmful to health."[58] That may have been a bit of an overstatement. But as the drug policy scholar Mark Kleiman observed in his 1992 book *Against Excess*, "Aside from the almost self-evident proposition that smoking anything is probably bad for the lungs, the quarter century since large numbers of Americans began to use marijuana has produced remarkably little laboratory or epidemiological evidence of serious health damage done by the drug."[59] The respiratory effects of smoking were also the main concern of the panel that analyzed the pros and cons of medicinal marijuana for the National Academy of Sciences in 1999.[60] Upon releasing a comprehensive report on marijuana in 2002, the chairman of the Canadian Senate's Special Committee on Illegal Drugs noted that "scientific evidence overwhelmingly indicates that cannabis is substantially less harmful than alcohol."[61]

Anti-pot propagandists are fond of pointing out that marijuana generates larger quantities of certain carcinogens than tobacco does. But since virtually no pot smokers consume anything like twenty cigarettes a day—the average intake for a tobacco smoker—this comparison is misleading. Because they typically smoke much less often, marijuana smokers absorb much smaller doses of potentially dangerous chemicals than cigarette smokers do. Heavy pot smoking has been linked to bronchitis, but elevated risks of lung cancer and emphysema have not been observed in people who smoke only marijuana.[62] Whatever the respiratory risks of pot smoking, they probably can be reduced through the use of vaporizers, which heat marijuana to release the THC rather than burning it. Water pipes, by contrast, filter out THC along with tar and therefore do not appear to make pot smoking any safer.[63] Marijuana users who are leery of smoking can eat it instead, although this delays the effect and makes the dose harder to calibrate.

Stronger Stuff

Because research on the health effects of marijuana has failed to turn up anything very alarming, recent warnings have focused on the alleged increase in marijuana's potency since the 1970s. Today's pot smokers are told, in effect, "This is not your father's marijuana." Such claims are doubly misleading.

First, commonly heard assertions that marijuana is ten to forty times as powerful as it used to be are based on spurious comparisons with small samples of low-grade Mexican marijuana seized in the early seventies. These samples were not representative of the marijuana available at the time, and it appears that they decayed before they were tested.[64] Since 1980 or so, when the federal government began testing broader samples and using better storage methods, the average THC content of confiscated marijuana has gone up and down within a range from around 2 percent to 4 percent.[65]

Second, even if average THC content is significantly higher now than it was in the seventies, it's not clear why this should be a cause for concern. It's essentially impossible to die from an overdose of marijuana; no deaths from acute toxicity have ever been documented, and based on research with mice a lethal dose of THC would be something like 40,000 times the amount it takes to get high.[66] Since marijuana users generally smoke until they achieve the effect they desire, higher potency would mean inhaling less smoke, which would tend to reduce health risks rather than increase them.

In light of these facts, warnings that marijuana is more dangerous today because it's much more potent than it used to be can best be understood as attempts to neutralize charges of hypocrisy. In a 1995 op-ed piece, for example, HHS secretary Donna Shalala warned that "more potent forms of marijuana are readily available."[67] Shalala has also declared that marijuana is "illegal, dangerous, and wrong."[68] Yet in 1992 she admitted smoking pot as a college student.[69] Public officials in her position can always say they've changed their minds, but this rings a bit hollow. It helps to argue that the marijuana smoked by today's college students is more dangerous (and, presumably, more "wrong") than the stuff Shalala, Al Gore, Bill Clinton, and Newt Gingrich once enjoyed.

Another sign of desperation among marijuana's detractors is the familiar claim that pot smoking leads to the use of more dangerous drugs. In the summer of 1985, when I was working as a reporter for my hometown newspaper, I covered a raid on a marijuana farm in northeastern Pennsylvania. Watching state troopers uproot the tall, bright green plants as the farm's owner looked on sorrowfully, I asked the officer in charge what all the fuss was about. "Marijuana may not be so bad," he said, "but it leads to harder drugs. I've seen it a thousand times." No doubt this trooper, like law-enforcement officers throughout the country, had known pot smokers who eventually became cocaine or heroin users. But in concluding that marijuana caused this progression, he was taking a leap.

The basic idea that one sort of drug use leads to another goes back at least a couple of centuries. The eighteenth-century physician Benjamin Rush claimed that chewing or smoking tobacco contributes to drunkenness by creating a peculiar kind of thirst: "This thirst cannot be allayed by water, for no sedative or even insipid liquor will be relished after the mouth and throat have been exposed to the stimulus of the smoke, or juice of tobacco. A desire of course is excited for strong drinks, and these when taken between meals soon lead to intemperance and drunkenness."[70] The anti-alcohol crusaders of the nineteenth century echoed Rush's charge that tobacco use encourages drinking.[71] In 1912 Charles B. Towns took this argument a step further, saying tobacco leads to alcohol and alcohol leads to morphine.[72]

Federal authorities did not start playing up the idea that marijuana was a "stepping stone" to other drugs until the 1950s. Federal Bureau of Narcotics Commissioner Harry Anslinger, who previously had rejected the idea, endorsed it in 1951 as a way of justifying increased penalties for marijuana offenses. He told a congressional committee: "Over 50 percent of those young addicts started on marihuana smoking. They started there and graduated to heroin; they took the needle when the thrill of marijuana was gone."[73] This became the main justification for putting marijuana in the same category as narcotics.

Half a century later, the same rationale can still be heard. "The statistical link between marijuana and other drugs like LSD, cocaine, or heroin is tighter than [those] between smoking and lung cancer, high cholesterol, and heart disease, and asbestos and lung cancer," the Center on Addiction and Substance Abuse announced in 1999. "For example, twelve- to seventeen-year-olds who smoke marijuana are eighty-five times more likely to use cocaine than those who do not."[74] That sounds impressive, until you realize that two things—tattoos and motorcycle riding, say—can be highly correlated even if one does not cause the other. It's true that most people who try cocaine have already tried marijuana, and it's true that people who try marijuana are more likely to try cocaine than people who never try marijuana. But it does not follow that smoking marijuana is what makes people try cocaine. Rather, these probabilities reflect the fact that people who experiment with several different drugs tend to use them in a particular order: first tobacco and alcohol (also identified by CASA as "gateway drugs"), then marijuana, then "LSD, cocaine or heroin."

One could observe similar correlations between recreational activities. People who go bungee jumping are probably more likely to try sky diving than people who don't go bungee jumping. Does bungee jumping cause sky diving, or is it just that a disproportionate number of people who like one activity also like the other, and tend to try the easier, less risky, and less expensive one first? By comparing "the statistical link between marijuana and other drugs" to the association between smoking and lung cancer, CASA implies not only that the correlation is strong but that there is a plausible biological explanation for it, one that fits the facts better than any other theory. But as the National Academy of Sciences observed, "There is no evidence that marijuana serves as a stepping stone on the basis of its particular drug effect."[75] The Canadian Senate's Special Committee on Illegal Drugs likewise concluded that "cannabis itself is not a cause of other drug use. In this sense, we reject the gateway theory."[76]

If smoking marijuana does make people more likely to use other illegal drugs, the connection is probably an artifact of prohibition. Once people violate the drug laws with impunity, they're apt to do it again. Once they've discovered that official warnings about marijuana are overblown, they're apt to think the same is true of official warnings about other illicit substances. As the psychiatrist Jerome Jaffe, Richard Nixon's drug czar, observed at a 1971 press conference, "Any time somebody steps over the bounds of using a drug which is not currently totally approved by society, he has broken a boundary, he has in fact put himself outside the conventional limits, and to the extent that one begins to experiment beyond the conventional limits, one is more susceptible to experiment with other non-conventional and non-socially approved illegal substances."[77]

However one views the progression from marijuana to other

drugs, it's clear that most pot smokers do not even experiment with cocaine or heroin, let alone become frequent users. The number of Americans who have tried marijuana is more than twenty-five times the number who have tried heroin and more than 600 times the number who have used heroin in the last month.[78] Even if everyone who tries heroin uses marijuana first, the percentage of pot smokers who are now regular heroin users is tiny. Although cocaine is much more popular than heroin, the number of people who have smoked pot is still fifty times the number who have used cocaine in the last month.[79] Thus, in addition to implicitly conceding that marijuana itself is not very dangerous, the warnings about its role as a "gateway" or "stepping stone" suggest that rare outcomes are much more common than they actually are. In an unintentional parody of this approach, CASA likens pot smoking to Russian roulette—a game in which there is at least a one-in-six chance of instant death.[80]

The Pot Smoker Next Door

Official warnings about pot, like anti-drug propaganda in general, offer a grotesquely distorted view of the typical user: Even if he somehow avoids overdosing on heroin, he's a burned-out slacker who amounts to nothing. In the case of marijuana, this sort of portrayal is hard to get away with because so many people have had personal experiences with the drug. If they haven't smoked pot themselves, the odds are they know people who have, or who still do, and nevertheless manage to lead successful lives.

Groups that support the decriminalization of marijuana try to build on this widely shared knowledge. In 1999 the National Organization for the Reform of Marijuana Laws (whose acronym reflects its quest for respectability) began testing a billboard campaign emphasizing that pot smokers are part of the mainstream. "Honk If You Inhale," said one, followed by the tag line, "Stop Arresting Responsible Pot Smokers." Another said, "A Pot Smoker Is Busted Every 45 Seconds—and You Wonder Why We're Paranoid." Keith Stroup, NORML's founder and executive director, was eager to break the hippie stereotype. "The reality is the average marijuana smoker is a middle-aged person who puts on a coat and tie and goes to work and raises a family," he said. "Our constituency is largely in the closet, and when you're in the closet you're invisible to elected officials and have very little power."[81]

Not surprisingly, most of the pot smokers I interviewed for this book were concerned that being publicly identified as illegal drug users would hurt their careers. One of the few who did not ask me to use a pseudonym was Bob Wallace, a software engineer who was an early employee of Microsoft, where he was the Pascal product manager, and founder of Quicksoft, which sold the DOS-based word processor PC-Write (created by Wallace) and pioneered the concept of shareware. Wallace, who died in September 2002 after a bout with pneumonia, had left Microsoft with stock worth millions of dollars, so he was not worried about keeping a job. And as operator of Mind Books, a mail-order business that sold titles related to psychedelic drugs, he was not shy about expressing his views on drug policy or discussing his own experiences.

Wallace first tried marijuana in 1967, when he was eighteen and about to start college. When I interviewed him, he'd been smoking it nearly every day for about fifteen years, generally taking a puff or two in the evening. "It's what I might put in the category of a habit—you know, while reading the newspaper or with a glass of wine," he said. In addition to unwinding with marijuana, he found it a useful adjunct to certain kinds of mental work, such as resolving design problems for the house he and his wife were building in Marin County, California. "It does provide a shift in perspective, kind of a new way of looking at things," Wallace said. "For programming I found it helpful so I could see the forest. I wasn't caught in the detail; I could get a little above it and sort of see the overall design." He said his drug use was never an issue at Microsoft, where he worked from 1978 until 1983: "There was the perception that if you were good at what you were doing, nothing else really mattered."[82]

William Gazecki, the documentarian who co-produced and co-wrote *Waco: The Rules of Engagement,* also reported that marijuana had sometimes helped with his work. As a sound engineer in the recording industry during the 1970s, he smoked pot every day. "I found marijuana to be conducive in some regards," he recalled. "I designed a recording mixing console—a big electronic device with hundreds of knobs, meters, and switches. I designed and built one from scratch, including all the circuit boards and the operational amplifying circuits and the entire wiring plan and the interconnecting system and the ergonomic layout—I did the whole thing stoned. It was quite a success and is still in operation today."[83]

In the early eighties, when Gazecki started working on films, he cut down on his marijuana consumption in response to different hours and expectations, smoking only in the evenings. When I talked to him he was hardly using marijuana at all. "The film I just finished is the first project I've done completely straight," he said, "and I'm pretty happy with it. I think that I managed to find in my own inner architecture a way of pretty much being as creative [without pot]. It feels like it's harder work, I will say that. It feels like it requires more effort. The insight and the sort of spontaneous visions, so to speak, don't come as naturally. So it takes more focusing; it takes more patience. But I think the net result is just as good."[84]

Like Wallace and Gazecki, a number of writers, artists, and musicians have reported that marijuana can facilitate creativity.[85] In general, though, pot smokers find that marijuana and work do not mix well. "I wouldn't use it to go to work or when I have to use my brain," said Alan Mattus, an MBA in his mid thirties who was working for a real estate developer. "I am not an artist. . . . If I have to be intelligent, I won't use it." Mattus first tried pot in high school and smoked it a few times a week for most of college. When he talked to me he was using it once a week or so, in the evening or on the weekend. "Pot is just really fun—that euphoric buzz you have," he said. "A crappy day isn't a crappy day anymore. . . . One of my favorite things is to go to a park. There's nothing better than toking up and going to look at some great scenery."[86]

Elizabeth Carr, a grandmother in her sixties who visits elderly people for a social service agency, likewise said she reserved marijuana for occasions when she did not need to be productive. "I would not turn on first thing in the morning," she said. "Generally speaking, if you have a lot of things that you need to do in a day and you need to stay active, smoking marijuana is stupid." Carr first tried marijuana in the late 1950s, and some of her early experiences involved music: going to a jazz club, hearing the New York Philharmonic. "I loved the intensity," she recalled. When I interviewed her she was smoking marijuana two or three times a week, usually in the evening. "There are occasional times when it's a beautiful spring day, and we'll be out on a hike or doing something out in nature, and we'll smoke," she said. "It can intensify and deepen visual and auditory experiences, the colors and the sense of beauty. . . . When I smoke at night, sometimes it's just because I'm feeling like I want to kick back, or there's a particular movie I'm watching that I think it might enhance. . . . Marijuana and food are so wonderful, and marijuana and sex are wonderful."[87]

The use of marijuana to enhance various kinds of experiences belies the notion that pot smokers do nothing but lie around in a stupor. At the same time, purists might argue that music, scenery, movies, food, and sex should be enjoyed on their own terms, without artificial improvement (or distortion, depending upon your perspective). There is something to be said for this position: If you can enjoy something only when you're under the influence of marijuana, you may have a problem. At the same time, a well-balanced person can use drugs to get more pleasure out of life without compromising his ability to sense and feel. People commonly use alcohol, caffeine, and tobacco to enhance activities—eating, socializing, sex, listening to music or comedy—that could also be enjoyed without drugs, and this is not usually considered morally problematic.

Marijuana's compatibility with a wide range of activities is one reason for its popularity: Measured by use in the past year, pot is five times as popular as cocaine, more than forty times as popular as heroin.[88] Walter Stevenson, a neuroscientist in his late twenties, has tried just about every drug you've heard of and a few you probably haven't, but his favorite is marijuana, which he first smoked when he was seventeen. When I interviewed him his habit was to smoke a little in the evening, and sometimes he would smoke before going on a hike or attending a concert. He said he liked marijuana because "it's completely amorphous. Your experience with it changes over time. It's very easy to procure large amounts of it or to create large amounts of it. . . . It's generally pleasurable. It's extremely safe. It doesn't interact poorly with anything. Nobody's ever died from it." For Stevenson, who was once arrested for marijuana possession, the drug's main disadvantage was its legal status. "It's threatening," he said. "It makes it often uncomfortable to use it in an otherwise perfectly comfortable situation," such as "going out to a park and enjoying myself, and having my heart pound every time I see a police officer."[89]

Marijuana's detractors call such feelings "paranoia," which they view as a side effect of the drug. It's hardly surprising that pot smokers, knowing that they're breaking the law and hearing that marijuana makes people paranoid, sometimes feel anxious after a toke or two. As we'll see in the next chapter, a similar dynamic helps account for the terrifying experiences that are often attributed to LSD and other psychedelics.

CHAPTER FOUR

CRAZY, MAN

The effects of LSD can be described as drug-induced psychosis.
—NATIONAL INSTITUTE ON DRUG ABUSE

Gonna Fly Now

In 1993 Ann Landers ran a letter from a reader who had recently seen an article "about how LSD is making a big comeback among the youth of America." (In retrospect, this "big comeback" looks more like a modest upward trend that peaked after a few years.) "I was a teenager in the 1960s," Landers's correspondent wrote, "and although I was never involved in the drug scene, I remember hearing a lot of horror stories about young people jumping in front of trains, off roofs, and out of windows while under the influence of LSD. I am very concerned for this new generation of LSD users." The reader urged Landers to publish accounts by former acid users of "how this drug ruined their youth and possibly their adult years as well," along with letters from people who had "lost loved ones because of LSD." Landers agreed there was cause for alarm. "The prospect of this dangerous drug making a comeback is bone-chilling," she replied. "This mind-altering drug has been responsible for many deaths."[1]

The exchange nicely illustrated how the conventional wisdom about LSD (and other illegal drugs) is propagated: People who don't know what they're talking about pass on hearsay and misinformation, blithely reinforcing each other's ignorance. With no foundation other than the "horror stories" to which her correspondent alluded, Landers felt free to assert that LSD had caused "many deaths." Her anxiety about irrational, life-threatening behavior triggered by "a mind-altering drug" reflects the perennial concern that certain potions have the power to drive people mad. According to voodoo pharmacology, drugs sever the user's connection to reality, transforming him into a raving lunatic.

During the last few decades such fears have been strongly associated with psychedelics, the class of "mind-manifesting" drugs whose effects resemble those of LSD. Aside from LSD itself (lysergic acid diethylamide), the best-known examples are psilocybin, the main psychoactive ingredient in "magic mushrooms" (*Psilocybe mexicana*), and mescaline, derived from peyote (the caps from cactuses of the *Lophophora* genus). There is some disagreement about which drugs belong in this category, but Lester Grinspoon and James Bakalar's rather unwieldy definition gives some sense of the criteria: "A psychedelic drug is one which, without causing physical addiction, craving, major physiological disturbances, delirium, disorientation, or amnesia, more or less reliably produces thought, mood, and perceptual changes otherwise rarely experienced except in dreams, contemplative and religious exaltation, flashes of vivid involuntary memory, and acute psychoses."[2]

Focusing on that last comparison, the National Institute on Drug

Abuse says, "The effects of LSD can be described as drug-induced psychosis—distortion or disorganization of a person's capacity to recognize reality, think rationally, or communicate with others." According to this view, LSD causes insanity by definition. If so, it's a kind of insanity the drug's users seem to like; otherwise, no one would ever drop acid more than once, and bad word of mouth would have eliminated LSD use long ago. Another warning in the same NIDA pamphlet is scarier: "Some LSD users experience devastating psychological effects that persist after the trip has ended, producing a long-lasting psychotic-like state. LSD-induced persistent psychosis may include dramatic mood swings from mania to profound depression, vivid visual disturbances, and hallucinations. These effects may last for years and can affect people who have no history or other symptoms of psychological disorder."[3]

In other words, LSD makes some people crazy not just for the duration of the trip (eight to twelve hours) but for a long time afterward: Drop a little acid, and you just might lose your mind. It's not surprising that "fears of insanity" figure prominently in the "bad trips" that NIDA also warns the public about. Government propaganda feeds those fears, fostering drug experiences that seem to confirm the propaganda. As NIDA acknowledges, the quality of an LSD trip depends largely on the user's expectations, and those expectations are shaped by official warnings.

Reefer Madness

Today's drug warriors are exploiting an age-old terror that at different times has been linked to different symbols, including alcohol. Benjamin Rush and his followers warned that habitual drinking leads to madness, a theme reflected in the anti-alcohol movement's posters and pamphlets. "King Alcohol" was depicted as a crowned skeleton seated on a barrel of whiskey, holding a banner that listed his accomplishments; "Insanity" was fifth, between "Poverty" and "Theft." Defenders of Prohibition thought it was "clear that sobriety increases a man's chance of keeping out of the insane hospital."[4] There was a kernel of truth in these warnings: Heavy drinkers who are malnourished may suffer memory loss (Korsakoff's syndrome), and chronic alcoholics who stop drinking suddenly sometimes experience delirium tremens, which includes disorientation and hallucinations. But such problems are associated only with the most extreme levels of consumption, so it is hardly reasonable for drinkers to worry that they are risking their sanity every time they raise a glass to their lips.

Likewise, while most Americans still consider it plausible that LSD causes insanity, they would probably be surprised, if not amused, to hear that the same charge was once leveled against marijuana. Even if marijuana doesn't drive you crazy, of course, it could be that LSD does (a question we'll consider later). But the discrediting of reefer madness at least shows that it's possible for the authorities to be wrong about such matters. It also shows that preconceptions and sinister anecdotes can be trumped by experience.

Back when marijuana was unfamiliar to white, middle-class Americans, its reputation was formed by stories about what it did to poor, dark-skinned people. With little more than their prejudices to guide them, politicians and journalists readily accepted the idea that blacks and Mexicans, like the inhabitants of backward countries such as India and Egypt, would eagerly consume a drug that drove a large percentage of its users crazy. (As Chapter 6 shows, claims that marijuana caused violence also found a credulous audience, for similar reasons.)

Those who believed in reefer madness often cited reports from abroad. An Egyptian delegate to a 1925 drug conference claimed, for example, that "the illicit use of hashish is the principal cause of most of the cases of insanity occurring in Egypt."[5] By 1931, Denver's director of safety was casually asserting that marijuana, "consumed over any period of time, drives the user insane."[6] An article published in the *Journal of Criminal Law and Criminology* in 1932 likewise insisted that madness was the predictable result of repeated marijuana use. "With smokers whether constant or infrequent," the authors wrote, "each experience aids in the destruction of brain tissues and nerve centers, and does irreparable damage. If continued, the inevitable result is insanity, which those familiar with it describe as absolutely incurable, and, without exception ending in death. Statistics show that from 17 to 20 percent of all males admitted to mental hospitals and asylums in India have become insane through the use of this drug."[7]

Lobbying for uniform state legislation against cannabis and later for a national ban, the Federal Bureau of Narcotics emphasized the connection between marijuana and madness. FBN Commissioner Harry J. Anslinger claimed that, while "it is extremely difficult" to cure an opium or cocaine addict, "The case of Marihuana addicts is well nigh hopeless as the Hasheesh or Marihuana user becomes insane."[8] The FBN was still promoting this view as late as 1950, despite increasing skepticism among scientists who studied pot smokers in the United States. The emerging consensus among these researchers was that foreign reports about the link between marijuana and insanity were greatly exaggerated. While marijuana might conceivably precipitate a "psychotic break" in susceptible individuals, they concluded, such incidents appeared to be very rare, and well-balanced users had little reason to fear that cannabis would drive them over the edge.

The current view of LSD among careful researchers (including several whose work has been funded by NIDA) happens to be quite similar. But unlike marijuana, LSD is still widely seen as a threat to sanity. Partly this is because public alarm about LSD is a relatively recent development. Although the drug was first synthesized in 1938 and its psychoactive effects were discovered in 1943, it received little attention until the 1960s, when an explosion in its popularity prompted state and federal bans. Hence calmer minds have had less time to prevail than in the case of marijuana, which has been a target of legislation in the United States since the 1920s.

Yet it must also be admitted that LSD is a more plausible agent of madness than marijuana. It is, to begin with, much more powerful, with doses measured in micrograms rather than milligrams. It is also longer-acting, with effects persisting not just a few hours but up to half a day. More important, although cannabis is sometimes considered a psychedelic, LSD has much more profound effects on perceptions, thoughts, and feelings. Users generally experience the world around them and their own emotions with a special intensity, noticing and becoming absorbed in details they would ordinarily ignore and acknowledging feelings they would otherwise suppress. They often perceive time as passing slowly, experience visual distortions (lingering after-images, undulating surfaces), see vivid abstract and phantasmagorical images with their eyes closed, and experience synthesthesia, a perceptual crossover in which they see sounds, feel colors, and so on. Their thoughts may be fanciful and dream-like, their mood giddy, wryly amused, reflective, or serene. They may relive long-neglected memories, reflect candidly on personal shortcomings, play out symbolic dramas inside their heads, experience ineffable feelings of transcendence or unity.

Many of these phenomena, of course, could be disturbing or frightening as well as interesting, enjoyable, or rewarding. People who deliberately take LSD understand what's going on, attribute it to the drug, and can reassure themselves that it will pass. (LSD-tinged perceptions therefore are not true hallucinations, which is why the term *hallucinogen,* frequently used by the government instead of *psychedelic,* is a misnomer.) But someone who was exposed to LSD unknowingly might very well think he was going crazy. Indeed, early LSD researchers hoped they could use the drug to simulate, and thereby study, the "psychotic" state of mind; they called LSD-like drugs "psychotomimetic," meaning "psychosis-imitating." Although this analogy was eventually rejected as inaccurate and unproductive, its lingering influence can be seen in official descriptions and public perceptions of LSD. Another early line of research, sponsored largely by the U.S. Army and the Central Intelligence Agency, approached LSD as a chemical weapon that could be used to confuse a target, loosen his tongue, or convince him he was losing his mind.[9] Needless to say, neither sort of research left much room for the LSD trip as a positive experience.

From the Couch to the Street

There's an interesting parallel here with a mind alteration technique that remains perfectly legal: the isolation tank. Early studies of sensory deprivation approached it as a form of brainwashing or an interrogation tool; not surprisingly, subjects generally reported unpleasant experiences. By contrast, the neuroscientist John Lilly saw sensory deprivation as a way to relieve stress, achieve self-insight, and expand one's consciousness. Lilly (who often used psychedelics in conjunction with sensory deprivation) popularized the concept of tanking in a series of books. By the late 1970s people were buying versions of his tank for home use or renting them by the hour at spas where they could float effortlessly in a body-temperature epsom-salt solution, cut off from sight, sound, and smell. Even those who did not see visions or think deep thoughts usually emerged deeply relaxed, with a heightened appreciation of their senses.

Lilly's work with isolation tanks helped recast the public image of sensory deprivation, transforming it from torture into recreation. Studies of LSD's usefulness in psychotherapy could conceivably do something similar, changing it from a trigger of insanity into a tool of mental health. In the 1950s and sixties, when the U.S. government was using LSD to discombobulate unwitting test subjects, other researchers were using it to help alcoholics straighten out their lives or help terminal cancer patients come to terms with death. Hundreds of psychiatrists gave it to their patients as a way of overcoming resistance and promoting insight. According to the actor Cary Grant, who underwent 100 LSD therapy sessions, "The first thing that happens is you don't want to look at who you are. Then the light breaks through; to use the cliché, you are enlightened. I discovered that I had created my own pattern, and I had to be responsible for it. . . . I went through rebirth."[10]

This period saw the publication of more than a thousand papers and dozens of books on the subject of psychedelic therapy. Reviewing the research in their book *Psychedelic Drugs Reconsidered*, Grinspoon and Bakalar find that early enthusiastic reports were often tempered by the more equivocal results of subsequent studies. The literature is full of testimonials and case histories but little that could be characterized as hard evidence. On the other hand, it's hard to imagine how a rigorous, controlled, double-blind experiment could be done with LSD: Given the drug's dramatic short-term effects, it would be obvious to both the subjects and the researchers who had taken the placebo and who had been given the real thing. In any event, as Grinspoon and Bakalar note, the evidence for LSD is at least as strong as the evidence for other approaches to psychotherapy, suggesting that further research would be worthwhile. The use of LSD with patients suffering terminal illnesses seems especially promising.[11]

The scientific investigation of LSD's potential, only recently revived in a tentative way, was cut short by its emergence as a popular street drug and countercultural symbol in the 1960s. No one embodied this shift more than Timothy Leary, the Harvard psychologist turned psychedelic guru, who switched from studying psychedelics in an academic setting to promoting the use of LSD as an agent of personal and social transformation. Four decades later, the mention of his name still provokes strong reactions. Some consider him a misunderstood visionary or astute social critic, while others see him as a cunning charlatan, reckless hedonist, or incoherent pseudo-mystic. There is evidence for each of these views in Leary's career and writings. His public statements are a puzzling mixture of esoteric ramblings, deliberate provocations, cautious qualifications, simplistic pronouncements, and wild predictions. It's often hard to tell whether he was being naive or simply putting people on. In a 1998 introduction to *The Politics of Ecstasy,* a collection of his writings from the sixties, Leary said, "Much of it was written in a state of rapturous delusion."[12]

In his responsible persona, Leary emphasized the importance of "set and setting"—expectations and environment—in shaping an LSD user's experience. He said only well-balanced individuals should try the drug, and only with the guidance of an experienced user in a secure, comfortable, supportive environment. He acknowledged that an LSD trip could be frightening and recommended ways to prevent people from freaking out and reassuring them when they did. At the same time, however, he was urging everyone to "turn on, tune in, drop out," a message with little room for caveats.

There was more than a whiff of disingenuousness in the way that Leary told his audiences what he thought they wanted to hear. Speaking to a group of Lutheran psychologists in 1964, he argued that the psychedelic experience was fundamentally religious. "From the theological standpoint," he said, "everyone must discover the seven faces of God within his own body." In a 1966 interview with *Playboy,* he declared that LSD's appeal was really all about sex. "There is no question that LSD is the most powerful aphrodisiac ever discovered by man," he said. "Compared with sex under LSD, the way you've been making love—no matter how ecstatic the pleasure you think you get from it—is like making love to a department-store-window dummy." In the same interview, he fawned over the baby boomers who represented the bulk of his following, insisting that "the present generation under the age of twenty-five is the wisest and holiest generation that the human race has ever seen."[13]

Despite his own rhetorical excesses, Leary rightly lampooned the overreaction against LSD, observing that "psychedelic drugs cause panic and temporary insanity in people who have not taken them."[14] He also noted, in one of his more sober moments, that "chemicals like LSD cause no specific response beyond their general tendency to speed up and drastically expand awareness. The specific effect is almost entirely due to the preparations for the session and the surroundings."[15]

Yet Leary also argued that LSD was inherently threatening to the existing social order, that it revealed the falsity of the "games" people play as consumers, employees, and citizens. "The nervous system can be changed, integrated, recircuited, expanded in its function," he wrote. "These possibilities naturally threaten every branch of the establishment. . . . LSD is more frightening than the bomb! . . . Make no mistake: the effect of consciousness-expanding drugs will be to transform our concepts of human nature, human potentialities, existence. The game is about to be changed, ladies and gentlemen. . . . Our favorite concepts are standing in the way of a flood tide 2 billion years building up."[16]

Depending on one's perspective, this sort of grandiosity made Leary either laughable or dangerous—and neither impression was good for the reputation of psychedelic drugs. "The most ardent enthusiasts," write Martin Lee and Bruce Shlain in *Acid Dreams,* "looked to LSD as something capable, in and of itself, of ushering in the Kingdom of Heaven on earth. The drug was hailed as an elixir of truth, a psychic solvent that could cleanse the heart of greed and envy and break the barriers of separateness."[17] In the thinking and rhetoric of LSD aficionados who were more overtly political than Leary, the drug was tied to particular views about the Vietnam War, the environment, race relations, and capitalism. Even more than marijuana, LSD came to represent an ideology, one that provoked hostility from much of America.

Holidays in Hell

Once the debate over LSD became charged with political and cultural meaning, the middle ground was a dangerous place to be. Anyone urging caution was siding with the establishment, while anyone suggesting that LSD had positive uses was casting his lot with the hippies. Where the counterculture saw enlightenment, the government saw only insanity. At congressional hearings in 1966, one year after Congress voted to prohibit unauthorized manufacture and sale of LSD and two years before it banned possession of the drug, witnesses warned that acid caused psychotic reactions that could persist after the trip or reappear as "flashbacks." According to a summary in the *Congressional Record,* "One of the most common recurrent reactions to LSD use is a psychotic breakdown of an extended but unknown duration. What this means, of course, is that many LSD abusers become insane in a few short hours under the influence of the drug."[18] The state senator who chaired the New Jersey Narcotic Study Commission called LSD "the greatest threat facing the country today . . . more dangerous than the Vietnam War."[19]

The alarming press coverage that had begun in 1963, when Leary was fired by Harvard for giving LSD to undergraduates, intensified after distribution of the drug was banned. The March 25, 1966, issue of *Life,* the cover of which trumpeted "THE EXPLODING THREAT OF THE MIND DRUG THAT GOT OUT OF CONTROL," warned that dropping acid "could be a one-way trip to an asylum, prison, or grave." *Life* said a user "can become permanently deranged through a single terrifying LSD experience. Hospitals report case after case where people arrive in a state of mental disorganization, unable to distinguish their bodies from their surroundings."[20] *Time* quoted a psychiatrist who said

LSD could cause "florid psychoses with terrifying visual and auditory hallucinations, marked depression, often with serious suicide attempts, and anxiety bordering on panic." Another psychiatrist warned that "LSD can kill you dead—by making you feel that you can walk on water, or fly."[21] Stories of bizarre behavior under the influence of LSD—some carried by the press, others by word of mouth—began to circulate: people who stared at the sun until they went blind, gouged out their own eyes, or tried to fly by jumping from windows.

As the letter to Ann Landers at the beginning of this chapter suggests, these stories still carry a lot of weight with many Americans, who remain convinced that taking LSD is a reckless gamble in which you can easily lose your mind. But that view is not supported by the evidence, even in research sponsored by the federal government. "The literature on LSD does document some bizarre episodes," writes epidemiologist Leigh A. Henderson in a collection of reports on LSD studies funded by NIDA. "Given the millions of doses of LSD that have been consumed since the 1950s, however, these are rare indeed."[22]

Henderson was able to locate a dozen cases of people who suffered eye damage from overexposure to sunlight after taking LSD; no one was blinded. "The condition is well known and by no means confined to LSD users," she notes. "It occurs among sunbathers and persons watching solar eclipses without eye protection." As for eye gouging, Henderson found that only twelve incidents of "self-enucleation" had been reported since 1846, and none involved people under the influence of LSD, although two psychiatric patients who plucked out their right eyes had used the drug at some point. Finally, "LSD has been detected (usually with other drugs) in the blood of persons killed . . . in jumping or falling from heights," and some of these fatalities could be due to LSD-impaired judgment—although this sort of hazard is hardly unique to psychedelics.[23]

On the broader question of how many LSD users go nuts after dropping acid, Henderson notes that impressions based on studies of psychiatric patients—one reason for some of the early concerns about LSD-induced psychosis—are likely to be misleading. These subjects tend to be unbalanced to begin with, making them more vulnerable to the stress of a bad trip and making it harder to know whether a setback they experience after they take LSD should be attributed to the drug. A 1960 study avoided these problems by surveying researchers who administered LSD to volunteers from the general population. They reported "a psychotic reaction lasting more than forty-eight hours" about 0.08 percent of the time. "Prolonged psychiatric illness appears to be a rare complication of LSD use," Henderson concludes. "If large numbers of such cases exist, they are not documented in the scientific literature."[24]

With LSD as with marijuana, observers will often be tempted to attribute concurrent or subsequent behavior changes to the drug, when these changes might have occurred anyway. Even when LSD does seem to worsen someone's psychological problems, it is not a simple cause-and-effect relationship, like turning on a switch or striking a spark. The long-term impact of LSD lies not in any lasting effect it has on the brain but in the reverberations from the experiences it facilitates. In this respect, the risks of an LSD trip are not fundamentally different from the risks of other intense emotional experiences. "We tend to misconceive drugs as something utterly different from and almost by definition more dangerous than other ways of changing mental processes," Grinspoon and Bakalar observe in their discussion of psychedelic therapy. "Actually the dangers in work with LSD do not seem obviously greater than in comparable forms of therapy aimed at emotional insight."[25]

Another lingering effect cited by LSD's detractors, the "flashback," is a vivid recollection of a trip that may occur several days, weeks, or months afterward and generally lasts a few seconds to a few minutes. A user may have a glimpse of things the way they looked during the trip or re-experience emotions he felt then. One-fifth to one-third of LSD users report flashbacks, which can be triggered by stress, fatigue, or marijuana use. (Contrary to popular belief, flashbacks are not caused by LSD residue in the brain.) One explanation of flashbacks holds that people who take LSD learn a new way of perceiving things and can later spontaneously recapture that frame of mind without the drug. "A large proportion of those experiencing flashbacks (35 to 57 percent) have reported finding them pleasant (a 'free trip')," writes Henderson. "Very few have sought psychiatric help because of the experience."[26]

No one denies that people sometimes have unpleasant, even harrowing experiences under the influence of psychedelics. Elizabeth Carr, a Californian in her sixties, remembered the time she took 600 micrograms of LSD, a hefty dose. "I was convinced that I went into this very bizarre underworld where I was fighting for my life before a tribunal of dead people," she said. "I was convinced that I was going to die."[27] Bruce Rogers, a Floridian in his forties, had a similar experience when he took a few too many psilocybin mushrooms. "I would go to places where creatures from the underworld with insects crawling all over their bodies sitting around the table playing poker would tell me that I'm going to enjoy being like that," he recalled. "When I die, that's where I'm going."[28] In such cases, the best response usually is to reassure the user that the situation is temporary, that the experience is symbolic rather than real, and that surrendering to it will cause no lasting harm. It may even be beneficial: Users often report that they gained self-insight as a result of emotionally painful psychedelic experiences. "I've always learned something from [bad trips]," Rogers said. "It's always a neat thing when you come out the other end of it."[29] And clearly the good generally outweighs the bad, or people would not continue to use psychedelics.

Several researchers have observed that the incidence of bad trips seemed to rise after LSD became a hot political issue. On the one hand, Leary and his followers raised people's expectations about what an LSD trip could accomplish: mystical insight, peace of mind, psychological metamorphosis. On the other hand, the government and its allies in the mainstream press harped on the dangers the drug allegedly posed to individual sanity and social order. The resulting crosscurrents of hope and anxiety probably were not conducive to the frame of mind one ought to have when taking a powerful psychoactive drug.

The drug policy historian Edward Brecher argued that "increased expectation of adverse effects" was one reason hospitalization rates for LSD users rose between 1962 and 1969. "Many who were warned that LSD would drive them crazy did in fact suffer severe panic reactions, fearing that LSD had driven them crazy," he wrote. "Thus the warnings became self-fulfilling prophecies, and enhanced the hazards of the drug."[30] Based on survey data, the sociologist Richard Bunce concluded that the frequency of bad trips dropped substantially between the mid-sixties and the mid-seventies, a decline he attributed to a calmer environment. (Another important factor was a decrease in the size of the typical dose, as users learned how much

LSD was optimal for a positive experience.[31]) "In [the] extremely polarized and politicized environment which defined LSD use in the 1960s," Bunce wrote, "it is predictable that anxiety and apprehension would often attend use, and that users keyed to risking 'insanity' and 'psychosis' in order to experience 'ecstasy' and 'expanded consciousness' would often have a volatile experience with psychedelics, including 'bad trips.'"[32]

The effects of many psychoactive substances (or of nondrug catalysts such as the isolation tank) can be viewed as a kind of madness. The sociologist Howard S. Becker argued that such an interpretation is more likely to prevail when a drug is unfamiliar and no culture has developed surrounding its use. "Users do not have a sufficient amount of experience with the drug to form a stable conception of it as an object," he wrote. "No drug-using culture exists, and there is thus no authoritative alternative with which to counter the possible definition, when and if it comes to mind, of the drug experience as madness." At this stage, "'psychotic episodes' occur frequently." But as a consensus develops among users "about the drug's subjective effects, their duration, proper dosages, predictable dangers and how they may be avoided," the frequency of "psychotic episodes" declines. Writing in 1967, Becker argued that such a pattern could be seen with marijuana and predicted that something similar would happen with LSD.[33]

Wild Ride

LSD has never been as popular as marijuana, presumably because its effects are so dramatic, unpredictable, and long-lasting. But since the 1960s it has consistently proved attractive to a small minority of Americans. By 1970, according to one widely cited estimate, between

1 and 2 million Americans had tried LSD.[34] Based on retrospective survey data, about 100,000 Americans first took a psychedelic (mainly LSD) in 1965 (the first year for which an estimate is available); that number rose to nearly 1 million in 1976.[35] A survey of high school seniors shows past-month LSD use at 2.3 percent in 1975; the figure fell to a low of 1.5 percent in 1984 and rose to a peak of 4 percent in 1995 before falling to 0.7 percent in 2002.[36] (This was the "big comeback" that worried Ann Landers.) In the 2001 National Household Survey on Drug Abuse, 0.1 percent of respondents over the age of twelve reported using LSD in the past month; 9 percent (which represents 20 million or so people) said they had tried it at some point in their lives.[37]

LSD use is mainly a phenomenon of late adolescence and early adulthood; the average age at which people first try it is around eighteen or nineteen.[38] Although LSD is inexpensive compared to other illegal drugs (a few dollars for a dose that lasts eight to twelve hours), a trip is time-consuming, physically tiring, and often emotionally intense, so frequent use is rare. Because tolerance to the drug develops quickly, even those determined to drop acid as often as possible would soon be forced to take a rest between trips. Among high school seniors who have used LSD in the last year, only 3 percent say they took it twenty or more times in the previous thirty days.[39] Users typically take the drug a few times in their late teens or early twenties and then stop. Among those who continue taking LSD, occasional use is the rule.

"Long-term chronic use of LSD rarely develops," writes Leigh Henderson. "Admission to drug treatment for abuse of LSD is extremely rare." And despite the warnings about neurological and genetic damage that were heard in the 1960s and seventies, "LSD appears to pose few if any risks to physical health." There's little evidence of permanent changes in the brain, and the "chromosome breaks" that LSD (like many other substances) can cause are temporary and have no impact on the user's offspring. Likewise, "LSD use during pregnancy does not appear to harm the developing fetus."[40]

The main risk posed by LSD, then, is the possibility of an unpleasant experience. Even so, many people find it hard to understand why anyone would take the chance of being stuck for hours in a chemically induced nightmare. Part of the answer is that any given trip is unlikely to be dominated by feelings of anxiety, fear, or paranoia, and users can take precautions to minimize the risk of a negative reaction. "I try to make sure that I have a good day beforehand, that I get some things out of the way and feel like I'm on top of things," said Walter Stevenson, a neuroscientist in his late twenties who has used a wide variety of psychedelics. "I try to relax and get rid of any nervousness I might have going into it."[41] Location as well as mood can have a strong effect on a psychedelic experience. "The setting is extremely important," said William Gazecki, who took LSD once every month or two in his late teens and continues to use psilocybin and other psychedelics from time to time. "It has to be an extremely safe environment, an environment for self-expression. I don't want to attract any interference. It has to be either in my home or out in the woods somewhere, where I won't be intruded upon. . . . It has to be aesthetically pleasing visually, [with] music, comfort, and warmth. . . . When I do it with a guide, I have to be very familiar with the guide, know them and trust them."[42]

Any risk of a bad trip, of course, would be unacceptable without some sort of payoff. Users offer several reasons for taking LSD and other psychedelics. First of all, it's interesting. Curiosity—as opposed to escape, rebellion, or peer pressure—was the most common initial motivation among the psychedelic users I interviewed. Peter Collins, a knowledge engineer in his early thirties who was earning a master's degree in psychology, said his interest in LSD was piqued by a college course on altered states of consciousness. Bruce Rogers, who first tried LSD in the late sixties, remembered seeing anti-drug films in school that "would show these hippies tripping and looking at themselves in the mirror and turning into gorillas. I remember this one where the chick reached out and touched this pretty flower, and it was a hot stove. As kids, we were just thinking, 'Wow, that's cool!' So those movies more than anything else made me want to try it."[43]

Walter Stevenson, who first tried LSD with some friends when he was a senior in high school, vividly remembered the fish that seemed to leap from the pattern of blue and white threads in his jeans, the Muppet character that appeared in one of his friend's penny loafers, the Pepsi bottle that seemed to sprout wings as it sank to the ground. Watching migrating birds silhouetted against the orange background created by the setting sun, "I got the distinct impression that I could follow their sense of each other. They were flying in several overlaid patterns of octagons. . . . They were kind of in a honeycomb pattern, several honeycomb patterns moving over each other. I thought it was incredibly interesting and felt I could account for what was happening."[44]

People can enjoy such visions whether or not they generate any useful insights, just as they can enjoy optical illusions created by natural conditions, a magician's tricks, or cinematic special effects. "I loved seeing stuff differently," said Elizabeth Carr of her first LSD trip in the early 1970s. "I loved looking at things and watching them transform into something else, the magical shape-shifting quality of the psychedelic experience."[45] Bill Santini, a psychiatrist in his late fifties, said that when he closed his eyes after taking mescaline, "it was one of the unique sensations of my life—patterns on patterns. Very interesting." With eyes open, "sounds had colors and colors had textures, and I very much liked that experience."[46]

In other words, psychedelics are *fun*. True, it's not the kind of fun that everyone enjoys, but that in itself does not make the experience morally suspect. As with other forms of recreation, the relevant standard has to be the value that psychedelics offer to a given individual, weighed against the risks they pose. "When a person is tripping on LSD," observe anthropologists James MacDonald and Michael Agar, "everything is touched with a patina of mystery and magic. You never know what will happen next. But as you are experiencing these distortions and illusions, there is always the knowledge that they are just that: illusions. The person on LSD never completely loses sight of the fact that the distortions are drug induced; the altered world never completely supplants the world one remembers. In fact, one must believe that when the drug wears off, things will return to normal. If the [LSD user] loses sight of this fact for too long, a bad trip—even a profoundly bad trip—may result. . . . The irony is that one objective of a trip is to lose control, but loss of control is the cause of a bad trip."[47] Recreational users of psychedelics seek a *controlled* loss of control, an experience something like a roller-coaster ride, where there is a predictable beginning and end, where surprises and a sense of danger are part of the thrill but the true risk is minimal.

The mystery and magic that make psychedelics fun may have something to teach us about how we think and perceive. "It was interesting to learn how much of our mental makeup can be shifted," said Bob Wallace, the software developer, recalling the first time he tried LSD, the summer between his freshman and sophomore years in college. Like many researchers, he argued that "psychedelics are an important and overlooked way of understanding the mind."[48]

In addition to their entertainment value and intellectual interest, psychedelic experiences can play a role in the creative process. Some psychedelic users, like some marijuana smokers, say their work has benefited from drug-facilitated shifts in perspective. Kary B. Mullis, the Nobel Prize–winning chemist who invented the polymerase chain reaction technique for replicating DNA segments, has credited LSD with helping him work out the ideas underlying a paper on astrophysics he published in 1968.[49] The software engineer Mark Pesce, co-inventor of Virtual Reality Modeling Language, says psilocybin mushrooms and LSD helped shape his career. "There was an opening up that came from the psychedelic experience, which resulted in my becoming attracted to certain types of ideas," he told an interviewer. Without psychedelics, "I'm not sure I'd be doing *any* of the work that I'm doing now."[50] The novelist Tom Robbins writes: "The plant genies don't manufacture imagination, nor do they market wonder and beauty—but they force us out of context so dramatically and so meditatively that we gawk in amazement at the ubiquitous everyday wonders that we are culturally disposed to overlook, and they teach us invaluable lessons about fluidity, relativity, flexibility, and paradox. Such an increase in awareness, if skillfully applied, can lift a disciplined, adventurous artist permanently out of reach of the faded jaws of mediocrity."[51]

Navel Gazing

More common than claims of enhanced creativity are reports of self-discovery assisted by psychedelics. The bans passed in the sixties have eliminated the open use of LSD in psychotherapy, but many people use psychedelics on their own for much the same purpose. They sort through personal problems, reflect on relationships, and take stock of their lives. It would be difficult to scientifically validate the utility of psychedelics for such purposes, but research does indicate that people often consider them useful. In one study, researchers gave questionnaires to subjects three to twelve months after they took a combination of LSD and mescaline. As described by Grinspoon and Bakalar, "83 percent said that the experience was of lasting benefit: 74 percent considered themselves happier, 66 percent less anxious, and 78 percent more able to love; 88 percent said that it gave them a better understanding of themselves and others, and 78 percent described it as 'the greatest thing that ever happened to me.'" In another study cited by Grinspoon and Bakalar, subjects were divided into three groups, receiving either a 200-microgram dose of LSD, a 25-microgram dose, or 20 milligrams of amphetamine. Fifty-eight percent of the high-dose LSD group, compared to none of the low-dose group and 13 percent of the amphetamine group, "reported lasting changes in personality, attitudes, and values after six months—especially enhanced understanding of self and others, more introspection, a tendency not to take themselves so seriously, more tolerance, less materialism, more detachment, and greater calmness in frustrating situations."[52]

It's possible, of course, that all these people are fooling themselves. Perhaps they would have been just as happy and well-adjusted if they had never taken any drugs. Perhaps the insights they think they gained are not really valid or helpful. But the same objections could be raised against any experience that people credit with improving their lives, whether it's conventional psychotherapy, meditation, philosophical study, or religious conversion. Given the difficulty of objectively assessing such deeply personal matters, we usually defer to an individual's judgment about what makes him happier. And when we are moved to criticize, it's because we see evidence that a friend or relative is not really the better person he claims to be. In such cases, it doesn't matter whether he used a chemical to achieve the transformation.

One reason people tend to doubt the authenticity of psychological breakthroughs achieved with the help of psychedelics is that they seem too easy. That is largely a misperception, since psychedelics serve not as happy pills but as catalysts for the hard work of self-improvement. The trip itself may be grueling, and the effort that follows may be no less demanding than the effort required to build on insights generated through other means. "I've had several very difficult trips," said Kenneth Donaldson, a thirtysomething executive with a global management consulting company. "Around the period when I was getting divorced, I was using the psychedelics a lot in a therapeutic sense—let's go in there, dig out the stuff, deal with it, move on to the next piece—so a lot of those experiences were very unpleasant [but] ultimately productive."[53] Peter Collins, who had used LSD half a dozen times, said, "Every time I've dropped, I've spent the next year processing things that had become clear to me during those experiences."[54]

Katrina Lubovic, a strategic marketer in her twenties who used psilocybin mushrooms several times in college, said, "They kind of opened my eyes to a lot of things. . . . Everything was deconstructed and then constructed again. . . . I started finding out about myself." Among other things, she realized the extent to which her parents shielded her from unpleasant realities. "For a lot of my life it felt like

I was walking in a cloud," she said. "I was quite spoiled." For her, psychedelics were not a method of escape or an obstacle to maturity but part of growing up. At the same time, she said she had no desire to use them again. "It was too intense," she said, "and as I got older I just didn't need mushrooms to analyze my life."[55]

Walter Stevenson said he finds psychedelics useful when "I'm feeling very confused about things and having a difficult time deciding what I'm going to do with my life, whether I'm doing what I ought to be doing or whether what I'm doing really interests me, whether I'm with the right person—things like that. . . . If I take LSD in a fairly controlled situation, then it kind of forces me to confront all of those things at once, to look at how those things fit together and why things are the way that they are, how the person that I'm with fits with the job that I have and the job that I have fits my interests, whether I could really be doing anything else that would be any more rewarding than what I am doing. It just forces me to take stock of my life as it is at the time and to come to terms with that."[56]

Sometimes this sort of reflection leads to concrete action. Peter Collins switched jobs after an LSD trip made him realize how unhappy he was in his current position. Elizabeth Carr, who started smoking cigarettes in high school, quit more than forty years later after an LSD-assisted encounter with a Hindu god. "I had this experience playing chess with Shiva, realizing the difference between good games and bad games, and I really got that smoking was not a good game," she recalled. "Afterwards, when I was getting ready to light up, all this stuff that had happened for me during the trip came flooding into my consciousness. It said, 'If you smoke this cigarette, all the insights that you gained during this day will be gone.' . . . I haven't smoked a cigarette since."[57]

Maybe Collins and Carr would have made the same decisions without the LSD. But maybe not. And if the drug did indeed help them change their lives in positive ways, their use of it, like their use of any other self-help technique, should be judged by those results.

Seeing God

Much the same could be said of the spiritual experiences reported by psychedelic users. "I think the first thing that I noticed was a feeling of awe," Walter Stevenson said of his first LSD trip, and many others have used similar language. Elizabeth Carr remembered "looking in the mirror and seeing all my skin come off and going down to the bones and watching my whole self disappear, except for the glimmer of consciousness that was there. . . . To me, that was a deeply religious experience." Through psychedelics, she said, "I've realized a lot about the transitory nature of life and yet the permanence of consciousness, the permanence of being. . . . These drugs do help you to see things in a deeper way." The first time he took LSD, Peter Collins said, "I felt like I met God and ended up sitting in a chair with him in a room having a conversation, asking him about all the things that had confused me about religion." He said using psilocybin mushrooms is "a very intense religious ritual for me," one that gives him a feeling of "transcendence and connection," a sense that "the universe is contained within me."[58]

Such reports can easily be dismissed as one more variety of nonsense by those who reject religion in general as irrational and absurd. Likewise, orthodox believers are bound to deny the validity of religious claims that contradict their own. In neither case does it matter how someone came by his false belief, whether tripping on acid or meditating on a mountaintop. But those who believe there is value in religion that goes beyond disputes over exactly what God said to whom cannot reject out of hand the spiritual epiphanies of psychedelic users. Whether one values religion because it reflects deep truths or because it helps keep people moral, the proof of a vision has to be the extent to which it satisfies those criteria, not the manner in which it was produced. People may hear religious messages while fasting or feverish, exhausted or dreaming. If these altered states of consciousness do not invalidate the message, it's hard to see why a psychedelic trip should.

The philosopher and psychologist William James rejected the idea that religious experiences could be nullified by explaining their organic basis. "Their value," he wrote in *The Varieties of Religious Experience,* "can only be ascertained by spiritual judgments directly passed upon them, judgments based on their own immediate feeling primarily; and secondarily on what we can ascertain of their experiential relations to our moral needs and the rest of what we hold true. . . . By their fruits ye shall know them, not by their roots."[59]

James was quoting the Sermon on the Mount, in which Jesus warns the people against false prophets.[60] Similarly, the Hebrew Bible sets forth two criteria for identifying a true prophet: 1) the accuracy of his predictions, and 2) the compatibility of his message with God's earlier commandments. If a self-proclaimed prophet tells the people to worship idols, they are to disregard him, even if he impresses them with "a sign or a wonder."[61] Psychedelic visions can likewise be judged by their usefulness (though perhaps not in foretelling the future) and their compatibility with preexisting moral values.

Conservatives may be put off by the New Agey, pantheistic, or Eastern flavor of the spiritual experiences reported by some psychedelic users. A few of the people I interviewed described themselves as pagans or Wiccans, and many acid droppers of the sixties turned to Hinduism or Buddhism. Some spiritual seekers look to the ritual use of ayahuasca in South America or iboga root in Africa as a model. But many others have found in the psychedelic experience a way of strengthening their connection to monotheistic Western religions.

In one classic experiment, Walter Pahnke, a physician and minister who was working toward a Ph.D. in religion and society from Harvard, gave either psilocybin or nicotinic acid (a placebo with noticeable physical effects) to twenty Protestant divinity students who were participating in a Good Friday service at Boston University's Marsh Chapel. "All of a sudden," one of the subjects who took psilocybin later recalled, "I felt sort of drawn out into infinity, and all of a sudden I had lost touch with my mind. I felt that I was caught up in the vastness of Creation. . . . The meditation was going on all during this time, and he [the minister leading the service] would say things about Jesus and you would have this overwhelming feeling of Jesus. . . . It was like you totally penetrated what was being said and it penetrated you."[62]

Based on written descriptions, questionnaires, and interviews, Pahnke assessed the extent to which the subjects and the controls had mystical experiences. He used eight criteria: a sense of unity, transcendence of time and space, a sense of sacredness, a sense of objective reality, deeply felt positive mood, ineffability, paradoxicality, and transience. He also asked about lingering positive effects. Pahnke reported that "eight out of ten of the experimental subjects experienced at least seven out of the nine categories. None of the control group, when each individual was compared to his matched partner, had a score which was higher." In every category, the average score of the students who took psilocybin was much higher than the average score of the students who took the placebo. On "transcendence," for example, the average score of the experimental group was seventy-eight at the six-month follow-up, compared to seven for the control group. When it came to "persisting positive changes in attitude and behavior," the average score for the experimental subjects was forty-eight, compared to fifteen for the controls.[63]

A quarter century after the Good Friday Experiment, psychedelic researcher Rick Doblin managed to get seven of the subjects and nine of the controls to fill out questionnaires again. Their scores and the gaps between them were remarkably similar. In the open-ended part of the questionnaire, "experimental subjects wrote that the experience helped them resolve career decisions, recognize the arbitrariness of ego boundaries, increase their depth of faith, increase their appreciation of eternal life, deepen their sense of the meaning of Christ, and heighten their sense of joy and beauty."[64]

The subjects' experiences were not all sweetness and light. Most also reported intense negative emotions such as fear and guilt; one became so agitated that the researchers gave him a tranquilizer. And as with tests of LSD as a psychotherapeutic tool, studies like the Good Friday Experiment cannot produce the sort of evidence the Food and Drug Administration would demand before certifying the effectiveness of, say, a new heart drug. Although the experiment was set up as a double-blind study, with neither the researchers nor the subjects knowing who got the psilocybin, the mystery was cleared up once the drug's dramatic psychoactive effects kicked in. It is therefore impossible to isolate the drug's contribution to the subjects' experiences from the influence of their expectations. But as Doblin notes, "Pahnke did not set out to investigate whether psilocybin was able to produce mystical experiences irrespective of preparation and context."[65]

Rather, he wanted to see whether psilocybin, when administered to religiously inclined individuals in a religious setting, would increase the odds of such experiences.

The Native American Church provides another example of how psychedelics can be combined with Christianity. Founded a century ago, the movement today claims about a quarter-million members, whose ritual use of the peyote cactus (the source of mescaline) is sanctioned under federal law and the laws of most states. Many credit the church, and in particular the insights gained through the use of peyote, with saving them from lives dominated by self-destructive, antisocial behavior. "To us [peyote] is a portion of the body of Christ," said Albert Hensley, a Winnebago member of the church, "even as the communion bread is believed to be a portion of Christ's body for Christians. In the Bible, Christ spoke of a comforter who was to come. Sent by God, this comforter came to the Indians in the form of this holy Medicine. . . . It cures us of our temporal ills, as well as ills of a spiritual nature. It takes away the desire for strong drink. . . . Hundreds of confirmed drunkards have been rescued from their downward ways." Here the psychotherapeutic and spiritual uses of psychedelics converge, a phenomenon that is not limited to the Native American Church. Bill Wilson, founder of Alcoholics Anonymous, likened his experience with LSD to the religious revelation that led him to sobriety.[66]

William James, too, recognized the resemblance between certain drug-induced states of consciousness and mystical experiences. He wrote that under the influence of nitrous oxide, "Depth upon depth of truth seems revealed to the inhaler. This truth fades out, however, or escapes, at the moment of coming to; and if any words remain over in which it seemed to clothe itself, they prove to be the veriest nonsense. Nonetheless, the sense of a profound meaning having been there persists; and I know more than one person who is persuaded that in the nitrous oxide trance we have a genuine metaphysical revelation."[67]

Even those who believe that people can in some sense communicate with God are inclined to dismiss messages received under the influence of drugs as "the veriest nonsense." But James was not so harsh in his judgment. Regarding his experiences with nitrous oxide, he wrote, "One conclusion was forced upon my mind at that time, and my impression of its truth has ever since remained unshaken. It is that our normal waking consciousness, rational consciousness as we call it, is but one special type of consciousness, whilst all about it, parted from it by the filmiest of screens, there lie potential forms of consciousness entirely different. We may go through life without their existence; but apply the requisite stimulus, and at a touch they are there in all their completeness, definite types of mentality which probably somewhere have their field of application and adaptation. No account of the universe in its totality can be final which leaves these other forms of consciousness quite disregarded."[68]

Compared to the vision championed by Timothy Leary and other LSD prophets in the sixties, this is a modest claim. It does not imply that certain drugs have the power to remake the world or change human nature. It does not mean that psychedelics are an infallible guide to the truth. It does not exclude the possibility that much of what people come to believe after using them will be silly, pernicious, or both. But it does suggest that psychedelics can help us learn about ourselves, about the human mind, and maybe even about God. As foolish as it is to assume that every LSD-inspired thought is a divine revelation, it is no less unreasonable to assume that nothing good can come from psychedelics. The experience of the sixties suggests that the first kind of dogmatism invites the second. The more LSD's boosters insisted that it would make the world a saner place, the more its opponents warned that it could lead to nothing but madness. As we'll see in the next chapter, the way MDMA, a.k.a. Ecstasy, was promoted in the 1980s likewise led to a predictable reaction against it, this time tied to sexual hedonism rather than insanity.

CHAPTER FIVE

RANDOM SEX ACTS

Ecstasy abuse can lead to prostitution and casual sex.
—*NEW STRAITS TIMES* (MALAYSIA), 2000

So-called Ecstasy . . . has been implicated nationally in the sexual assaults of approximately 5,000 teen-age and young adult women.
—PEDIATRICIAN PETER D. ROGERS IN THE *COLUMBUS DISPATCH*, 2000

Wild Parties

In 2001 the Chicago City Council decided "to crack down on wild rave parties that lure youngsters into environments loaded with dangerous club drugs, underage drinking, and sometimes predatory sexual behavior," as the *Chicago Tribune* put it. The newspaper described raves as "one-night-only parties . . . often held in warehouses or secret locations where people pay to dance, do drugs, play loud music, and engage in random sex acts." Taking a dim view of such goings-on, the city council passed an ordinance threatening to jail building owners or managers who allowed raves to be held on their property.

Mayor Richard Daley took the occasion to "lash out at the people who produce the huge rogue dance parties where Ecstasy and other designer drugs are widely used." In Daley's view, rave promoters were deliberately seducing the innocent. "They are after all of our children," he warned. "Parents should be outraged by this."[1]

The reaction against raves reflects familiar anxieties about what the kids are up to, especially when it comes to sex. As the chemical symbol of raves, MDMA, a.k.a. Ecstasy, has come to represent sexual abandon and, partly through association with other "club drugs," sexual assault. These are not the only fears raised by MDMA. The drug, whose full name is methylenedioxymethamphetamine, has also been accused of causing brain damage and of leading people astray with ersatz feelings of empathy and euphoria (concerns discussed later in this chapter). But the sexual angle is interesting because it has little to do with the drug's actual properties, a situation for which there is considerable precedent in the history of reputed aphrodisiacs. As the phenomenal success of Viagra shows, sex-promoting drugs can be respectable. When they're seen in a more sinister light, however, they represent another variation on voodoo pharmacology, inciting lust and turning people into sex maniacs.

A relative of both amphetamine and mescaline, MDMA is often described as a stimulant with psychedelic qualities. But its effects are primarily emotional, without the perceptual changes caused by LSD. Although MDMA was first synthesized by the German drug company Merck in 1912, it did not gain a following until the 1970s, when the psychonautical chemist Alexander Shulgin, a Dow researcher turned independent consultant, tried some at the suggestion of a graduate student he was helping a friend supervise. "It was not a psychedelic in the visual or interpretive sense," he later wrote, "but the lightness and warmth of the psychedelic was present and quite remarkable." MDMA created a "window," he decided. "It enabled me to see out, and to see my own insides, without distortions or reservations."[2]

After observing some striking examples of people who claimed to have overcome serious personal problems (including a severe stutter and oppressive guilt) with the help of MDMA, Shulgin introduced the drug to a psychologist he knew who had already used psyche-delics as an aid to therapy. "Adam," the pseudonym that Shulgin gave him (also a nickname for the drug), was on the verge of retiring but was so impressed by MDMA's effects that he decided to continue working. He shared his techniques with other psychologists and psychiatrists, and under his influence thousands of people report-edly used the drug to enhance communication and self-insight.[3] "It seemed to dissolve fear for a few hours," said a psychiatrist who tried MDMA in the early eighties. "I thought it would have been very use-ful for working with people with trauma disorders."[4] (Nearly two decades later, the Food and Drug Administration approved a study of MDMA-assisted psychotherapy for people diagnosed with posttrau-matic stress disorder.[5]) Shulgin concedes that there was "a hint of snake-oil" in MDMA's reputed versatility, but he himself considered it "an incredible tool." He quotes one psychiatrist as saying, "MDMA is penicillin for the soul, and you don't give up penicillin, once you've seen what it can do."[6]

Ecstatic Reception

Shulgin did not see MDMA exclusively as a psychotherapeutic tool. He also referred to it as "my low-calorie martini," a way of loos-ening up and relating more easily to others at social gatherings.[7] This aspect of the drug came to the fore in the 1980s, when MDMA became popular among nightclubbers in Texas, where it was marketed as a party drug under the name *Ecstasy*. The open recreational use of Ecstasy at clubs in Dallas and Austin brought down the wrath of the Drug Enforcement Administration, which decided to put MDMA in the same legal category as heroin. The ban was opposed by researchers who emphasized the drug's psychotherapeutic potential. "We had no idea psychiatrists were using it," a DEA pharmacologist told *Newsweek* in 1985.[8] Nor did they care: Despite an administrative law judge's recommendation that doctors be allowed to prescribe the drug, a permanent ban on MDMA took effect the following year.

Thus MDMA followed the same pattern as LSD, moving from discreet psychotherapeutic use to the sort of conspicuous consumption that was bound to provoke a government reaction. Like LSD, it became illegal because too many people started to enjoy it. Although the DEA probably would have sought to ban any newly popular intoxicant, the name change certainly didn't help. The distributor who claimed to have originated the name *Ecstasy* said he picked it "because it would sell better than calling it 'Empathy.' 'Empathy' would be more appropriate, but how many people know what it means?"[9] In its traditional sense, *ecstasy* has a spiritual connotation, but in common usage it simply means intense pleasure—often the kind associated with sex. As David Smith, director of the Haight-Ashbury Free Clinic, observed, the name "suggested that it made sex better."[10] Some marketers have been more explicit: A 1999 article in the *Journal of Toxicology* (headlined "SEX on the Streets of Cincinnati") reported an analysis of "unknown tablets imprinted with 'SEX'" that turned out to contain MDMA.[11]

Hyperbolic comments by some users have reinforced Ecstasy's sexual connotations. "One enthusiast described the feeling as a six-hour orgasm!" exclaimed the author of a 2000 op-ed piece in Malaysia's *New Straits Times,* picking up a phrase quoted in *Time* a couple months before.[12] A column in the *Toronto Sun,* meanwhile, stated matter-of-factly that MDMA "can even make you feel like a six-hour orgasm."[13] If simply taking MDMA makes you feel that way, readers might reasonably have concluded, MDMA-enhanced sex must be indescribably good.

Another reason MDMA came to be associated with sex is its reputation as a "hug drug" that breaks down emotional barriers and brings out feelings of affection. The warmth and candor of people who've taken MDMA may be interpreted as flirtatiousness. More generally, MDMA is said to remove fear, which is one reason psychotherapists have found it useful. The same effect could also be described as a loss of inhibitions, often a precursor to sexual liaisons. Finally, users report enhanced pleasure from physical sensations, especially the sense of touch. They often trade hugs, caresses, and back rubs.

Yet the consensus among users seems to be that MDMA's effects are more sensual than sexual. According to a therapist quoted by Jerome Beck and Marsha Rosenbaum in their book *Pursuit of Ecstasy,* "MDMA and sex do not go very well together. For most people, MDMA turns off the ability to function as a lover, to put it indelicately. It's called the love drug because it opens up the capacity to feel loving and affectionate and trusting." At the same time, however, it makes the "focusing of the body and the psychic energy necessary to achieve orgasm . . . very difficult. And most men find it impossible. . . . So it is a love drug but not a sex drug for most people."[14] Michael Buchanan, a retired professor in his early seventies, has used MDMA several times with one or two other people. "It's just wonderful," he said, "to bring closeness, intimacy—not erotic intimacy at all, but a kind of spiritual intimacy, a loving relationship, an openness to dialogue that nothing else can quite match."[15]

Although this distinction is widely reported by users, press coverage has tended to perpetuate the connection between MDMA and sex. In 1985 *Newsweek* said the drug "is considered an aphrodisiac," while *Maclean's* played up one user's claim of "very good sexual possibilities."[16] *Life* also cited "the drug's reputation for good sex," even while noting that it "blocks male ejaculation."[17] More recently, a story about MDMA in *Time* began by describing "a classic Southeast Asian den of iniquity" where prostitutes used Ecstasy so they could be "friendly and outgoing." It warned that "because users feel empathetic, ecstasy can lower sexual inhibitions. Men generally cannot get erections when high on e, but they are often ferociously randy when its effects begin to fade." The article cited a correlation between MDMA use and "unprotected sex."[18] Celebrity psychologist Joyce Brothers picked up on this theme a few months later, observing that "kids on drugs that lower inhibitions (MDMA included) are . . . more likely to indulge in unprotected sex."[19] In a similar vein, a cautionary article in *Cosmopolitan* began with the account of "a 28-year-old lawyer from Los Angeles" who brought home a man with whom she felt "deeply connected" under the influence of MDMA. "We would have had sex, but he couldn't get an erection," she reported. "The next day, I was horrified that I had let a guy I couldn't even stand into my bed!"[20]

Rape Drugs

MDMA has been linked not just to regrettable sexual encounters but to rapes in which drugs are used as weapons. The connection is usually made indirectly, by way of other drugs whose effects are quite different but which are also popular at raves and dance clubs. In particular, the depressants GHB and Rohypnol have acquired reputations as "date rape drugs," used to incapacitate victims to whom they are given surreptitiously. Needless to say, this is not the main use for these substances, which people generally take on purpose because they like their effects. It's not clear exactly how often rapists use GHB or Rohypnol, but such cases are surely much rarer than the hysterical reaction from the press and Congress (which passed a Date Rape Drug Prohibition Act in 2000) would lead one to believe. In a 1998 study of 578 rape victims who said they'd been drugged before they were attacked, only 1 percent of their urine samples tested positive for Rohypnol, compared to 36 percent for alcohol.[21] The public nonetheless has come to view Rohypnol and GHB primarily as instruments of assault, an impression that has affected the image of other "club drugs," especially MDMA.

Grouping MDMA with GHB and Rohypnol, a 2000 Knight Ridder story warned that the dangers of "club drugs" include "vulnerability to sexual assault."[22] Similarly, the *Chicago Tribune* cited Ecstasy as the most popular "club drug" before referring to "women who suspect they were raped after they used or were slipped a club drug."[23] In a *Columbus Dispatch* op-ed piece, pediatrician Peter D. Rogers further obscured the distinction between MDMA and the so-called rape drugs by saying that "Ecstasy . . . comes in three forms," including "GHB, also called liquid Ecstasy," and "Herbal Ecstasy, also known as ma huang or ephedra" (a legal stimulant), as well as "MDMA, or chemical Ecstasy." He asserted, without citing a source, that "so-called Ecstasy"—it's not clear which one he meant—"has been implicated nationally in the sexual assaults of approximately 5,000 teen-age and young adult women." Rogers described a sixteen-year-old patient who "took Ecstasy and was raped twice. She told me that she remembers the rapes but, high on the drug, was powerless to stop them. She couldn't even scream, let alone fight back."[24] If Rogers, identified as a member of the American Academy of Pediatrics' Committee on Substance Abuse, had trouble keeping the "club drugs" straight, it's not surprising that the general public saw little difference between giving a date MDMA and slipping her a mickey.

As the alleged connections between MDMA and sex illustrate, the concept of an aphrodisiac is complex and ambiguous. A drug could be considered an aphrodisiac because it reduced resistance, because it increased interest, because it improved ability, or because it enhanced enjoyment. From a traditional perspective on sex that sees men as aggressive and women as reluctant, aphrodisiacs are given to women primarily for the first two reasons and taken by men for the second two. A particular drug could be effective for one or two of these purposes but useless (or worse) for the others. Shakespeare observed that alcohol "provokes the desire, but it takes away the performance."[25] Something similar seems to be true of MDMA, except that the desire is more emotional than sexual, a sense of closeness which may find expression in sex that is apt to be aborted because of difficulty in getting an erection or reaching orgasm. Also like alcohol, MDMA is blamed for causing people to act against their considered judgment. The concern is not just that people might have casual sex but that they might regret it afterward.

Surely this concern is not entirely misplaced. As Ogden Nash observed, "Candy is dandy, but liquor is quicker."[26] When drinking precedes sex, there may be a fine line between seducing someone and taking advantage, between lowering inhibitions and impairing judgment. But the possibility of crossing that line does not mean that alcohol is nothing but a trick employed by cads. Nor does the possibility of using alcohol to render someone incapable of resistance condemn it as a tool of rapists.

The closest thing we have to a genuine aphrodisiac—increasing interest, ability, and enjoyment—is Viagra, the avowed purpose of which is to enable people to have more and better sex. Instead of being deplored as an aid to hedonism, it is widely praised for increasing the net sum of human happiness. Instead of being sold on the sly in dark nightclubs, it's pitched on television by a former Senate majority leader and presidential candidate. The difference seems to be that Viagra is viewed as a legitimate medicine, approved by the government and prescribed by doctors.

But as Joann Ellison Rodgers, author of *Drugs and Sexual Behavior,* observes, "there is great unease with the idea of encouraging sexual prowess. . . . At the very least, drugs in the service of sex do seem to subvert or at least trivialize important aspects of sexual experiences, such as love, romance, commitment, trust and health."[27] If we've managed to accept Viagra and (to a lesser extent) alcohol as aphrodisiacs, it may be only because we've projected their darker possibilities onto other substances, of which the "club drugs" are just the latest examples.

Where There's Smoke

During the twentieth century the cigarette acquired strong sexual connotations, especially in the hands and mouths of seductive movie stars. It played a role before sex, as part of the mating ritual, and afterward, as a postcoital prop. But the cigarette was understood as an expression of eroticism rather than a cause of it, a sexual totem rather than an aphrodisiac. Centuries before the cigarette became popular, tobacco itself was rumored to ignite passion—a belief that fit well with the critique of smoking as a hedonistic rite of wild heathens. ("Shall we . . . abase ourselves so farre, as to imitate these beastly *Indians?*" wrote King James I in his 1604 *Counterblaste to Tobacco.* "Why doe we not as well imitate them in walking naked as they doe? . . . yea why doe we not denie God and adore the Devill as they doe?"[28]) The anthropologist Alexander Von Gernet suggests that the rumors of tobacco's aphrodisiac properties "may have been initiated or fortified by colonizers who explained the alleged ardency of native Nicaraguan women by citing their addiction to cigar-smoking."[29] Defenders of the habit insisted that, far from releasing sexual impulses, smoking helped control them. Benedetto Stella, author of a 1689 treatise on the weed, argued that "the use of tobacco, taken moderately, not only is useful, but even necessary for the priests, monks, friars and other religious who must and desire to lead a chaste life, and repress those sensual urges that sometimes assail them. The natural cause of lust is heat and humidity. When this is dried out through the use of tobacco, these libidinous surges are not felt so powerfully."[30]

Some of tobacco's foes continued to condemn it for inciting lust as late as the nineteenth century, when an American polemicist declared that "tobacco-eating and deviltry are both one, because the fierce passions of many tobacco chewers, as regards the other sex, are immensely increased by the fires kindled in their systems, and of course in their cerebellums, by tobacco excitement."[31] By the late twentieth century, however, anti-tobacco crusaders were warning not that smoking might stir up amorous feelings but that it could stop you from following through on them. One memorable anti-smoking ad showed cigarettes wilting in the mouths of would-be Lotharios rendered impotent by tobacco.

The link between tobacco and sexual license perceived by some European observers of American Indian habits was an early manifestation of a recurring stereotype involving drugs identified with outsiders. A similar pattern can be seen in descriptions of opium use by Chinese immigrants to the United States. The country's first anti-opium laws, passed by Western states in the late nineteenth century, were motivated largely by hostility toward the low-cost Chinese laborers who competed for work with Americans of European descent. Supporters of such legislation, together with a sensationalist press, popularized the image of the sinister Chinaman who lured white women into his opium den, turning them into concubines, prostitutes, or sex slaves. Although users generally find that opiates dampen their sex drive, "it was commonly reported that opium smoking aroused sexual desire," writes historian David Courtwright, "and that some shameless smokers persuaded 'innocent girls to smoke in order to excite their passions and effect their ruin.'"[32] San Francisco authorities lamented that the police "have found white women and Chinamen side by side under the effects of this drug—a humiliating sight to anyone who has anything left of manhood."[33] In 1910 Hamilton Wright, a U.S. diplomat who played a key role in the passage of federal anti-drug legislation, told Congress that "one of the most unfortunate phases of the habit of smoking opium in this country" was "the large number of women who [had] become involved and were living as common-law wives or cohabiting with Chinese in the Chinatowns of our various cities."[34]

Fears of miscegenation also played a role in popular outrage about cocaine, which (as discussed in the next chapter) was said to make blacks uppity and prone to violence against whites, especially sexual assault. In 1910 Christopher Koch, a member of the Pennsylvania

Pharmacy Board who pushed for a federal ban on cocaine, informed Congress that "the colored people seem to have a weakness for it. . . . They would just as leave rape a woman as anything else, and a great many of the southern rape cases have been traced to cocaine."[35] A few years later, presumably after conducting more extensive research, Koch declared that "*most* of the attacks upon white women of the South are a direct result of a cocaine-crazed Negro brain."[36] Describing cocaine's effect on "hitherto inoffensive, law abiding negroes," Edward Huntington Williams likewise warned that "sexual desires are increased and perverted."[37]

Marijuana, another drug that was believed to cause violence (see Chapter 6), was also linked to sex crimes and, like opium, seduction. Under marijuana's influence, according to a widely cited 1932 report in the *Journal of Criminal Law and Criminology*, "sexual desires are stimulated and may lead to unnatural acts, such as indecent exposure and rape." The authors cited a newspaper account of "a Kansas hasheesh eater" who "thinks he is a white elephant" and was found wandering naked down a road. They also quoted an informant who "reported several instances of which he claimed to have positive knowledge, where boys had induced girls to use the weed for the purpose of seducing them."[38] The Federal Bureau of Narcotics, which collected anecdotes about marijuana's baneful effects to support a national ban on the drug, cited "colored students at the Univ. of Minn. partying with female students (white) smoking [marijuana] and getting their sympathy with stories of racial persecution. Result pregnancy." The bureau also described a case in which "two Negroes took a girl fourteen years old and kept her for two days in a hut under the influence of marijuana. Upon recovery she was found to be suffering from syphilis."[39]

Drug-related horror stories nowadays are rarely so explicitly racist. A notable and surprising exception appears in the 2000 film *Traffic*, which is critical of the war on drugs but nevertheless represents the utter degradation of a middle-class white teenager who gets hooked on crack by showing her having sex with a black man. Whether related to race or not, parental anxieties about sexual activity among teenagers have not gone away, and drugs are a convenient scapegoat when kids seem to be growing up too fast. The link between drugs and sex was reinforced by the free-love ethos of the sixties counterculture that embraced marijuana and LSD. In the public mind, pot smoking, acid dropping, and promiscuous sex were all part of the same lifestyle; a chaste hippie chick was a contradiction in terms. When Timothy Leary extolled LSD's sex-enhancing qualities in his 1966 *Playboy* interview—notwithstanding his emphasis on monogamy—he fueled the fears of parents who worried that their daughters would be seduced into a decadent world of sex, drugs, and rock 'n' roll. The Charles Manson case added a sinister twist to this scenario, raising the possibility of losing one's daughter to an evil cult leader who uses LSD to brainwash his followers, in much the same way as Chinese men were once imagined to enthrall formerly respectable white girls with opium.

Signal of Misunderstanding

The alarm about the sexual repercussions of "club drugs," then, has to be understood in the context of warnings about other alleged aphrodisiacs, often identified with particular groups perceived as inferior, threatening, or both: American Indians, Chinese immigrants, blacks, hippies, teenagers. The fear of uncontrolled sexual impulses, of the chaos that would result if we let our basic instincts run wild, is projected onto these groups and, by extension, their intoxicants. In the case of "club drugs," adolescents are both victims and perpetrators. Parents fear for their children, but they also fear them. When Mayor Daley warned that "they are after all of our children," he may have been imagining predators in the mold of Fu Manchu or Charles Manson. But the reality is that raves—which grew out of the British "acid house" movement, itself reminiscent of the psychedelic dance scene that emerged in San Francisco during the late sixties—are overwhelmingly a youth phenomenon.

The experience of moving all night to a throbbing beat amid flickering light has been likened to tribal dancing around a fire. A similar exuberance, sense of community, and trance-like state of consciousness can also be observed in traditional Jewish dancing, in which the same verse is sung over and over again while everyone whirls around in a circle. But for most people over thirty, the appeal of dancing for hours on end to the fast, repetitive rhythm of techno music is hard to fathom. "The sensationalist reaction that greets every mention of the word Ecstasy in this country is part of a wider, almost unconscious fear of young people," writes Jonathan Keane in the British *New Statesman,* and the observation applies equally to the United States. For "middle-aged and middle-class opinion leaders . . . E is a symbol of a youth culture they don't understand."[40]

This is not to say that no one ever felt horny after taking MDMA. Individual reactions to drugs are highly variable, and one could probably find anecdotes suggesting aphrodisiac properties for almost any psychoactive substance. And it is no doubt true that some MDMA users, like the woman quoted in *Cosmo,* have paired up with sexual partners they found less attractive the morning after. But once MDMA is stripped of its symbolism, these issues are no different from those raised by alcohol. In fact, since MDMA users tend to be more lucid than drinkers, the chances that they will do something regrettable are probably lower.

Jasmine Menendez, a public-relations director in her twenties who was using MDMA every weekend for a while, decided to cut back because she didn't like the after-effects. But her most serious drug-related scrape occurred when she was sixteen, the night she was nearly raped after she drank so much peppermint schnapps that she passed out. "I swore to myself that if I ever drank like that again, it would be with people I knew in an environment that wasn't shady," she said.[41] You won't be reading Menendez's story in *Cosmo,* of course, because alcohol is legal and familiar. It doesn't even count as a "club drug."

I Love You Guys

Another alcohol-related hazard, one that seems to be more characteristic of MDMA than the risk of casual sex or rape, is the possibility of inappropriate emotional intimacy. The maudlin drunk who proclaims his affection for everyone and reveals secrets he might later wish he had kept is a widely recognized character, either comical or pathetic depending upon your point of view. Given MDMA's reputation as a "love drug," it's natural to wonder whether it fosters the same sort of embarrassing behavior.

Tom Cowan, a systems analyst in his thirties, has used MDMA a few times, and he doesn't think it revealed any deep emotional truths. "For me," he said, "it was almost too much of a fake. . . . It was too artificial for me. . . . I felt warm. I felt loved. All of those sensations came upon me. . . . I had all these feelings, but I knew that deep down I didn't feel that, so at the same time there was that inner struggle as far as just letting loose and just being. . . . That was difficult because of the fakeness about it for me."[42] More typically, MDMA users perceive the warm feelings as real, both at the time and in retrospect. Some emphasize an enhanced connection to friends, while others report a feeling of benevolence toward people in general.

"I was very alert but very relaxed at the same time," said Alison Witt, a software engineer in her twenties. "I didn't love everybody. . . . It's a very social drug, and you do feel connected to other people, but I think it's more because it creates a sense of relaxation and pleasure with people you're familiar with."[43] Walter Stevenson, a neuroscientist in his late twenties, gave a similar account: "I felt really happy to have my friends around me. I just enjoyed sitting there and spending time with them, not necessarily talking about anything, but not to the degree that I felt particularly attracted or warm to people I didn't know. I was very friendly and open to meeting people, but there wasn't anything inappropriate about the feeling."[44] Adam Newman, an Internet specialist in his twenties, believes his MDMA use helped improve his social life. "It kind of catapulted me past a bunch of shyness and other mental and emotional blocks," he said. Even when he wasn't using MDMA, "I felt a lot better than I had in social interactions before."[45] Bruce Rogers, a horticulturist in his forties, said one thing he likes about MDMA is that "you can find something good in somebody that you dislike." He thinks "it would make the world a better place if everybody did it just once."[46]

That's the kind of assertion, reminiscent of claims about LSD's earthshaking potential, that tends to elicit skeptical smiles. But the important point is that many MDMA users believe the drug has lasting psychological benefits, even when it's taken in a recreational context—the sort of thing you don't often hear about alcohol.

For those who turn to MDMA for help with serious problems,

these benefits are the main point, rather than merely a welcome side effect. Sue Stevens and her husband, Shane, who was diagnosed with kidney cancer at the age of twenty-two, used MDMA to deal with the emotions raised by his illness. "We didn't know about the emotional process," she said. "We didn't know about the fears. We developed huge walls around us . . . so we didn't have to deal with it. . . . We avoided it, and in doing so we started destroying [our marriage]."[47]

At a friend's suggestion, Sue and Shane tried MDMA. "We were able to sit down and open up," she said, "and talk about everything we'd been avoiding—all of the pain, all of the anger, all the fear. And we were able to do it without fear of being judged by each other, without fear of hurting each other. It was just amazing. I never knew that you could reach levels like that, such openness and honesty between two people. One night . . . changed our life permanently. . . . We woke up to the same people we had fallen in love with. . . . There were no barriers between us, no fears, no anger. . . . Anytime he had an issue [related to his illness], he would come to me without fear of hurting me, and vice versa; I could go to him without fear of crying in front of him and getting his walls up. . . . We learned that night how to become a team, how to fight the cancer together rather than separate ourselves from the cancer and each other."[48]

Sue and Shane had their first MDMA session around the time his doctors had predicted he would die. His health was failing, and he was cutting back on his work, sleeping late, and relying heavily on painkillers. He was moody and irritable. After the session, Sue said, "He decided to live." He threw away the Vicodin and became physically active again, riding his bike and playing basketball with the kids. "You'd never [have known] anything was wrong with him," she said. "Emotionally, physically, he overcame it." Shane finally died three years later, in the fall of 1999. He and Sue used MDMA again a month before his death. "We wanted one last night," she said. "We spent the next six hours recapping our lives together. We talked about everything. . . . We lived our entire life together in that night, plus we lived fifty more years. We kind of took back what the cancer had robbed. We took time." At one point, she recalled, "he looked at me and said, 'You know, it's really great not to have cancer tonight.'"[49]

Adam vs. Ecstasy

It's hard to believe that the life-changing catalyst described by Sue Stevens is the same drug taken by ravers and clubbers for fun. (In many cases, since other substances are often passed off as "Ecstasy," it may not be. But independent tests suggest that most pills sold as Ecstasy do contain the real thing, and this was certainly the case when MDMA was still legal.[50]) MDMA can be Adam, a powerful tool for personal transformation, or it can be Ecstasy, the party drug that helps you dance the night away. "I don't understand how the kids can use it that way," said Michael Buchanan, the retired academic who had taken MDMA only in intimate settings.[51] In one context, the drug is used to enhance communication; in the other, the music is so loud that communication is barely possible. Not surprisingly, people who use MDMA in clubs and at raves emphasize its sensual and stimulant properties, the way it enhances music and dancing. But they also talk about a sense of connectedness, especially at raves. Jasmine Menendez, who had used MDMA both at raves and with small groups of friends, said it provides "a great body high. I lose all sense of inhibition and my full potential is released. . . . It allows me to get closer to people and to myself."[52]

Euphoria is a commonly reported effect of MDMA, which raises the usual concerns about the lure of artificial pleasure. "It was an incredible feeling of being tremendously happy where I was and being content in a basic way," Walter Stevenson recalled of the first time he felt MDMA's effects.[53] He used it several more times after that, but it never became a regular habit.

Menendez, on the other hand, found MDMA "easy to become addicted to" because "you see the full potential in yourself and others; you feel like you won the lottery." She began chasing that feeling one weekend after another, often taking several pills in one night. "Doing e as much as I did affected my relationship with my mother," she said. "I would come home 'cracked out' from a night of partying and sleep the whole day. She couldn't invite anyone over because I was always sleeping. She said that my party habits were out of control. We fought constantly. I would also go to work high from the party, if I had to work weekends. The comedown was horrible because I wanted to sleep and instead I had to be running around doing errands."[54]

Menendez decided to cut back on her MDMA consumption, eventually using it only on special occasions. "I think I've outgrown it finally," she said. "I used e to do some serious soul searching and to come out of my shell, learning all I could about who I really am. I'm grateful that I had the experiences that I did and wouldn't change it for the world. But now, being twenty-three, I'm ready to embrace mental clarity fully. Ecstacy is definitely a constructive tool and if used correctly can benefit the user. It changed my life for the better, and because of what I learned about myself, I'm ready to start a new life without it."[55]

Sustained heavy use of MDMA is rare, partly because it's impractical. MDMA works mainly by stimulating the release of the neurotransmitter serotonin. Taking it depletes the brain's supply, which may not return to normal levels for a week or more. Some users report a hangover period of melancholy and woolly-headedness that can last a few days. As frequency of use increases, MDMA's euphoric and empathetic effects diminish and its unpleasant side effects, including jitteriness and hangovers, intensify. Like LSD, it has a self-limiting quality, which is reflected in patterns of use. In the 2001 National Household Survey on Drug Abuse, less than 4 percent of the respondents said they had tried MDMA. Within this group, 38 percent had used it in the previous year, 8 percent in the previous month.[56] In a 2002 survey, about 7 percent of high-school seniors reported using MDMA in the previous year. About a third of the past-year users said they had taken it in the previous month, and less than 1 percent of them reported "daily" use (defined as use on twenty or more occasions in the previous thirty days). To parents, of course, any use of MDMA is alarming, and the share of high-school seniors who said they'd ever tried the drug nearly doubled between 1996 and 2001, when it was about 12 percent.[57]

Parental fears have been stoked by reports of sudden fatalities among MDMA users. Given the millions of doses consumed each year, such cases are remarkably rare: The Drug Abuse Warning Network counted nine MDMA-related deaths in 1998.[58] The most common cause of death is overheating and dehydration. MDMA impairs the ability to regulate body temperature, which can be especially dangerous for people dancing vigorously in crowded, poorly ventilated spaces for hours at a time. The solution to this problem, well-known to experienced ravers, is pretty straightforward: avoid clubs and parties where conditions are stifling, take frequent rests, abstain from alcohol (which compounds dehydration), and drink plenty of water. (Ironically, this last bit of advice can be risky if followed too enthusiastically: A few deaths among MDMA users have been attributed to water intoxication, which occurs when people drink so much water that the sodium level in their blood drops significantly, causing their brains to swell.) MDMA also may interact dangerously with some prescription drugs (including monoamine oxidase inhibitors, a class of antidepressants), and it raises heart rate and blood pressure, of special concern for people with cardiovascular conditions.

Another hazard is a product of the black market created by prohibition: Tablets or capsules sold as Ecstasy may in fact contain other, possibly more dangerous drugs. In tests by private U.S. laboratories, more than one-third of "Ecstasy" pills turned out to be bogus.[59] (The samples were not necessarily representative, and the results may be on the high side, since the drugs were submitted voluntarily for testing, perhaps by buyers who had reason to be suspicious.) Most of the MDMA substitutes, which included caffeine, ephedrine, and aspirin, were relatively harmless, but one of them, the cough suppressant dextromethorphan (DXM), has disturbing psychoactive effects in high doses, impedes the metabolism of MDMA, and blocks perspiration, raising the risk of overheating. Another drug that has been passed off as MDMA is paramethoxyamphetamine (PMA), which is potentially lethal in doses over 50 milligrams, especially when combined with other drugs. In 2000 the DEA reported ten deaths tied to PMA.[60] Wary Ecstasy users can buy test kits or have pills analyzed by organizations such as DanceSafe, which sets up booths at raves and nightclubs.

Nervous Breakdown

Generally speaking, the short-term dangers of MDMA can be avoided by a careful user. Of more concern is the possibility of long-term brain damage. In animal studies, high or repeated doses of MDMA cause degeneration of serotonin nerve terminals, and some of the changes appear to be permanent. The relevance of these studies to human use of MDMA is unclear because we don't know whether the same changes occur in people or, if they do, at what doses and with what practical consequences.

Charles S. Grob, a professor of psychiatry at UCLA and a leading authority on MDMA, notes that the appetite suppressant fenfluramine has neural effects "virtually identical" to those seen in animal studies of MDMA. Yet although fenfluramine was taken by some 25 million people over a period of more than thirty years, "no clinical syndrome of fenfluramine neurotoxicity [was ever] described." When the drug was removed from the market in 1997, it was because of its suspected role in cardiac valve damage, not because of neurotoxicity concerns.[61]

There is little evidence of significant behavior changes in animals exposed to MDMA. A number of studies have found that heavy MDMA users perform worse on certain cognitive tests than nonusers, and one study using positron emission tomography (PET) reported evidence that heavy users' neurons were less able to transport serotonin. In a review of the research, Grob cites serious weaknesses in all of these studies. One major problem is that MDMA use may not be the only relevant difference between subjects and controls. The raver lifestyle, involving the use of other drugs, overexertion, inadequate sleep, and poor nutrition, could account for some or all of the (usually modest) differences in test performance. Then, too, there may be preexisting cognitive or neural differences that make people more apt to use MDMA. Grob also questions whether the results of the PET scan study can reasonably be interpreted as evidence of brain damage.[62]

"Virtually all research efforts to date have been directed at establishing through laboratory animal investigations and retrospective human Ecstasy user models the neurotoxic dangers of MDMA," Grob writes. "After fifteen years, however, the case has yet to be made. Although long-term alterations of neuronal architecture in animals ranging from rats to human primates have been consistently demonstrated, the functional consequences have remained obscure. Furthermore, efforts to extrapolate evidence of MDMA-induced neuropathology from retrospective examinations of heavy Ecstasy users have consistently manifested serious methodological flaws."[63]

A 2001 study, reported after Grob's review of the literature, muddied the waters further. A team of Dutch researchers found that the density of serotonin receptors in cortical neurons was, on average, 9 percent lower in twenty-two recent MDMA users than in thirteen controls who had never used the drug. But they found no differences in sixteen former MDMA users (who had not used the drug in more than a year), suggesting that any neural changes are reversible. On the other hand, both recent and former MDMA users had lower scores than the controls on a word recall test. In other words, the differences in performance were not related to the neural changes—a puzzling result if MDMA was responsible for the gap.[64]

Still, the possibility of lasting damage to memory should not be lightly dismissed. There's enough reason for concern that MDMA should no longer be treated as casually as "a low-calorie martini." If the fears about memory impairment prove to be well-founded and a safe dose cannot be estimated with any confidence, a prudent person would need a good reason—probably better than a fun night out—to take the risk. On the other hand, the animal research suggests that it may be possible to avoid neural damage by preventing hyperthermia or by taking certain drugs (for example, fluoxetine, a.k.a. Prozac) in conjunction with MDMA.[65] In that case, such precautions would be a requirement of responsible use.

The morality of using MDMA hinges mostly on how it affects the brain over the long term. The drug's immediate effects pose issues no different in principle from those associated with alcoholic intoxication. If anything, drinking seems to be more problematic, given its effects on judgment and its reputation for encouraging violence.

Brawling is one thing MDMA has never been charged with causing. Even when it has been accused, along with other "club drugs," of making life easier for rapists, no one has suggested that Ecstasy brings out a man's violent impulses. But as the next chapter shows, a surprisingly wide range of other drugs have been cast as Dr. Jekyll's potion.

CHAPTER SIX

KILLER DRUGS

The drug crack causes unpredictable, violent behavior.
—FORMER PROSECUTOR ROBERT E. PETERSON AT A 1990 DRUG POLICY CONFERENCE

Crack Shots

On November 9, 1986, Phillip Hall stole $20 from his parents to buy crack. After getting high, the twenty-year-old returned to his family's three-bedroom apartment in the Bedford-Stuyvesant section of Brooklyn and beat his sleeping parents to death with a metal baseball bat. Then he took another $80 to buy more crack. On his way out, he woke up his thirteen-year-old nephew and used the bat to kill him as well.

Three years later, after Hall pleaded guilty, a judge imposed a sentence of twenty years to life for the triple homicide. "I always felt Mr. Hall was a victim of his drug abuse," he said. The prosecutor seemed to agree, although he asked for a longer sentence to help deter other people from using drugs. "People should know that the use of crack can have these type of consequences," he said "An entire family can be wiped out with this kind of drug use."[1]

Confronted by savage, seemingly irrational violence, we are tempted to explain the perpetrator's behavior by reference to some external force that took control of him. In another age, people might have said that Phillip Hall was possessed by evil spirits. Nowadays, drugs often serve the role that demons once did. Thus, Phillip Hall did not kill his family; crack did. People find this explanation comforting, because it means they do not have to think too much about the dark side of human nature. The fear that drugs will make people violent, like the fear that drugs will make people lazy, crazy, or easy, is a familiar element of voodoo pharmacology. The implication—that we can eliminate the evil by getting rid of the chemicals—has obvious appeal.

The idea that crack leads to murder was etched into the public consciousness by a flood of press coverage that began in 1986 and did not abate until the early 1990s. One story after another linked "drug-related violence" to crack, a cheap, smokable form of cocaine first marketed in the early 1980s. "Wherever it appears," *Newsweek* reported in June 1986, crack "spawns vicious violence among dealers and dopers," creating "an epidemic of urban lawlessness."[2] Referring to "the crime it has loosed in our city streets," *Newsweek* editor-in-chief Richard M. Smith called crack use "an authentic national crisis—an assault on the law and the peace, a waste of life and treasure."[3] In the late 1980s newspapers and magazines routinely quoted law-enforcement sources who blamed crack for rising homicide rates, especially in Washington, D.C., the nation's "murder capital."

Since crack users were described as paranoid and hyperactive, casual readers probably assumed that the typical "crack murder" was committed under the drug's influence by someone intoxicated or desperate for more—someone like Phillip Hall. That impression was reinforced by occasional reports of cases that resembled his: the young man in New York City who stabbed his mother to death in an argument about his crack habit, the transit authority maintenance worker charged with killing a subway token clerk during a robbery aimed at obtaining money to buy crack.[4] And it seemed to be confirmed by the testimony of cocaine users seeking help. In a 1989 survey of callers to a toll-free cocaine hotline (including snorters as well as smokers), nearly a third cited "uncontrollable violence" as one effect of their drug use.[5]

Yet a closer look at the press coverage revealed that "crack-related" homicides were usually committed by participants in the drug trade as a way of settling disputes or eliminating competitors. Two 1987 articles in *The New York Times Magazine,* for instance, gave a detailed account of a case in which a dealer was shot repeatedly in the head, neck, and chest, apparently by the henchmen of a former mentor whose territory he was trying to take over. Although there was no evidence that any of the perpetrators were using cocaine at the time of the shooting, this case was still identified as a "crack murder."[6] A 1989 *Newsweek* article on "drug-related violence in Washington" conceded that "these homicides are, for the most part, cases of drug dealers killing other drug dealers." Revealingly, the article began by introducing an emergency room physician who likened a recent night of gun violence in D.C. to the 1929 Saint Valentine's Day Massacre, in which Al Capone's men struck back at a gangster who had been hijacking his shipments of illicit whiskey.[7] Those murders could be described as "alcohol-related," but not because the killers were drunk.

An analysis of New York City homicides committed in 1988 and identified as "crack-related" found that 85 percent grew out of black-market disputes, while about 7 percent occurred during crimes committed to support a crack habit. Only one homicide out of 118 involved a perpetrator who was high on crack. The most common motive for the black-market homicides was "territorial dispute," followed by "robbery of drug dealer," "assault to collect debt," "punishment of worker," "dispute over drug theft," and "dealer sold bad drugs."[8] These kinds of killings, which were also seen during alcohol prohibition, are a predictable result of bans that leave a business with no legal protection and no peaceful way to resolve disputes. Far from preventing such violence, crackdowns on drug trafficking actually encourage it by creating unsettled conditions that lead to more conflict. When a major drug dealer is arrested, there is a struggle to take his place; when dealers are cleared from one corner, they're apt to set up shop on another already claimed by competitors. One of the reasons the crack trade seemed especially violent was that the market emerged quickly, with dealers scrambling to build organizations and claim territory.

Controllable Violence

Given that homicides committed under the influence of crack seem to be quite rare, what should we make of cocaine hotline callers who said the drug made them violent? Perhaps the effect they reported is not strong enough to cause many murders, or perhaps blaming the drug is a convenient way of dodging responsibility for antisocial behavior. In any case, it may be risky to draw conclusions about cocaine's effects from the reports of users who are desperate enough to call a hotline.

Trying to find a sample that was more representative of frequent cocaine users than the self-identified addicts who are usually presented as typical, sociologists Craig Reinarman, Dan Waldorf, and Sheigla Murphy interviewed more than fifty heavy consumers of crack and freebase (another form of smokable cocaine) who were not in treatment, in jail, or living on the streets. Although many had experienced problems as a result of their drug use, "almost none engaged in any criminal behavior other than using or sharing illicit drugs. . . . The two most criminal of our freebasers and crack users were a lawyer who embezzled and a payroll clerk who filed a false insurance claim. They spent their proceeds smoking cocaine. They committed crimes they knew how to do; they did not become burglars." Many of the cocaine smokers in the study decided to give up the habit because of its financial consequences. "For our respondents," write Reinarman et al., "the idea that they could solve their money problems and get more crack or base through street crime simply did not occur to them. In the culture of most working- and middle-class people, serious crime is not a thinkable option, not part of their behavioral repertoire."[9] Any connection between crack use and crime, then, depends on the user's values and circumstances; it is not a pharmacological effect.

The same could be said for other kinds of drug use. Alcohol is the drug that is most strongly associated with violence. But as McAndrew and Edgerton showed in their classic study *Drunken Comportment* (discussed in the Introduction), the fact that some people get into fights after drinking does not mean alcohol makes them behave that way. Variations in responses to alcohol across individuals, cultures, and situations show that drinking does not necessarily beget violence.

At first glance, statistics about drinking by criminals seem to provide compelling evidence that alcohol predisposes people to commit antisocial acts. One in four victims of violent crime reports that his attacker seemed to be under the influence of alcohol. About a third of convicted criminals are thought to have been drinking at the time of their offense.[10] Assuming these figures are accurate, they do not necessarily indicate that drinking fosters crime. For one thing, it seems likely that the sort of people who are apt to commit crimes are also apt to be heavy drinkers. In particular, they may be apt to drink before committing a crime to get their courage up. Then, too, intoxicated criminals may be more likely to get caught, in which case they would be overrepresented among convicts. To better assess the risk that drinking will lead to crime, you would want to know not what percentage of criminals are drinkers but what percentage of drinkers are criminals. Even then, it would be hard to disentangle intoxication from personal and environmental factors that make both drinking and crime more likely.

Since the angry drunk who beats his wife is one of the first images that comes to mind when people think about alcoholism, they tend to assume that drinking must play an important role in domestic violence, if not in crimes against strangers. The numbers for this sort of crime are especially striking: Two-thirds of people attacked by current or former spouses or lovers say their assailant had been drinking.[11] But as the sociologists Richard Gelles and Murray Straus observe, "Drinking (or claiming to be drunk) provides the perfect excuse for instances of domestic violence. 'I didn't know what I was doing when I was drunk' is the most frequently heard excuse by those who counsel violent families. When women claim their husbands are like 'Dr. Jekyll and Mr. Hyde,' they are actually providing the excuse their husbands need to justify their violent behavior. In the end, violent parents and partners learn that if they do not want to be held responsible for their violence, they should drink and hit, or at least say they were drunk."[12]

If there is a connection between alcohol and crime, it is neither inevitable nor straightforward. And if that is true of alcohol, where the correlations are strongest, it is also true of other intoxicants. As one review of the literature noted, "Research on the nexus between substance use and aggression consistently has found a complex relation, mediated by the type of substance and its psychoactive effects, personality factors, and the expected effects of substances, situational factors in the immediate settings where substances are used, and sociocultural factors, that channel the arousal effects of substances into behaviors that may include aggression."[13] The pharmacologist John P. Morgan and the sociologist Lynn Zimmer put it this way: "No drug *directly causes* violence simply through its pharmacological action."[14]

Yet the temptation to ascribe such powers to drugs is strong, especially when demonizing a drug serves a political agenda. Long before Americans started to worry about crazed, homicidal crackheads—typically portrayed as inner-city blacks—anti-drug campaigners were warning the public about the menace posed by "Negro cocaine fiends" in the South. "Many of the horrible crimes committed in the Southern States by the colored people can be traced directly to the cocaine habit," Colonel J. W. Watson of Georgia told the *New York Tribune* in 1903.[15] Under cocaine's influence, according to a 1914 article in the *Medical Record,* "peaceful negroes become quarrelsome, and timid negroes develop a degree of 'Dutch courage' that is sometimes almost incredible." The article's author, Edward Huntington Williams, claimed that "a large proportion of the wholesale killings in the South during recent years have been the result of cocaine." Williams also attributed superhuman strength to "cocainized" blacks, reporting that police officers had been forced to carry higher-caliber guns because "the cocaine nigger is sure hard to kill."[16]

As historian Joseph F. Spillane has shown, such claims helped "explain" particularly outrageous crimes, even when there was no evidence that the perpetrators had taken cocaine. They allowed white Southerners to blame a drug for any hostility they sensed from blacks, even while justifying continued repression. Stories about cocaine-crazed rapists and murderers also helped overcome Southern resistance to federal anti-drug legislation. "Violent cocaine fiends," Spillane writes, "appear to have been more a terrifying social fiction than an empirical reality and one with a sharp racial overtone. Especially in the racially tense South, but also in the cities of the North, such fears flourished and shaped the prevalent image of the cocaine user as an unpredictable menace to social order."[17]

Marijuana Murder

Since cocaine is a stimulant that enhances confidence, the idea that people would take it before committing daring crimes was at least superficially plausible. But anyone familiar with the effects of marijuana will have a hard time understanding how it ever could have been blamed for inciting violence. Part of the answer is that, like cocaine and opium, marijuana was perceived as a drug used by outsiders. Although oral cannabis preparations were available as medicines in the United States during the nineteenth century, Americans were unfamiliar with marijuana smoking. Starting around 1900, Mexican immigrants brought the practice across the border into Texas and New Mexico. As they moved to other Western states, so did the use of marijuana as an intoxicant. Marijuana was also introduced to New Orleans and other Gulf of Mexico ports by sailors and immigrants from the West Indies. It spread from there to cities in the Northeast, where use was concentrated among blacks. From the beginning, then, marijuana was associated with minorities who were believed to have criminal tendencies.

The link between marijuana and violent crime was first drawn by local law enforcement officials. In a 1917 report, an investigator from the U.S. Department of Agriculture quoted a Texas police captain who said marijuana produces a "lust for blood." The captain claimed habitual users "become very violent, especially when they become angry, and will attack an officer even if a gun is drawn." He added that they "seem to have no fear," are "insensible to pain," and display "abnormal strength," so that "it will take several men to handle one man." According to a 1925 account from a U.S. Army botanist, the superintendent of the prison in Yuma, Arizona, having observed inmates who used marijuana, reported that "under its baneful influence reckless men become bloodthirsty, trebly daring and dangerous to an uncontrollable degree." The botanist also cited an American diplomat in Mexico who said marijuana "causes the smoker to become exceedingly pugnacious and to run amuck without discrimination."[18]

Such descriptions helped build support for anti-marijuana laws, which thirty-three states passed between 1915 and 1933. In 1931, when Texas banned marijuana possession, the *San Antonio Light* editorialized: "At last the state legislature had taken a definite step toward suppression of traffic in a dangerous and insanity-producing narcotic easily compounded of a weed indigenous to this section. . . . This newspaper has urged the passage of prohibitory legislation and is gratified that the solons at Austin have acted, even if tardily, in the suppression of traffic in a drug which makes the addict frequently a dangerous or homicidal maniac."[19]

At least two different versions of the "killer weed" thesis were propagated in the 1920s and thirties. According to one, either marijuana intoxication or the long-term effect of the habit drove people crazy, causing them to commit otherwise inexplicable acts of violence. A 1932 article in the *Journal of Criminal Law and Criminology* quoted Joseph F. Taylor, the Los Angeles Police Department's chief of detectives, who said "we have had officers of this department shot and killed by Marihuana addicts and have traced the act of murder directly to the influence of Marihuana, with no other motive. Numerous assaults have been made upon officers and citizens with intent to kill by Marihuana addicts which were directly traceable to the influence of Marihuana."[20]

In the other version of the marijuana murder theory, criminals took the drug to steel their nerves before carrying out an attack. "In some eastern cities," a Tulsa prosecutor reported in 1943, "the gunman has discovered that the weed offers him something new in the way of courage—courage to kill. . . . A few whiffs of a marihuana cigarette, mixed with tobacco, and he loses all sense of fear."[21] New Orleans Public Safety Commissioner Frank Gomila described a "crime wave" in the late 1920s in which "youngsters known to be 'muggleheads' fortified themselves with the narcotic and proceeded to shoot down police, bank clerks and casual bystanders." He said the district attorney "declared that many of the crimes in New Orleans and the south were thus committed by criminals who relied on the drug to give them false courage and freedom from restraint."[22]

The Anslinger File

Harry J. Anslinger, who headed the Federal Bureau of Narcotics from 1930 to 1962, latched onto the alleged connection between marijuana and crime in his campaign for a Uniform State Narcotic Drug Act banning cannabis. "Instances of criminals using the drug to give them courage before making brutal forays are occurrences commonly known to the narcotics bureau," he told the commission charged with drawing up the statute in 1931.[23] Anslinger began to keep a file of reports on crimes—the grislier, the better—in which the perpetrator was said to be a marijuana user, and he encouraged newspapers and magazines to run articles reinforcing the belief that cannabis fostered violence.

In a 1936 pamphlet, the FBN claimed that "prolonged use of Marihuana frequently develops a delirious rage which sometimes leads to high crimes, such as assault and murder. Hence Marihuana has been called the 'killer drug.' . . . Marihuana sometimes gives man the lust to kill, unreasonably and without motive. Many cases of assault, rape, robbery, and murder are traced to the use of Marihuana."[24] The bureau began circulating an often-repeated estimate that "50 percent of the violent crimes committed in districts occupied by Mexicans, Turks, Filipinos, Greeks, Spaniards, Latin-Americans and Negroes may be traced to the abuse of marihuana."[25] Anslinger also liked to describe cases from his marijuana murder file. One of his favorites involved a young man in Florida named Victor Licata who was "addicted to smoking marihuana cigarettes." One day Licata "seized an axe and killed his father, mother, two brothers and a sister, wiping out the entire family except himself."[26] As in the case of Phillip Hall,

Licata's drug use was treated as a sufficient explanation for his monstrous crime.

Anslinger's propaganda campaign achieved his goal of encouraging states to pass their own marijuana bans; all had done so by 1937. It also stirred up enough alarm among politicians to win easy passage of the Marihuana Tax Act of 1937, a national ban disguised as a revenue measure. At the legislative hearings, Anslinger happily confirmed both versions of the "killer weed" story: that it drove unwilling perpetrators to violence and that it helped criminals carry out their plans. He also trotted out his favorite examples of marijuana-induced violence, which led to one bit of gruesome comedy. Anslinger presented a photograph of the victim in a case where "one colored young man killed another, literally smashing his head and face to a pulp." An inattentive senator, misunderstanding the significance of the picture, asked, "Was there in this case a blood or skin disease caused by marihuana?" Anslinger corrected him: "No. This is a photograph of the murdered man, Senator. It shows the fury of the murderer."[27]

Having accomplished what he wanted with his scare stories, Anslinger started backing away from the claim that marijuana caused violence. Now that the FBN had jurisdiction over the drug, hysterical reports about out-of-control marijuana addicts would not reflect well on the bureau. Furthermore, the idea of cannabis-induced violence did not sit well with prosecutors, who did not want to see criminals get off the hook by claiming that marijuana made them do it. New Orleans District Attorney Eugene Stanley reported that "many prosecuting attorneys in the South and Southwest have been confronted with the defense that, at the time of the commission of the criminal act, the defendant was irresponsible, because he was under the influence of marihuana to such a degree he was unable to appreciate the difference between right and wrong, and was legally insane."[28]

In the 1950s, when the main rationale for controlling marijuana became its alleged link to opiate use, Anslinger publicly downplayed the crime angle. During congressional hearings in 1955, one senator asked, "Is it or is it not a fact that the marijuana user has been responsible for many of our most sadistic, terrible crimes in this Nation, such as sex slayings, sadistic slayings, and matter of that kind?" Anslinger's response injected a note of caution that had been notably lacking from his statements on the subject in the thirties. "There have been instances of that, Senator," he said. "We have had some rather tragic occurrences by users of marijuana. It does not follow that all crimes can be traced to marijuana. There have been many brutal crimes traced to marijuana. But I would not say that it is the controlling factor in the commission of crimes."[29]

Given marijuana's current reputation as a drug that leaves its users sedate, if not docile, it's hard to believe that anyone could have thought that it drove people to violence. But marijuana was banned before it gained any sort of mainstream acceptance, so most people simply had no experience with it. This lack of familiarity is reflected in an exchange that occurred on the floor of the House when the Marihuana Tax Act came up for a vote. "I do not know anything about the bill," said one representative who complained that it was too late in the day to bring up important legislation. "It has something to do with something that is called marihuana," a colleague informed him. "I believe it is a narcotic of some kind."[30]

For those who believed that blacks and Mexicans were prone to crime, the fact that marijuana use was concentrated in these groups lent credibility to the charge that it fostered violence. "I wish I could show you what a small marihuana cigaret can do to one of our degenerate Spanish-speaking residents," a Colorado newspaper editor wrote in a 1936 letter to the FBN. "That's why our problem is so great; the greatest percentage of our population is composed of Spanish-speaking persons, most of whom are low mentally, because of social and racial conditions."[31]

Finally, a distorted bit of folklore about eleventh-century Muslim fanatics whose leader gave them hashish was cited as evidence that cannabis makes people aggressive. As Marco Polo told the story, the "Old Man of the Mountain" (identified in other accounts as Hasan ibn Sabah) would drug his followers and bring them to a beautiful valley that was meant to resemble Paradise. He told them this was a taste of their reward for following his orders, a reward they would receive whether or not they survived their missions. So motivated, they became fearless killers. Marco Polo did not identify the drug used by the Old Man of the Mountain, but it was later reputed to be hashish. Hence the killers were known as Hashishin (hashish eaters), thought to be the root of the word *assassin*. But even assuming the drug was hashish (rather than, say, opium), its role was to put the Hashishin to sleep before they were enticed with the promise of Paradise. By contrast, the version of the legend popularized by marijuana's opponents in the 1920s and thirties had the Hashishin taking the drug in preparation for their missions of murder.[32]

Terror of a Drug

Beginning in the 1970s, the anesthetic PCP (phencyclidine, a.k.a. angel dust) acquired a reputation strikingly similar to that of cocaine in 1914 or marijuana in 1937. It was said to induce feelings of invulnerability, give its users superhuman strength, and cause outbursts of vicious, irrational violence. "It's a real terror of a drug," Robert DuPont, director of the National Institute on Drug Abuse, told *Time* in 1977. "Everything people used to say about marijuana is true of angel dust." *Time* reported that "angel dust has been linked to hundreds of murders, suicides and accidental deaths." One example: "A user in California walked into a house that he had picked at random, killed a baby and stabbed a pregnant woman in the stomach."[33] Other stories described "the superhuman physical strength and tolerance to pain that PCP precipitates," requiring several police officers to subdue a single man.[34]

This image of PCP users became so well accepted that, like marijuana in the 1930s, the drug could be offered as an excuse, or at least as a mitigating factor, in criminal cases. Defendants began to argue that they were not in their right minds when they assaulted the victim because they had (perhaps unknowingly) just smoked a PCP-laced joint. Barry Braeseke, a California man who conspired with a neighbor to murder his mother, father, and grandfather in 1976, apparently to get his hands on the family's money, blamed PCP for the killings. "It had to have been the constant saturation of my brain [with] that drug that actually made me go along with the idea," he said.[35] The perception that PCP turns men into uncontrollable brutes also played a role in the Rodney King case. The Los Angeles police officers who beat King tried to explain the length and intensity of their assault by claiming they thought he was high on PCP. One of them described King as a "monster" with "Hulk-like strength."[36]

But in a review of 350 journal articles on PCP in humans, the psychiatrist Martin Brecher and his colleagues found scant evidence for "the assumption that [PCP] provokes violent behavior in humans with predictable regularity." High doses of PCP can produce "severe agitation and hyperactivity," coupled with "cognitive disorganization, disorientation, hallucinations, and paranoia." Combined with the drug's anesthetic effect, which makes users less sensitive to pain and therefore harder to restrain, such acute reactions have contributed to PCP's reputation for transforming people into Incredible Hulks. Yet in their search of the literature, Brecher and his coauthors found only three documented cases in which people under the influence of PCP alone had committed acts of violence. They also noted that between 1959 and 1965, when PCP was tested as a human anesthetic, it was given to hundreds of patients, but "not a single case of violence was reported." They concluded that "PCP does not live up to its reputation as a violence-inducing drug."[37]

The fact that PCP showed no sign of precipitating violence when it was given to patients illustrates the importance of context in determining how people act after taking a drug. When a substance is used mainly by disaffected individuals with antisocial tendencies, for example, its effects may seem different than when it is used by middle-class dabblers with stable lives. Bruce Rogers, who went to high school in Florida in the early 1970s, remembered that PCP was popular there—it gave you "a lot of bang for the buck"—and reported that he himself used it perhaps thirty times. He said stories about "chopping your grandmother up with an ax" were "laughable because I never even saw anyone experience a psychotic episode and never even treaded near one at all dosage levels. . . . It seemed more likely to calm somebody down."[38] Bob Wallace, the software developer turned psychedelic researcher, noted that ketamine, another anesthetic with dissociative effects similar to PCP's, does not have a reputation for causing aggression. "PCP is more associated with people who are kind of struggling," he said. "They're on the edges of society, and they may be more violent."[39]

Speed Kills

The history of methamphetamine also illustrates how a drug's reputed effects may depend on who is using it and how. For decades methamphetamine (Methedrine) was widely used in oral form, along with amphetamine (Benzedrine) and dextroamphetamine (Dexedrine). These drugs were given to soldiers during World War II, taken by students cramming for exams and truck drivers trying to stay awake on long hauls, and precribed by doctors for weight loss, narcolepsy, depression, and hyperactivity. Until 1954, amphetamines were available in the United States without a prescription. The drug policy historian Edward M. Brecher concluded that "enormous quantities of oral amphetamines were consumed in the United States during the 1940s and 1950s with apparently little misuse."[40] Contrary to current expectations, the widespread use of amphetamines during this period was not accompanied by an epidemic of violence. It was not until the mid sixties, following a rise in thrill-seeking, intravenous use of amphetamines, that the image of the paranoid, aggressive "speed freak" began to eclipse that of the hardworking student or truck driver.

In the 1990s, the speed freak returned to the public stage, angrier, meaner, crazier, and better-armed. Attorney General Janet Reno described methamphetamine as "a very dangerous, very violence-inciting drug, certainly as dangerous as crack cocaine."[41] Assistant U.S. Attorney David Risley went her one better, saying "the level of violence associated with meth users surpasses that associated with crack."[42] Thomas Constantine, head of the Drug Enforcement Administration, agreed: "The violence can be incredible."[43] An undercover narcotics officer in Washington state told a local newspaper: "Methamphetamine users are probably the most dangerous people to deal with in the drug subculture. They're unpredictable, paranoid and prone to violence. They like guns and knives."[44]

Methamphetamine was tied to "a wave of unspeakable acts of violence."[45] There was the California man who beat his four-year-old stepdaughter to death, the Olympia, Washington, teenager who shot a convenience store clerk after she refused to sell him beer, the Arizona man who cut off his teenage son's head and tossed it out the window of his van. Press accounts described the drug in diabolical terms. A 1994 story in *Reader's Digest* was entitled "A Demon Stalks the Land."[46] Denver's *Rocky Mountain News* called methamphetamine "the devil in a drug, a substance so seductive and so destructive that using it is like selling your soul." The article quoted a local prosecutor who said, "In a sense, methamphetamine is the devil's key to your soul. Once that's opened up, the devil can get to work. . . . It's an evil drug."[47]

Predictably, methamphetamine became popular as an excuse as well as an explanation. A man who shot a Mesa County, Colorado, sheriff's deputy claimed he was "too high [on methamphetamine] to know what he was doing."[48] A California burglar accused of using a shotgun to kill two accomplices after smoking methamphetamine with them reportedly said: "I think I might have done some things that aren't like me. . . . [I] hope it was all a bad dream." He claimed "that drug makes me the evilest person in the world."[49]

As in the case of PCP, there was an element of truth to the stories about methamphetamine-inspired violence. Heavy, prolonged use of methamphetamine (like heavy, prolonged use of cocaine) can lead to jitteriness, irritability, and paranoia, all aggravated by the effects of staying awake for days at a time. These symptoms are apt to appear sooner and be more severe when the drug is snorted or smoked, the sort of use that attracted official attention when methamphetamine was dubbed "the crack of the nineties." And it was certainly true that some methamphetamine users, albeit a tiny percentage of them, did commit "unspeakable acts of violence."

The extent to which such crimes can be blamed on methamphetamine use is debatable, however. Consider the case of Eric Starr Smith, who was arrested in 1995 for beheading his fourteen-year-old son and later told police he thought the boy was "possessed by the devil." Smith's sister said he had been up for twenty-four hours, high on methamphetamine, before he killed his son, and the murder was cited repeatedly as evidence of the drug's mind-warping, conscience-obliterating power. But Smith was also under the influence of alcohol at the time of the attack, and he had a history of violence, often after drinking. A former co-worker said Smith "had a fierce temper and a history of getting in bar fights." His two sisters accused Smith of molesting them when they were children, and his ex-wife cited "a pattern of domestic violence sparked by alcohol" when she sought a protective order against him after he was arrested for assaulting her in 1993. Whatever else it might be, the Smith case is not the story of a peaceful, law-abiding man turned into a monster by methamphetamine.[50]

But the demon drug proved so irresistible as an explanation for otherwise inexplicable acts that its presence could almost be assumed if a crime was sufficiently heinous. In 1991 a California man named Ricky Lee Earp was convicted of raping and murdering an eighteen-month-old girl whom he was babysitting at the time of her death. The Nexis database includes seventeen newspaper articles about Earp's arrest, trial, and sentencing; none mentions methamphetamine, and neither does the California Supreme Court's eighty-seven-page decision rejecting Earp's appeal of his death sentence.[51] Julio Moran, who covered the case for the *Los Angeles Times,* said, "I don't recall drugs being involved, even off the record."[52] Yet *Reader's Digest* still put the case on a list of "meth-related child killings."[53]

Qat-Crazed Killers

The need to understand shocking acts of violence also gave rise to one of the most bizarre drug scares in recent decades. In 1992, prior to the U.S. military intervention in Somalia, news reports suggested that qat, a mild stimulant plant that has been chewed in parts of Africa and the Middle East for centuries, was contributing to that country's civil war. "It is considered generally unwise to move around Mogadishu at night," the *New York Times* reported, "because by then the narcotic effect of the [teenage nomads'] two-bunch-a-day habit has taken hold. Since the mixture of qat and guns has proved such a lethal combination (the addiction often generates the looting), some desperate Somali elders have facetiously suggested a 'qat for guns' swap to empty the town of weapons."[54]

Similarly, the *Washington Times* paraphrased a psychiatrist's statement that "chewing qat is one of the factors causing much of the seemingly senseless violence." The article, headlined "Drug Gives Young Gunmen Courage," reported that U.S. troops would face Somalis "chemically wired from chewing qat, a twig that gives its users a sense of euphoria and potency."[55] In a similar vein, an aid worker told CNN that after chewing qat the machine-gun-wielding teenagers "all think they're Rambo. . . . They think they can conquer the country."[56]

Perhaps the most extreme example of qat hype was a *New Republic* article by a Nairobi-based freelancer. "After taking the drug," he wrote, "restless adolescents become more and more agitated and less and less rational. A drug-conjured insistence on personal supremacy turns pubescent energy into casual, cheap violence. Raw tempers are released in the form of reckless driving, senseless arguments, and the playful exchange of gunfire. Gunshot wounds in Mogadishu . . . peak in the early evening hours, when the young gunmen are at the apex of their qat sprees."[57]

Observers of the unrest in Somalia accurately reported what they saw: teenagers with guns who chewed qat and committed "seemingly senseless violence." But in concluding that qat was a cause of the violence, they went beyond anything they could have witnessed. Too much of any stimulant can make people edgy. But because qat chewers slowly absorb the plant's main active ingredient, cathinone, and metabolize it quickly, there's a built-in limit to how much can accumulate in the bloodstream. Given qat's typical effects and its traditionally sociable function, blaming it for the breakdown of law and order in Somalia is rather like blaming coffee for murder and mayhem in the United States.

If qat chewing routinely led to violence, of course, the practice would rightly be condemned, but it probably would not have caught on to begin with. This is one reason to be skeptical of accounts implying that a drug used repeatedly by large numbers of people often causes violent outbursts: People, by and large, do not enjoy getting into fights (and those who do will find a pretext no matter what drug they take). However one views the nexus between drugs and violence, it's clear that drug users typically control their aggressive impulses.

In their review of the research on PCP, Martin Brecher and his colleagues noted that amphetamines, LSD, and barbiturates had also been implicated in assault and homicide, but "the reports linking these compounds with violence offer even less documentation than the PCP literature." For alcohol, by contrast, "there is a well-documented linkage between ingestion and violence that dwarfs any other drug's linkage with violent behavior."[58] Despite that association, we recognize that alcohol does not boost aggression in the same mechanistic way that adrenaline boosts one's heart rate, and we do not consider it unreasonable to expect people to refrain from violence even after they've had a few drinks.

Coke Bugs and Speed Traps

The risk of violence is not the only thing that people worry about in connection with stimulants such as cocaine and amphetamines. Heavy use can lead to insomnia, restlessness, paranoid delusions, and hallucinations (such as "coke bugs," the sensation of insects under the skin). The most common physical complaint among cocaine users is the runny nose and inflamed nasal tissue that come from snorting the powder regularly, but more serious reactions are possible. Both cocaine and amphetamines affect the cardiovascular system and in high doses can cause irregular heartbeats, strokes, and seizures.

Fatal overdoses of stimulants are rare. The federal government's Drug Abuse Warning Network reported that cocaine, used by about 3.7 million Americans in 1999, was mentioned by medical examiners in 4,864 cases that year. Methamphetamine, used by about 1.1 million Americans, was mentioned in 690 cases. Even assuming that each user took the drug only once, these numbers are modest. Furthermore, only a small fraction of the cases where a given drug was mentioned involved deaths that were directly caused by the drug. The cocaine "mentions," for example, include cases where other drugs were also present and where cocaine was detected but did not necessarily play a direct role. Only 308 deaths (6 percent of the total) were listed as caused by an overdose of cocaine alone.[59]

In the late 1980s and early nineties, concerns about cocaine's effects on its users were eclipsed by dramatic reports of its allegedly devastasting impact on children exposed to the drug in the womb. "Crack babies" were said to be permanently impaired, incapable of learning or forming social attachments. But the early studies on which these reports were based often used ratings by observers who knew which children had been exposed to cocaine and which had not. More important, the studies failed to take into account all the ways in which cocaine users differed from other mothers. Since factors such as nutrition, prenatal care, and the use of other drugs (tobacco and alcohol, for example) may affect the health of newborns, this was a crucial shortcoming. Likewise, the home environment of children raised by crack users might affect their development independent of any lingering impact from what their mothers did during pregnancy. Subsequent studies that controlled for such variables painted a much less alarming picture, although some researchers still believe in utero exposure to cocaine may have subtle effects on intelligence.[60]

While the extent to which the problems of "crack babies" (or "crack kids") could be attributed to cocaine was by no means clear, the reaction from the press, the public, and the government was unambiguous. Women who used cocaine during pregnancy were condemned, stripped of custody, forced into treatment, and, in some jurisdictions, sent to jail. Yet the evidence against them was far less substantial than the evidence against pregnant women who drink heavily, which is clearly linked to mental retardation and facial deformities, or who smoke cigarettes, which is associated with premature birth, low birth weight, stillbirth, and defects such as cleft palate. The point is not that all of these women should be thrown in jail—or that nothing a woman does during pregnancy should be cause for criticism. A pregnant woman's risky behavior, like anything that exposes one's children to danger, raises serious moral issues. But the resolution of those issues hinges on the nature of the risk, its magnitude, and the reasons for taking it, not the legality of the substance involved.

One reason people found the "crack baby" story so compelling was that it supposedly showed how the drug's allure could overwhelm maternal instincts. The next chapter examines claims about the addictiveness of crack and methamphetamine in more detail. But even without dissecting such claims, it's clear that most people who use cocaine and amphetamines manage to avoid anything that could reasonably be described as addiction. Of the 28 million or so Americans who have used cocaine, only about 1.7 million, or 6 percent, have used it in the last month. For crack, said to be more addictive than cocaine powder, the percentage is about the same. And past-month use is not necessarily a sign of a serious drug habit (unless everyone who drinks a beer now and then is an alcoholic). In a 1993 survey of young adults, only 7 percent of past-month cocaine users were taking the drug every day. The picture is similar for users of prescription-type stimulants generally and methamphetamine in particular: Only a small percentage have used them in the last month, and only a small percentage of past-month users take them every day.[61]

Such numbers offer only a snapshot, of course. They do not tell us what percentage of cocaine or amphetamine users may once have had drug problems they have since overcome (although, as we'll see in the next chapter, the ability to cut back or quit itself suggests these substances are not as powerful as they are said to be). But even over the long term, problem users are far from typical. A 1994 study, based on a nationally representative sample, estimated that 17 percent of cocaine users and 11 percent of other stimulant users had ever experienced "drug dependence."[62]

Control Keys

One way to keep the use of stimulants under control is to take them for a specific purpose, such as completing a time-sensitive project in school or at work. Kenneth Donaldson, a computer system designer in his early thirties, said he did not use amphetamines recreationally but added, "If you really need to stay awake and alert, amphetamine is far better than caffeine for that."[63] Alison Witt, a software architect in her twenties, used amphetamines two or three times a week during her sophomore year in college, usually for studying. "It would focus my energy," she said. "I would just be able to focus on one thing for long periods of time." Since then, she has used such stimulants "very, very rarely."[64]

When she was in college, Katrina Lubovic, a marketing specialist in her twenties, had a few friends diagnosed with attention deficit disorder who had prescriptions for Ritalin, a stimulant with effects similar to those of amphetamines. "Ritalin is very big in college around finals," she said. "We would crush it up, snort it. It made you concentrate like crazy. I finished *Crime and Punishment* in a matter of two hours, and I understood it fully. I could recite lines to you. . . .

The only times I used Ritalin [were] when I had a lot of reading to do, I had slacked off on my school work, and I had a big final coming up." Afterward, she said, "you're drained. . . . I would just get really, really involved with my work, and I would be emotionally drained, physically drained."[65]

Larry Seguin, a truck driver in his fifties, snorted and injected methamphetamine on weekends for a while. "You just went a hundred miles an hour," he recalled. "There wasn't anything you couldn't do. You wanted to pull an engine from a car, you'd do it real quick—swish, swish, swish." Eventually, he said, "I just lost my interest in it." Although he never used the drug heavily, he said injecting meth was "one of those things that could start running into trouble." On the other hand, "I wouldn't see anything wrong if you could go to a liquor store and get a couple of pills for the weekend that would boost you up to get some of your work done. I think people could do that without running into addiction."[66]

Cocaine, which wears off faster than amphetamines, is more likely to be taken in a recreational context. Commonly reported effects include increased energy, greater confidence, brighter mood, and easier conversation—all assets at a party. Rick Root, a Californian in his early fifties who was working as a production planner for a machinery manufacturer, said he used cocaine perhaps 100 times, mostly at parties, in the 1980s. "It gave a very pleasant high," he said. "It gave me the impression that I could dig deeper into my mind. . . . It gave me the ability to look at things in a much broader view." On cocaine, he was "more hyper, more talkative." He confessed, though, that he also used it "because it was cool," and he hasn't had any since the early nineties.[67]

"I have a lot of friends who party with [cocaine]," said Katrina

Lubovic. "They do not get hooked." But Lubovic herself, who used cocaine with her boyfriend every weekend for about six months when she was in college, decided she did not care for its effects. "I'm a very aggressive person naturally," she said. "For a while it made me even more outgoing, even more aggressive, and I don't know if I ever really liked it."[68] Larry Seguin was even less impressed. "I can't see why people get so excited about cocaine," he said. "I don't see any excitement in it at all."[69]

By contrast, Alan Mattus, an MBA in his mid-thirties, said he might like cocaine a little too much. "You are jazzed," he said, "and what I like about it now is you can stay awake. I'm older now, and midnight comes, that's it for me. . . . I've used it recreationally a few times, and I'm scared of it. I don't think I would be able to control myself with it. . . . It is a greedy kind of a thing. You can never get enough, but it is easy to have too much. You don't share it as much [as other drugs]. While it makes you feel good, it makes you feel bad at the same time."[70] Several other drug users I interviewed expressed similar sentiments. But having decided that cocaine could easily be used to excess, they all managed to stay away from it or use it only occasionally. The fear of losing control can itself be a source of control.

Contrary to the widespread impression that occasional cocaine use inevitably escalates to addiction, several researchers have found that people can maintain patterns of moderate use for years. Dan Waldorf, Craig Reinarman, and Sheigla Murphy interviewed a group of twenty-seven cocaine users in 1974 and 1975, then followed up with twenty-one of them more than a decade later. "Casual use was the norm among these users, and they experienced remarkably few negative effects," they write, summarizing their initial findings. "For nearly all of the follow-up subjects," they add, "regular ingestion of cocaine over an eleven-year period did not result in a pattern of compulsive use or addiction." In a separate study, Waldorf et al. interviewed more than 200 heavy consumers of cocaine, and even in this group they found many examples of controlled use. "While control over cocaine use is not easy for everyone and is no doubt difficult for most," they write, "the possibility cannot and should not be denied. Our respondents were among the heaviest users in the nation and, if many of them are controlled users, then surely most of the other 25 million Americans who have tried cocaine are too."[71]

The Dutch researchers Peter Cohen and Arjan Sas have reported similar findings. They interviewed 160 experienced cocaine users in 1987 and followed up with 64 of them in 1991, when the average period since first regular use was ten years. "One of the main conclusions of our 1987 cocaine study was that a very large majority of the investigated users gave no evidence of ever losing control," they write. "After analyzing longitudinal data on our 64 follow-up respondents we conclude that the main tendency of experienced cocaine users over time is towards decreasing levels of use, stability of low level use, and abstinence." About half of the follow-up subjects were using cocaine at a lower, stable level, and about half had given it up. Only four of them (about 6 percent) had considered asking for help in quitting, and only one had actually done so.[72]

Several keys to controlled consumption emerge from interviews with moderate users of stimulants. One is reserving the drug for particular uses or special occasions, so that it complements rather than crowds out other valued activities. Another is what Waldorf and his colleagues call "a stake in conventional life": work and relationships that the user does not want to jeopardize. "Jobs, families, friends— the ingredients of a normal identity—turned out to be the ballast that allowed many users to control their use or to return from abuse to occasional, controlled use," they write.[73] But if such assets commonly protect people from destructive entanglements with a substance as powerful as cocaine is reputed to be, what are we to make of claims that certain drugs destroy free will, compelling people to continue taking them? The next chapter considers that question, beginning with the drug that is widely considered to be the gold standard for addiction.

CHAPTER SEVEN

TOO GOOD

It's so good, don't even try it once.
—EMMANUEL, "A YOUNG MIDDLE-CLASS ADDICT"
  QUOTED IN THE TITLE OF A 1972 BOOK ON HEROIN

Breaking Eggs

"This is your brain," says a sexy young woman in a white tank top, holding an egg between two fingers. She lifts a frying pan. "This is heroin." She puts the egg on a kitchen counter and slams it with the frying pan. "This is what happens to your brain after snorting heroin." She displays the egg goo and bits of shell dripping down the back of the frying pan. "And this is what your body goes through." But "it's not over yet," she warns. She begins swinging the frying pan wildly, her short brown hair flying back and forth as she smashes a rack of dishes, a clock, glassware, and appliances while shouting, "This is what your family goes through! And your friends! And your money! And your job! And your self-respect! And your future!" She drops the frying pan and faces the camera, calm again. "Any questions?" she asks.

This familiar spot, unveiled by the Partnership for a Drug-Free America and the Office of National Drug Control Policy in 1998, draws on imagery popularized by an even better-known public service announcement that aired a decade before. In the earlier PSA, the egg/brain was cracked into a sizzling frying pan while a male voice said, "This is your brain on drugs. Any questions?" The ad was so vague, sweeping, and over the top that any thoughtful viewer had plenty of questions, starting with, "Huh?" (At least one politician, Senator Orrin Hatch, seemed to take the ad literally. "Do we really want a society of people with fried eggs as brains?" the Utah Republican asked at a 1996 anti-drug conference.[1]) Insofar as the message was intelligible, it was clearly false, since drug use does not typically cause brain damage. The fried egg entered the culture not as a stark warning but as an object of ridicule. Soon you could buy T-shirts and posters that showed pictures of breakfast foods with captions like, "This is your brain on drugs with orange juice, bacon, and toast."

Given this history, you might think the ad writers who contribute their work to the Partnership for a Drug-Free America would have been keen to avoid references to eggs and frying pans. Instead, they not only revisited the theme but took it up a few notches (and many decibels), replacing a sedate off-screen announcer with a screaming, frying-pan-wielding lunatic. Apparently, they thought they could preserve the credibility of their message by narrowing the focus from drugs in general to heroin, drawing on widely shared assumptions about the special dangers of opiates. Even people who are skeptical of the claim that marijuana will fry your brain are apt to believe that heroin will ruin your life. This is primarily because, unlike marijuana, heroin is considered inherently and inevitably addictive, causing an attachment that can be severed only at great physical cost. As the psychologist Stanton Peele notes, beginning early in the twentieth century heroin "came to be seen in American society as the nonpareil drug of addiction—as leading inescapably from even the most casual contact to an intractable dependence, withdrawal from which was traumatic and unthinkable for the addict."[2]

The conventional wisdom about heroin, which shapes the popular understanding of addiction, is nicely summed up in the journalist Martin Booth's 1996 history of opium. "Addiction is the compulsive taking of drugs which have such a hold over the addict he or she cannot stop using them without suffering severe symptoms and even death," he writes. "Opiate dependence . . . is as fundamental to an addict's existence as food and water, a physio-chemical fact: an addict's body is chemically reliant upon its drug for opiates actually alter the body's chemistry so it cannot function properly without being periodically primed. A hunger for the drug forms when the quantity in the bloodstream falls below a certain level. . . . Fail to feed the body and it deteriorates and may die from drug starvation." Booth also declares that "everyone . . . is a potential addict"; that "addiction can start with the very first dose"; and that "with continued use addiction is a certainty."[3]

Booth's description, which passed muster with his editors in England and the United States, probably fit the preconceptions of most readers. Yet it is wrong or grossly misleading in every particular. To understand why is to recognize the fallacies underlying a reductionist, drug-centered view of addiction in which chemicals force themselves on people—a view that iconoclasts such as Stanton Peele and maverick psychiatrist Thomas Szasz have long criticized.[4] The idea that a drug can compel the person who consumes it to continue consuming it, in essence forcing him to be a glutton, is the most important tenet of voodoo pharmacology, because this power makes possible all the other evils to which drug use supposedly leads.

Withdrawal Penalty

In Booth's gloss, as in other popular portrayals, the potentially fatal agony of withdrawal is the gun that heroin holds to the addict's head. These accounts greatly exaggerate both the severity and the importance of withdrawal symptoms. Heroin addicts who abruptly stop using the drug commonly report flu-like symptoms, which may include chills, sweating, runny nose and eyes, muscular aches, stomach cramps, nausea, diarrhea, or headaches. While certainly unpleasant, the experience is not life-threatening.[5] Indeed, addicts who have developed tolerance (needing higher doses to achieve the same effect) often voluntarily undergo withdrawal so they can begin using heroin again at a lower level, thereby reducing the cost of their habit.[6] Another sign that fear of withdrawal symptoms is not the essence of addiction is the fact that heroin users commonly drift in and out of their habits, going through periods of abstinence and returning to the drug long after any physical discomfort has faded away. Indeed, the observation that detoxification is not tantamount to overcoming an addiction, that addicts typically will try repeatedly before successfully kicking the habit, is a commonplace of drug treatment.

More evidence that withdrawal has been overemphasized as a motivation for using opiates comes from patients who take narcotic painkillers over extended periods of time. Like heroin addicts, they develop "physical dependence" and experience withdrawal symptoms when they stop taking the drugs. But studies conducted during the last two decades have consistently found that patients in pain who receive opioids (opiates or synthetics with similar effects) rarely become addicted. In 1980 researchers at Boston University Medical Center reported that they had reviewed the records of 11,882 patients treated with narcotics in the hospital and found "only four cases of reasonably well documented addiction in patients who had no history of addiction."[7] A 1982 study of 10,000 burn victims who had received narcotic injections for weeks or months found no cases of drug abuse that could be attributed to pain treatment.[8] In a 1986 study of 38 chronic pain patients who were treated with opioids for years, only two misused their medication, and both had histories of drug problems.[9]

Pain experts emphasize that physical dependence should not be confused with addiction, which requires a psychological component: a persistent desire to use the substance for its mood-altering effects. Critics have long complained that unreasonable fears about narcotic addiction discourage adequate pain treatment.[10] In 1989 Charles Schuster, then director of the National Institute on Drug Abuse, confessed, "We have been so effective in warning the medical establishment and the public in general about the inappropriate use of opiates that we have endowed these drugs with a mysterious power to enslave that is overrated."[11]

Although popular perceptions lag behind, the point made by pain specialists—that "physical dependence" is not the same as addiction—is now widely accepted by professionals who deal with drug problems. But under the heroin-based model that prevailed until the 1970s, tolerance and withdrawal symptoms were considered the hallmarks of addiction. By this standard, drugs such as nicotine and cocaine were not truly addictive; they were merely "habituating."

That distinction proved untenable, given the difficulty that people often had in giving up substances that were not considered addictive.

Having hijacked the term *addiction,* which in its original sense referred to any strong habit, psychiatrists ultimately abandoned it in favor of *substance dependence.* "The essential feature of Substance Dependence," according to the American Psychiatric Association, "is a cluster of cognitive, behavioral, and physiological symptoms indicating that the individual continues use of the substance despite significant substance-related problems. . . . Neither tolerance nor withdrawal is necessary or sufficient for a diagnosis of Substance Dependence." Instead, the condition is defined as "a maladaptive pattern of substance use" involving at least three of seven features. In addition to tolerance and withdrawal, these include using more of the drug than intended; trying unsuccessfully to cut back; spending a lot of time getting the drug, using it, or recovering from its effects; giving up or reducing important social, occupational, or recreational activities because of drug use; and continuing use even while recognizing drug-related psychological or physical problems.[12]

One can quibble with these criteria, especially since they are meant to be applied not by the drug user himself but by a government-licensed expert with whose judgment he may disagree. The possibility of such a conflict is all the more troubling because the evaluation may be involuntary (the result of an arrest, for example) and may have implications for the drug user's freedom. More fundamentally, classifying substance dependence as a "mental disorder" to be treated by medical doctors suggests that drug abuse is a disease, something that happens to people rather than something that people do. Yet it is clear from the description that we are talking about a pattern of behavior. Addiction is not simply a matter of introducing a chemical into someone's body, even if it is done often enough to create tolerance and withdrawal symptoms. Conversely, someone who takes a steady dose of a drug and who can stop using it without physical distress may still be addicted to it.

Simply Irresistible?

Even if addiction is not a physical compulsion, perhaps some drug experiences are so alluring that people find it impossible to resist them. Certainly that is heroin's reputation, encapsulated in the title of a 1972 book: *It's So Good, Don't Even Try It Once.*[13] When Martin Booth tells us that anyone can be addicted to heroin, that it may take just one dose, and that it will certainly happen to you if you're foolish enough to repeat the experiment, he is drawing on a long tradition of anti-drug propaganda. As we saw in Chapter 2, the original model for such warnings was not heroin but alcohol. The dry crusaders of the nineteenth and early twentieth centuries taught that every tippler was a potential drunkard, that a glass of beer was the first step on the road to ruin, and that repeated use of distilled spirits made addiction virtually inevitable. Today, when a wrecked kitchen is supposed to symbolize the havoc caused by a snort of heroin, similar assumptions about opiates are even more widely held, and they likewise are based more on faith than facts.

The fact that heroin use is so rare—involving, according to the government's data, something like 0.2 percent of the U.S. population in 2001—suggests that its appeal is much more limited than we've been led to believe. If heroin really is "so good," why does it have such a tiny share of the illegal drug market? Marijuana is more than forty-five times as popular. The National Household Survey on Drug Abuse indicates that about 3 million Americans have used heroin, 15 percent of them in the last year and 4 percent in the last month.[14] These numbers suggest that the vast majority of heroin users either never become addicted or, if they do, manage to give the drug up. A survey of high school seniors found that 1 percent had used heroin in the previous year, while 0.1 percent had used it on twenty or more days in the previous month.[15] Assuming that daily use is a reasonable proxy for opiate addiction, one in ten of the students who had taken heroin in the last year might have qualified as addicts. These are not the sort of numbers you'd expect for a drug that's irresistible.

True, these surveys exclude certain groups in which heroin use is more common and in which a larger percentage of users probably could be described as addicts. The household survey misses people living on the street, in prisons, and in residential drug treatment programs, while the high school survey leaves out truants and dropouts. But even for the entire population of heroin users, the estimated addiction rates do not come close to matching heroin's reputation. A 1976 study estimated there were 3 or 4 million heroin users in the United States, perhaps 10 percent of them addicts. "Of all active heroin users," the authors wrote, "a large majority are not addicts: they are not physically or socially dysfunctional; they are not daily users and they do not seem to require treatment."[16] A 1994 study estimated that 23 percent of heroin users *ever* experience substance dependence.[17]

The comparable rate for alcohol in that study was 15 percent, which seems to support the idea that heroin is more addictive: A larger percentage of the people who try it become heavy users, even though it's harder to get. At the same time, the fact that using heroin is illegal, expensive, risky, inconvenient, and almost universally condemned means that the people who nevertheless choose to do it repeatedly will tend to differ from people who choose to drink. They will be especially attracted to heroin's effects, the associated lifestyle, or both. In other words, heroin users are a self-selected group, less representative of the general population than alcohol users are, and they may be more inclined from the outset to form strong attachments to the drug.

The same study found that 32 percent of tobacco users had experienced substance dependence. Figures like that one are the basis for the claim that nicotine is "more addictive than heroin." After all, cigarette smokers typically go through a pack or so a day, so they're under the influence of nicotine every waking moment. Heroin users typically do not use their drug even once a day. Smokers offended by this comparison are quick to point out that they function fine, meeting their responsibilities at work and home, despite their habit. This, they assume, is impossible for heroin users. We'll take a closer look at that assumption later, but it's true that nicotine's psychoactive effects are easier to reconcile with the requirements of everyday life. Indeed, nicotine can actually enhance concentration and improve performance on certain tasks. So one important reason why most cigarette smokers consume their drug throughout the day is that they can do so without running into trouble. And because they're used to smoking in so many different settings, they may find nicotine harder to give up than a drug they use only with certain people in secret. In one survey, 57 percent of drug users entering a Canadian treatment program said giving up their problem substance (not necessarily heroin) would be easier than giving up cigarettes. In another survey, thirty-six heroin users entering treatment were asked to compare their strongest cigarette urge to their strongest heroin urge. Most said the heroin urge was stronger, but two said the cigarette urge was, and eleven rated the two urges about the same.[18]

In a sense, nicotine's compatibility with a wide range of activities makes it more addictive than, say, alcohol. But this is not the sort of thing people usually have in mind when they worry about addiction. Indeed, if it weren't for the health effects of smoking (and the complaints of bystanders exposed to the smoke), nicotine addiction probably would be seen as no big deal, just as caffeine addiction is. As alternative sources of nicotine that do not involve smoking (gum, patches, inhalers, beverages, lozenges, oral snuff) become popular not just as aids in quitting but as long-term replacements, it will be interesting to see whether they will be socially accepted. Once the health risks are dramatically reduced or eliminated, will daily consumption of nicotine still be viewed as shameful and déclassé, as a disease to be treated or a problem to be overcome? Perhaps so if, as Mormon teaching suggests, addiction per se is the issue. But not if it's the medical, social, and psychological consequences of addiction that really matter.

Although many smokers have a hard time quitting, those who succeed generally do so without formal treatment.[19] Surprisingly, the same may also be true of heroin addicts. In the early 1960s, based on records kept by the Federal Bureau of Narcotics, the sociologist Charles Winick concluded that narcotic addicts tend to "mature out" of the habit in their thirties. He suggested that "addiction may be a self-limiting process for perhaps two-thirds of addicts."[20] Subsequent researchers have questioned Winick's assumptions, and other studies have come up with lower estimates.[21] But it's clear that "natural recovery" is much more common than the public has been led to believe.[22] In a 1974 study of Vietnam veterans, only 12 percent of those who were addicted to heroin in Vietnam took up the habit again during the three years after their return to the United States. (This was not because they couldn't find heroin; half of them used it at least once after their return, generally without becoming addicted again.) Those who had undergone treatment (half of the group) were just as likely to be re-addicted as those who had not. Since those with stronger addictions were more likely to receive treatment, this does not necessarily mean that treatment was useless, but it clearly was not a prerequisite for giving up heroin.[23]

Despite its reputation, then, heroin is neither irresistible nor inescapable. Only a very small share of the population ever uses it, and a large majority of those who do never become addicted. Even within the minority who develop a daily habit, most manage to stop using heroin, often without professional intervention. Yet heroin remains the paradigmatic voodoo drug, ineluctably turning its users into zombies who must obey its commands.

Instantaneous Addiction

No substance can be taken seriously as an addictive drug until it is compared to heroin. That is why *Newsweek,* when it sought to stir up alarm about crack cocaine in 1986, called it "intensely addictive, a drug whose potential for social disruption and individual tragedy is comparable only to heroin." Three paragraphs later, the magazine cited a Los Angeles detective who "readily compares rock [i.e., crack] to heroin." Having established crack as heroin's equal, *Newsweek* immediately announced that in fact it was worse. "While a typical heroin addict shoots up once or twice a day," the article said, "crack addicts need another hit within minutes."[24] In the same issue, the magazine's editor-in-chief declared crack "the newest, purest and most addictive commodity now on the market."[25] *Newsweek* also quoted the psychopharmacologist Arnold Washton, who claimed, "Crack is the most addictive drug known to man," causing "almost instantaneous addiction."[26]

As we saw in the last chapter, however, crack users typically do not become addicted, instantly or otherwise. A 1994 survey of young adults found that 4.4 percent of them had tried crack, 1.1 percent had used it in the last year, and 0.3 percent had used it in the last month. In other words, 93 percent of the people who had tried a drug said to be instantly addictive were not using it even as often as once a month. The percentage using crack on twenty or more days in the previous month was so small that it was not reported.[27]

It's not even clear that crack is more addictive than cocaine powder. This claim is based mainly on the observation that smoking cocaine provides a brief, intense high, followed by a precipitous emotional drop. But while that experience might encourage binges, pharmacologist John P. Morgan and sociologist Lynn Zimmer note, "bingeing per se is not evidence of *drug dependence*. Most people who meet the diagnostic criteria for cocaine dependence probably *do* engage in episodes of bingeing. However, both cocaine [powder] and crack users may binge occasionally—and experience 'craving' and 'compulsion' during the binge—*without becoming dependent*."[28] In their study of fifty heavy cocaine smokers, Craig Reinarman and his colleagues found that they often went days or weeks without using the drug, then went on binges in which they felt out of control. This pattern of "repeatedly returning to bingeing" is quite different from what is usually meant by addiction, a constant craving that results in daily use.[29]

Animal research was also frequently cited as evidence of crack's allure. "A laboratory study with monkeys concluded that they preferred cocaine to life itself," *Newsweek* reported.[30] In this sort of research, animals were tethered to an apparatus that injected cocaine when they pressed a lever. Some of them chose the drug over food, while others took so much that they went into convulsions. Since injection was the route of administration, it's odd that such studies were cited as evidence that cocaine is especially addictive when smoked. In any case, as the psychologist Bruce Alexander has pointed out, such studies (which have also been conducted with heroin) tell us little about animal behavior in more naturalistic settings, let alone human behavior in the real world. Traumatized by the implantation of the catheter, the animals are kept in isolated cages with little to stimulate or soothe them except the drug running through the tube. Alexander and other researchers have found that rats kept in more comfortable, interesting, and sociable quarters are less attracted to drugs.[31]

As Stanton Peele points out, a similar pattern can be observed in people.[32] When they are bored, lonely, and in pain, they are more apt to use drugs heavily. And since humans can look to the future, the prospects they perceive for improving their situation also affect their drug use. People who find little satisfaction or meaning in life and do not expect things to get better are more prone to addiction than people with good jobs, strong attachments to family and community, and the "stake in conventional life" that Craig Reinarman and his colleagues found was important in controlling cocaine use. It is not surprising that heavy crack use during the 1980s was concentrated in neighborhoods where poverty, hopelessness, and alienation were also concentrated. Even there, however, most people did not become obsessed with the drug, and the example provided by those who did discouraged imitation, eventually leading to a decline in use. Unlike rats and monkeys, people have values—self-respect, ambition, duty to others—that help counteract the temptation to excess.

If these values are important enough, people will stop engaging in behavior that conflicts with them. Bob Wallace, the software developer, injected cocaine for a while but decided to give it up because the pleasure he got from it was not worth the anxiety about the needle's effect on his body and the feeling that his use was out of control. "It would be like a binge once a month," he recalled. "The worst thing is if you're injecting all night, toward the end of the evening your hands are trembling, and then trying to get a vein is very hard. You might stick yourself five or six times to find a vein, and this is like your twentieth time trying to do it, and my whole arm would turn purple. I was really worried about screwing up my arms. . . . The injection was dangerous and I wasn't really getting any benefit. [But] even though my higher mind was saying this is not a good thing to be taking, my lower mind and body would be reaching for it." After using cocaine in his twenties and thirties, "I finally decided I had a bad relationship with that and had to force myself to not take it anymore." He stopped cold and never used it again.[33]

Bruce Rogers, a horticulturist in his forties, likewise did not have much trouble giving up cocaine once he decided it wasn't worth the cost. He snorted it every day for a couple of years in his late twenties but stopped because of financial and health concerns. He remembered "taking out cash advances to go binge, and then you'd wake up the next day and [wonder], 'How am I going to pay that $500 cash advance on my credit card?' . . . I don't like something to be in control of me. After a while, it was very obvious that I was not the one in the driver's seat. That spelled evil to me, and I didn't want to be involved with anything evil. . . . I woke up one morning and said, 'This is going nowhere.' . . . I just walked away from it and never looked back. I don't see why people have to go to rehab."[34]

Wallace and Rogers both talked about loss of control, conventionally seen as the sine qua non of addiction, but their accounts made it clear that they were ultimately in charge of their behavior. They did not like the fact that they found themselves acting against their considered judgment so often. Aside from the practical consequences, it undermined their sense of themselves as individuals in control of their own destinies. And so they stopped. That doesn't mean that giving up cocaine might not be harder for different people in different circumstances, but it does show that the chemical does not neutralize free will.

The Crack of the Nineties

Although cocaine, whether snorted, smoked, or injected, was never as powerful as its press implied, that did not stop it from becoming a new touchstone of addictiveness. So when President Clinton wanted to scare the public about methamphetamine, he warned that the drug could become "the crack of the nineties."[35] The same title had earlier been given to gambling and, oddly, heroin.[36] Less than two years later, with just a couple years to go in the decade, drug czar Barry McCaffrey was reassuring the public that methamphetamine would *not* become "the crack cocaine of the nineties," thanks to "drug education programs."[37]

But for a while there, methamphetamine was "the most malignant, addictive drug known to mankind," as a physician told the *New York Times*.[38] A federal prosecutor declared it "more addictive than crack."[39] The head of the Drug Enforcement Administration, officially charged with *discouraging* drug use, said the meth high "is about ten times more pleasurable than any other sensual experience."[40] *U.S. News & World Report* began a story by describing a Phoenix beautician for whom "the seductive allure of methamphetamine took hold almost immediately." As she put it, "The first line I ever did, I thought, 'My God, this is it. This is the answer to all the world's problems.' . . . It's the ultimate high. You're like Wonder Woman. It makes you feel so powerful. You have tons of energy. You feel like you can do anything. I loved it. I craved it. It was total euphoria." As if to make up for this breathless advertising, *U.S. News* quickly added that "methamphetamine turned her euphoria into a free-fall nightmare"— "as it almost always does."[41]

This image of an instantly, inevitably addicting drug was familiar to anyone who had followed the news media's crack coverage. But while crack was said to be especially addictive because the high was so brief, meth was said to be even worse because the high lasted so long.[42] That was not the only clue that the alarm about methamphetamine was overblown. As we saw in the last chapter (and as several of the stories about the new menace acknowledged), methamphetamine (Methedrine) was widely used for decades in the United States and other countries, along with amphetamine (Benzedrine) and dextroamphetamine (Dexedrine), which have similar effects. Yet there was little evidence that taking such stimulants commonly led to addiction. A Swedish survey found that less than 0.1 percent of the people who received amphetamine prescriptions in 1942 (totaling about 6 million doses) could be accurately described as abusers (taking the drug every day, often in large quantities). In the United States, amphetamines were available without a prescription until 1954, and they were not moved to the most restrictive prescription drug category until 1970. As late as 1963, however, the American Medical Association's Council on Drugs reported: "At this time compulsive use of amphetamines constitutes . . . a small problem."[43]

Studies since then have not indicated that amphetamine use is especially hard to control. In a survey of young men conducted in the mid-1970s, one-third of those who had ever used amphetamines reported using them during the previous year. Within this group, nine out of ten had used them thirty or fewer times during the year—two or three times a month at most. Methamphetamine is said to be more addictive than the other amphetamines, especially when it's snorted or smoked. Yet of the 10 million or so Americans who have used it, only 6 percent report doing so in the last month. It's not clear whether frequent use is more common among smokers. In a 1994 survey of young adults, one-fifth of those who had ever smoked meth were past-month users, compared to one-tenth of those who had used "stimulants" generally. But in a 2002 survey of high-school seniors, past-month use was reported by a quarter of the meth smokers, compared to a third of all amphetamine users. If meth smokers are more prone to heavy use, it's hard to say whether this is due to the route of administration or to the sort of people who find it attractive. Like heroin injectors and crack smokers, they are a self-selected group, drawn to an extreme, notorious practice. In any case, it's striking that less than 7 percent of the high-school seniors who said they'd smoked meth in the previous year reported using it on twenty or more days in the previous month. Such heavy use apparently was so rare in the survey of young adults that the researchers did not include it in their tables. There is no support in these data for the claim that methamphetamine use "almost always" results in addiction.[44]

Methamphetamine's power was validated by reference to crack, while crack's power was validated by reference to heroin. Crack was said to be just as addictive as heroin, if not more so. Meth was like crack, only worse. And throughout this period, public health officials and anti-smoking activists were emphasizing that nicotine was "more addictive than heroin."[45] So even as heroin served as a model for addictiveness, its reputed power was implicitly downgraded. More recently, however, heroin has been making a comeback in the press, with reporters warning that it is "more addictive than crack cocaine."[46] Since heroin was perceived as the chief drug menace in the 1970s, crack could be described as the heroin of the eighties. Then methamphetamine was the crack of the nineties, and it looked like heroin could become the meth of the next decade.

Watching the title of Most Addictive Drug rotate from one substance to another, one starts to wonder how much the honor really means. Addiction hinges not just on the drug itself but on the user's personality, expectations, values, and circumstances—what the psychiatrist Norman Zinberg called "set and setting."[47] A person who likes heroin's sedating effect won't necessarily like the intense stimulation provided by crack or crystal meth. A patient in pain or a soldier at war can use a strong narcotic for particular reasons and give it up without much trouble once those reasons no longer apply. A happy person can take or leave the same drug that a miserable person turns to every day. A person who uses a drug to excess during an especially troubled period may find that he can use it in moderation after his situation improves. Given these differences, it makes little sense to talk about a drug's "addictiveness" as if it were a chemical property. Indeed, drugs are not even a necessary component of addiction, if by that term we mean a hard-to-break habit that often has negative consequences. Just about anything that provides pleasure or relieves stress—including eating, sex, gambling, shopping, jogging, TV watching, and Web surfing—can be the focus of an addiction.[48]

Heroin in Moderation

The idea that drugs cause addiction was rejected in the case of alcohol because it was so clearly at odds with everyday experience, which showed that the typical drinker was not an alcoholic. But what Bruce Alexander calls "the myth of drug-induced addiction" is still widely accepted in the case of heroin—and, by extension, the drugs compared to it—because moderate opiate users are hard to find. That does not mean they don't exist; indeed, judging from the government's survey results, they are a lot more common than addicts. It's just that people who use opiates in a controlled way are inconspicuous by definition, and keen to remain so.

In the early 1960s, however, researchers began to tentatively identify users of heroin and other opiates who were not addicts. "Surprisingly enough," one psychiatrist wrote in 1961, "in some cases at least, narcotic use may be confined to weekends or parties and the users may be able to continue in gainful employment for some time. Although this pattern often deteriorates and the rate of use increases, several cases have been observed in which relatively gainful and steady employment has been maintained for two to three years while the user was on what might be called a regulated or controlled habit."[49]

A few years later, Norman Zinberg and David C. Lewis described five categories of narcotic users, including "people who use narcotics regularly but who develop little or no tolerance for them and do not suffer withdrawal symptoms." They explained that "such people are usually able to work regularly and productively. They value the relaxation and the 'kick' obtained from the drug, but their fear of needing more and more of the drug to get the same kick causes them to impose rigorous controls on themselves."[50]

The example offered by Zinberg and Lewis was a forty-seven-year-old physician with a successful practice who had been injecting morphine four times a day, except weekends, for twelve years. He experienced modest discomfort on Saturdays and Sundays, when he abstained, but he stuck to his schedule and did not raise his dose except on occasions when he was especially busy or tense. Zinberg and Lewis's account suggests that morphine's main function for him was stress relief: "Somewhat facetiously, when describing his intolerance of people making emotional demands on him, he said that he took one shot for his patients, one for his mistress, one for his family and one to sleep. He expressed no guilt about his drug taking, and made it clear that he had no intention of stopping."[51]

Zinberg eventually interviewed sixty-one controlled opiate users. His criteria excluded both dabblers (the largest group of people who have used heroin) and daily users. One subject, for example, was a forty-one-year-old carpenter who had used heroin on weekends for a decade. Married sixteen years, he lived with his wife and three children in a middle-class suburb. Another was a twenty-seven-year-old college student studying special education. He had used heroin two or three times a month for three years, then once a week for a year. The controlled users said they liked "the 'rush' (glow or warmth), the sense of distance from their problems, and the tranquilizing powers of the drug." Opiate use was generally seen as a social activity, and it was often combined with other forms of recreation. Summing up the lessons he learned from his research, Zinberg emphasized the importance of self-imposed rules dictating when, where, and with whom the drug would be used.[52]

Other researchers have reported similar findings. After interviewing twelve occasional heroin users, one concluded that "it seems possible for young people from a number of different backgrounds, family patterns, and educational abilities to use heroin occasionally without becoming addicted." The subjects typically took heroin with one or more friends, and the most frequently reported benefit was relaxation. One subject, a twenty-three-year-old graduate student, said it was "like taking a vacation from yourself. . . . When things get to you, it's a way of getting away without getting away." These occasional users were unanimous in rejecting addiction as inconsistent with their self-images. A British study of fifty-one opiate users likewise found that distaste for the junkie lifestyle was an important deterrent to excessive use.[53]

While these studies show that controlled opiate use is possible, the Vietnam veterans study mentioned earlier in this chapter gives us some idea of how common it is. "Only one-quarter of those who used heroin in the last two years used it daily at all," the researchers reported. Likewise, only a quarter said they had felt dependent, and only a quarter said heroin use had interfered with their lives. Regular heroin use (more than once a week for more than a month) was associated with a significant increase in "social adjustment problems" (including crime, violence, divorce, alcohol abuse, transience, credit difficulties, and unemployment or frequent job changes), but occasional use was not.[54]

Many of these occasional users had been addicted in Vietnam, so they knew what it was like. Paradoxically, a drug's attractiveness, whether experienced directly or observed secondhand, can reinforce the user's determination to remain in control. (Presumably, that is the theory behind all the propaganda warning how wonderful certain drug experiences are, except that the aim of those messages is to stop people from experimenting at all.) Walter Stevenson, a neuroscientist in his late twenties, smoked heroin a couple of times in college. He said it was "nothing dramatic, just the feeling that everything was OK for about six hours, and I wasn't really motivated to do anything." Having observed several friends who were addicted to heroin at one time or another, he understood that the experience could be seductive, but "that kind of seduction . . . kind of repulsed me. That was exactly the kind of thing that I was trying to avoid in my life."[55]

Similarly, Bruce Rogers first snorted heroin in the mid 1980s and thought "it was too nice." As he described it, "you're sort of not awake and you're not asleep, and you feel sort of like a baby in the cradle, with no worries, just floating in a comfortable cocoon. That's an interesting place to be if you don't have anything else to do. That's Sunday-afternoon-on-the-couch material." Rogers did have other things to do, and after that first experience he used heroin only "once in a blue moon." But he managed to incorporate the regular use of another opiate, morphine pills, into a busy, productive life. For years he had been taking them once a week as a way of unwinding and relieving the aches and pains from the hard manual labor required by his landscaping business. "We use it as a reward system," he said. "On a Friday, if we've been working really hard and we're sore and it's available, it's a reward. It's like, 'We've worked hard today. We've earned our money, we paid our bills, but we're sore, so let's do this. It's medicine.'"[56]

Better Homes & Gardens

Evelyn Schwartz learned to use heroin in a similar way: as a complement to rest and relaxation rather than a means of suppressing unpleasant emotions. A social worker in her fifties, she injected heroin every day for years but was using it intermittently when I interviewed her. Schwartz originally became addicted after leaving home at fourteen because of conflict with her mother. "As I felt more and more alienated from my family, more and more alone, more and more depressed," she said, "I started to use [heroin] not in a recreational fashion but as a coping mechanism, to get rid of feelings, to feel OK. . . . I was very unhappy . . . and just hopeless about life, and I was just trying to survive day by day for many years."[57]

But after Schwartz found work that she loved and started feeling good about her life, she was able to use heroin in a different way. "I try not to use as a coping mechanism," she said. "I try very hard not to use when I'm miserable, because that's what gets me into trouble. It's set and setting. It's not the drug, because I can use this drug in a very controlled way, and I can also go out of control." To stay in control, "I try to use when I'm feeling good," she said, such as on vacation with friends, listening to music, or before a walk on a beautiful spring day. "If I need to clean the house, I do a little heroin, and I can clean the house, and it just makes me feel so good."[58]

Many people are shocked by the idea of using heroin so casually, which helps explain the controversy surrounding a 2001 BBC documentary that explored why people use drugs. "Heroin is my drug of choice over alcohol or cocaine," said one user interviewed for the program. "I take it at weekends in small doses, and do the gardening."[59] Given that addiction is an unlikely outcome, it's hard to see a moral distinction between such uses of heroin and smoking a joint at a concert or drinking beer at a football game. Using heroin to enliven housework or gardening is surely wiser than using it to alleviate grief, dissatisfaction, or loneliness. It's when drugs are used for emotional management that a destructive habit is apt to develop.

Even daily opiate use is not necessarily inconsistent with a productive life. One famous example is the pioneering surgeon William Halsted, who led a brilliant career while secretly addicted to morphine.[60] On a more modest level, Schwartz said that even during her years as a self-described junkie she always held a job, always paid the rent, and was able to conceal her drug use from people who would have been alarmed by it. "I was always one of the best secretaries at work, and no one ever knew, because I learned how to titrate my doses," she said. She would generally take three or four doses a day: when she got up in the morning, at lunchtime, when she came home from work, and perhaps before going to sleep. The doses she took during the day were small enough so that she could get her work done. "Aside from the fact that I was a junkie," she said, "I was raised to be a really good girl and do what I'm supposed to do, and I did."[61]

Schwartz's worst crime was shoplifting a raincoat for a job interview. "I never robbed," she said. "I never did anything like that. I never hurt a human being. I could never do that. I went sick a lot as a consequence. When other junkies would commit crimes, get money, and tighten up, I would be sick. Everyone . . . used to say: 'You're terrible at being a junkie.' I'm not going to hit anybody over the head. I'm sorry."[62]

Schwartz, a warm, smart, hardworking woman, is quite different from the heroin users you generally read about in the mainstream press. But once in a while, a challenge to junkie stereotypes appears in a surprising place. In 1992 the *New York Times* carried a front-page story about a successful businessman who happened to be a regular heroin user. It began: "He is an executive in a company in New York, lives in a condo on the Upper East Side of Manhattan, drives an expensive car, plays tennis in the Hamptons and vacations with his wife in Europe and the Caribbean. But unknown to office colleagues, friends and most of his family, the man is also a longtime heroin user. He says he finds heroin relaxing and pleasurable and has seen no reason to stop using it until the woman he recently married insisted that he do so. 'The drug is an enhancement of my life,' he said. 'I see it as similar to a guy coming home and having a drink of alcohol. Only alcohol has never done it for me.'" The *Times* noted that "nearly everything about the 44-year-old executive . . . seems to fly in the face of widely held perceptions about heroin users."[63]

The reporter who wrote the story and his editors seemed uncomfortable about contradicting official anti-drug propaganda. The headline read, "Executive's Secret Struggle With Heroin's Powerful Grip," which sounds more like a cautionary tale than a success story. And the *Times* hastened to add that heroin users "are flirting with disaster." It conceded that "heroin does not damage the organs as, for instance, heavy alcohol use does."[64] But it cited the risk of arrest, overdose, AIDS, and hepatitis—without noting that all of these risks are created or exacerbated by prohibition, which makes users subject to arrest, drives them to a black market where doses and purity are uncertain, and encourages them to share needles by limiting access to injection equipment.

The general thrust of the piece was: Here is a privileged man who is tempting fate by messing around with a very dangerous drug. He may have escaped disaster so far, but unless he quits he will probably end up dead or in prison.

That is not the way the businessman saw his situation. He said he had decided to give up heroin only because his wife did not approve of the habit. "In my heart," he said, "I really don't feel there's anything wrong with using heroin. But there doesn't seem to be any way in the world I can persuade my wife to grant me this space in our relationship. I don't want to lose her, so I'm making this effort."[65]

Legal Complications

Although not every addict resembles the shifty, shiftless thieves portrayed on TV, the Vietnam veterans study did find that crime and other "social adjustment problems" were more common among regular heroin users. This does not necessarily mean that heroin use caused these problems. Using a questionnaire designed to assess early warning signs of antisocial behavior, the researchers determined that "the men who used heroin were those who were especially disposed to adjustment problems even before they used the drug." While regular heroin use seemed to have an additional effect, it wasn't clear whether this was "because of the drug itself or because of its legal status."[66]

Both of these complications make it hard to assess heroin's direct contribution to the problems heavy users often experience or cause: Troubled or antisocial people may be especially attracted to the drug, and its legal status makes it more dangerous to use. The law's role goes beyond the risk of arrest and the handicap of a criminal record. The drug's legal status helps make it the focus of an oppositional identity—the junkie at odds with straight society—that users who have little else to define themselves with are reluctant to give up. As the sociologist Harold Alksne and his colleagues suggested in the late 1960s, "the process of becoming an addict and being an addict in our culture may well be as much a social process and condition as it is physical and psychological."[67] The importance of heroin addiction as a basis for identity is perhaps best illustrated by "pseudo-junkies," who claim to be addicted even though they have only dabbled in the drug.[68] Then, too, the difficulty of obtaining heroin creates anxiety that would not exist if it were readily available, so that many addicts organize their lives around getting the next fix. Users are exposed to violence because they have to get the drug from criminals. The artificially high price of heroin, perhaps forty or fifty times what it would otherwise cost, may lead to heavy debts, housing problems, poor nutrition, and theft.[69] The inflated cost also encourages users to inject the drug, a more efficient but riskier mode of administration. The legal treatment of injection equipment, including restrictions on distribution and penalties for possession, encourages needle sharing, which spreads diseases such as AIDS and hepatitis. The unreliable quality and unpredictable purity associated with the black market can lead to poisoning and accidental overdoses.

Without prohibition, then, a daily heroin habit would be far less burdensome and hazardous. Heroin itself is much less likely to kill a user than the reckless combination of heroin with other depressants, such as alcohol or barbiturates. The federal government's Drug Abuse Warning Network counted 4,820 mentions of heroin or morphine (which are indistinguishable in the blood) by medical examiners in 1999. Only 438 of these deaths (9 percent) were listed as directly caused by an overdose of the opiate. Three-quarters of the deaths were caused by heroin/morphine in combination with other drugs.[70] Provided the user avoids such mixtures, has access to a supply of reliable purity, and follows sanitary injection procedures, the health risks of long-term opiate consumption are minimal.[71]

The psychological and spiritual consequences are harder to assess. An occasional "vacation from yourself" is one thing, a perpetual holiday something else. A drug that makes you feel everything's OK has obvious perils, especially when it's not. Such a drug can help you avoid problems that ought to be dealt with and ease the discontent that might otherwise impel you to improve your situation. Even addicts who stay healthy and make an honest living may later regret the time and opportunities they wasted.[72]

Then again, it's widely accepted, even by the same people who see heroin addiction as an unmitigated evil, that some individuals suffer from biochemical imbalances that make them unhappy. These imbalances, we're told, can and should be treated with drugs. As Thomas Szasz and other critics of psychiatry have observed, such beliefs create a double standard: If an unhappy person takes heroin, he is committing a crime. If he takes Prozac, he is treating his depression. The next chapter explores the assumptions underlying that distinction.

CHAPTER EIGHT

BODY AND SOUL

All marijuana use is medical.
—DRUG REFORM ACTIVIST DENNIS PERON, 1996

Doctor's Orders

In the *Star Trek* episode "Specter of the Gun," a landing party from the *Enterprise* is transformed into the Clanton Gang and trapped in a re-creation of nineteenth-century Tombstone, Arizona. To avoid reenacting the shootout at the O.K. Corral, Spock suggests knocking out the Earps and Doc Holliday with an improvised gas grenade. Just before he tests the weapon on Scotty, the engineer gulps a glass of whiskey. "To kill the pain," he explains in response to Spock's puzzled look. "But this is painless," says Spock. "You should have warned me sooner, Mr. Spock," says Scotty with a sheepish smile.

The joke, which recalls the liberal use of alcohol as an anesthetic in westerns, suggests that even in the twenty-third century people will still be looking for an excuse to have a drink. This particular excuse reflects the dual role, as both medicine and intoxicant, that alcohol retained well into the twentieth century. At least since St. Paul's prescription of "a little wine for thy stomach's sake," alcohol has been seen as a balm for men's bodies as well as their souls, preventing illness, speeding recovery, and soothing pain. Over the centuries, it has been used for a wide variety of medical applications: to warm and invigorate the body, to resuscitate the injured, to counteract snake venom, to treat fevers and infections, to stimulate the heart, to aid digestion, and to ward off communicable diseases such as bubonic plague and malaria. Many of today's familiar alcoholic beverages, including gin, various liqueurs, and the mint julep, were invented as preventatives or treatments.[1] Alcohol was a leading ingredient in the patent medicines of the nineteenth and early twentieth centuries. Even if it didn't cure anyone, it made a lot of people feel better, at least temporarily.

This mixture of motives made anti-alcohol campaigners uncomfortable. Even Lyman Beecher, the minister who signaled the temperance movement's shift from moderation to abstinence, had left room for medicinal use. But his successors saw that the exception gave alcohol a patina of respectability and provided cover for intoxication. Under dry pressure, distilled spirits were removed from the *Pharmacopeia of the United States* in 1915. Two years later, the American Medical Association passed a resolution that said "the use of alcohol as a therapeutic agent should be discouraged."[2] Yet many physicians continued to view alcohol as a useful remedy, a fact reflected in the exemption for medical use during Prohibition. Because the drug still had vocal supporters, the tenth revision of the *Pharmacopeia,* published in the 1920s, again included whiskey and brandy. The AMA's 1926 guide called alcohol "a narcotic widely used as a stimulant" but warned that "it may do more harm than good."[3] Whiskey and brandy were finally removed from the *Pharmacopeia* in its thirteenth revision, which took effect in 1947.[4]

Among other things, the die-hard medical proponents of alcohol thought it was good for the heart. As we saw in Chapter 2, that intuition has been verified by epidemiological research during the last few decades. But even though a drink or two a day may be about as effective at reducing the risk of heart disease as some widely prescribed pharmaceuticals (and a lot easier than sticking to a new diet or exercise program), the idea of using alcohol as a medicine is highly controversial.[5] It smacks too much of the self-help approach that prevailed until the early twentieth century, when Congress began passing laws classifying drugs by their approved uses. Since then, self-medication has given way to treatment by experts. Keen to contrast their professional, scientific methods with the haphazard therapies of amateurs, doctors of medicine favored increasingly specific remedies. They became suspicious of panaceas, which often were drugs that did not cure illness so much as make it easier to bear. Such drugs not only could mask symptoms and thereby discourage more effective treatment; they could lead to long-term habits that came to be viewed as diseases in themselves. The evolution of modern medicine gave us our current, bifurcated view of drugs: the good ones that treat illness and the bad ones that people use to change their minds and moods.[6] We are not comfortable with drugs that straddle those two categories, which is one reason alcohol is not likely to be accepted as a medicine again.

Like alcohol, opium, coca, and cannabis all have long histories of medical use, and all were ingredients in remedies and tonics that were once readily available in the United States. Opiates could be consumed in preparations such as laudanum and Mrs. Winslow's

Soothing Syrup; coca was included in popular beverages such as Vin Mariani and Coca-Cola; and tincture of hemp was sold in drugstores. People used these products for a variety of reasons, including physical symptoms accompanied by low spirits and emotional problems accompanied by bodily complaints. The government did not try to police the boundary between medicine and intoxication. But with the rise of medical doctors as pharmacological gatekeepers, this situation could no longer be tolerated. Cocaine and morphine (the most powerful drug in opium) were classified as medicines, to be used only with a doctor's permission. Cannabis—which was not injectable and did not satisfy the new preference for isolated chemicals—was banned entirely, forbidden for therapy and for fun.

Today the government considers any nonmedical use of a prescription drug to be abuse. Bruce Rogers, the horticulturist quoted in the last chapter, may call it "medicine" when he uses morphine both to relieve pain and to relax, but such ambiguity is radically at odds with the modern system of legal controls. Although that system benefits physicians by enhancing their status and power, it also constrains them. Doctors are taught to be suspicious of patients in pain because prescribing narcotics to the wrong person can jeopardize their careers. They have to make sure that the patient really is suffering physically, not just emotionally. At the same time, however, psychiatrists have been defining an ever-lengthening list of mental states as disorders to be treated with psychoactive substances. The medical excuse for drug use is so powerful that it can justify giving stimulants to inattentive schoolboys, tranquilizers to anxious travelers, and happy pills to melancholy teenagers—provided an M.D. approves. (As we saw in Chapter 5, it can also justify giving an aphrodisiac to people who are dissatisfied with their sex lives.) Taking MDMA to overcome shyness is drug abuse, but prescribing Paxil to treat "social anxiety disorder" is good medicine. Legally, the distinction between medical and nonmedical is clear. Conceptually, it has never been blurrier.

Dirty Brains

The experience of Jim Dahl, a physician whose career was nearly ruined by a combination of bureaucratic intransigence and his own naiveté, illustrates the arbitrariness of the criteria for legitimate medical use. In 1998, when he was working for a health center in southwestern Pennsylvania, Dahl was feeling anxious because of conflicts with his boss. He began taking the antidepressant Zoloft, which "worked OK, not great," he recalled; he was "still feeling a lot of anxiety." On Thanksgiving Day he was putting up a satellite TV dish on his roof when he slipped and sprained his ankle. He took Vicodin, a combination of acetaminophen and the narcotic hydrocodone, for the pain. After the ten days or so that it took the injury to heal, he said, "I realized the stress that I was feeling from this job was gone, and it was the medicine I had been using." He continued using the painkiller for about nine months, taking two pills three times a day. After he resigned from his position in July 1999, planning to take a job in Texas, "the stress levels were going way down," and his consumption gradually declined. By then, however, his orders for painkillers had aroused suspicion, and in August two agents from the Drug Enforcement Administration came to his door.[7]

The DEA pressured Dahl to surrender his federal prescription license, which put an end to the job in Texas. To avoid criminal charges that carried a mandatory minimum sentence of more than two years, he agreed to undergo "rehabilitation," even though he did not consider himself an addict. He was already tapering off his use when the DEA came knocking, he stopped cold afterward, and he never experienced withdrawal symptoms. In his view, he never met the diagnostic criteria for substance dependence. But he eventually realized that resisting the addict label was not winning him any points because "then I'm in denial, which is a symptom of the disease." The diagnosis hinged not on any problems caused by the Vicodin but on Dahl's failure to get a psychiatrist's prescription and his unfashionable choice of a drug that is generally used to treat pain rather than anxiety. "Anybody who uses a controlled substance is deemed to be impaired," he said. "And since I was impaired, I needed treatment."[8]

The PDR Pocket Guide to Prescription Drugs warns: "Vicodin may make you drowsy, less alert, or unable to function well physically. Do not drive a car, operate machinery, or perform any other potentially dangerous activities until you know how this drug affects you."[9] But Dahl noted that many people take Vicodin regularly for pain and still do their jobs. He recalled telling his lawyer: "I give this to people every day. . . . They're working construction and they're driving big rigs, and they need this for their back. I would not give this to them if I thought that it would be impairing them."[10] Dahl believed the drug actually improved his job performance by relieving his anxiety and enabling him to focus better on his patients. Neither the DEA nor the state medical board cited complaints from patients or any other evidence of incompetence.

Dahl was appalled by what passed for "treatment" in the six-week rehab program he attended. "Your brains are defective—you need to have them washed," one speaker told the program's participants. "People are just sitting there eating this up," Dahl recalled, "because it gives them a chance to excuse their own bad behavior. . . . I was ready to scream every day." But he went through the motions, painting rocks to represent his feelings and confessing his sins to a bunch of strangers. Afterward, the state wanted him to attend Alcoholics Anonymous meetings every day, a demand he rejected because he viewed the program as a form of religious indoctrination. "I used the medicine for nine months," he said, "and I'm now sentenced for the rest of my life to this kind of crap." He was willing to be randomly tested to show that he was not using drugs, but he insisted that "I will not be monitored by somebody who's going to judge my serenity." Dahl ultimately got his prescription privileges back, and the state let him continue to practice medicine provided he submit to urinalysis for five years. It did not require participation in any twelve-step programs, which Dahl had argued would violate his First Amendment right to freedom of conscience.[11]

In a revealing footnote to this episode, Dahl underwent a vasectomy while he was still being watched closely by state regulators. Afterward he suffered from a painful hematoma that his doctor treated with Percocet, a combination of acetaminophen and the narcotic oxycodone. He took the Percocet for two weeks, and "the state didn't seem to have any problem with this," he said. "It is curious that my surgeon didn't feel the need to preclude me from practicing medicine while I was 'under the influence' of oxycodone. Apparently, the state feels there is a big difference between self-prescription of a less potent opiate, hydrocodone, and my urologist's recommendation that I [take] oxycodone. Am I missing something? Perhaps I am blinded by my severe 'disease of addiction.'"[12]

Whatever one may think of Dahl's drug use, which certainly was foolish given the potential legal and professional repercussions, it's clear that the government did not step in because Vicodin was inter-fering with his ability to do his job. If he had obtained another doc-tor's prescription first, he could have taken any number of drugs that might have made him sleepy or impaired his concentration, and he never would have attracted the DEA's attention. The piece of paper would have transformed addiction into treatment, drug abuse into legitimate medicine.

Pot Prescription

The power of the prescription can also be seen in the controversy over "medical marijuana." It's beyond serious dispute that marijuana, which has been used therapeutically for thousands of years, helps re-lieve nausea and restore appetite. Marinol, a capsule containing THC (tetrahydrocannabinol, marijuana's main active ingredient), is ap-proved by the Food and Drug Administration as a treatment for AIDS wasting syndrome and the side effects of cancer chemotherapy. But smoked marijuana has several advantages over Marinol: It doesn't have to be swallowed and kept in the stomach (a feat for people with severe nausea); it takes effect right away, so relief comes quickly and the dose is easy to calibrate; and its psychoactive effects are less dis-turbing. Many patients find that marijuana works better for them than any legal alternative. In addition to its use as an anti-emetic, marijuana shows promise in treating glaucoma, migraines and other painful conditions, and muscle spasms associated with epilepsy and multiple sclerosis.[13] In 2001 the DEA authorized studies investigat-ing marijuana as a treatment for muscle spasticity in MS patients and peripheral nerve pain in HIV patients.

But the public debate about the medical use of marijuana was never really about the adequacy of the scientific evidence. For reformers, it was an opportunity to show how the war on drugs punishes innocent people, causing needless suffering through blind adherence to political orthodoxy. More controversially, it was a chance to improve marijuana's image by showing that its benefits were not limited to getting high. Taking marijuana seriously as a medicine also meant considering its potential side effects, which turned out to be far less serious than the government had long claimed.[14] Finally, the example set by thousands of patients openly smoking pot would be bound to puncture myths about the drug's impact on behavior.

Like the dry activists who sought to expunge alcohol from the list of recognized medicines, federal officials worried that the therapeutic use of marijuana would give the drug legitimacy and offer an excuse for intoxication. They were also concerned that state initiatives endorsing marijuana as a medicine implicitly challenged the national government's authority to define the limits of acceptable medical practice (an authority with a shaky constitutional basis). These stakes help explain why the drug warriors felt they could not yield an inch on this issue. Beginning with the 1996 initiatives in Arizona and California, they came out with guns blazing, categorically denying that marijuana had any medical utility, accusing reformers of bad faith, and threatening to punish doctors who dared recommend marijuana to their patients.

"There is not a shred of scientific evidence that shows that smoked marijuana is useful or needed," Barry McCaffrey, then director of the Office of National Drug Control Policy, told the *San Francisco Chronicle* in August 1996. "This is not medicine. This is a cruel hoax that sounds more like something out of a Cheech and Chong show."[15] That December, a CNN correspondent asked McCaffrey whether there was "any evidence . . . that marijuana is useful in a medical situation." His reply was unequivocal: "No, none at all."[16] These statements, which were contradicted by the 1999 National Academy of Sciences report that McCaffrey himself commissioned, suggested that the drug czar could not bring himself to admit that smoking pot could lead to anything but trouble.[17] He knew marijuana was bad, and he knew medicine was good. Therefore marijuana simply could not be medicine, no matter what the evidence showed.

The next administration seemed equally determined to act on this conviction. Just weeks after the September 11 terrorist attacks, DEA agents in California, where state law allows the medicinal use of marijuana, were destroying plants grown by patients, seizing medical records, and raiding clubs that distributed cannabis to sick people.[18] During the next year, the federal government continued to pursue a strategy of shutting down medical marijuana clubs through civil injunctions, thereby avoiding juries who might be sympathetic to the clubs' members.

By 2002 nine states had passed laws, either by initiative or through the legislature, permitting patients to use marijuana, and reformers continued to campaign for such measures. Yet it seemed likely that the medical marijuana debate eventually would be rendered moot by the development of inhalers for THC (and possibly other useful cannabinoids), which would have marijuana's advantages over oral preparations without the hazards of smoking. (Vaporizers that heat marijuana to release THC are a step in this direction, but they still use whole cannabis. Inhalers would reassure doctors who are leery of raw plant matter, with its inconsistent strength and additional components.) It was not clear which side would emerge stronger from the struggle over medical marijuana. The drug warriors seemed cruelly stubborn, but the reformers could ultimately be perceived as disingenuous, using the medical argument to advance the cause of decriminalization, then switching to a new tack once better therapeutic alternatives were available.

Anxious not to look like potheads hiding behind patients, the reformers emphasized that a doctor's recommendation would be required to exempt marijuana users from prosecution. They put patients and physicians on TV. They did not talk about a broader agenda (indeed, many did not have one), and they distanced themselves from activists who were less discreet. One of these was Dennis Peron, one of the main activists behind California's medical marijuana proposition. "I believe all marijuana use is medical," he told the *New York Times* in 1996, arguing that stress relief is therapeutic.[19]

Such statements embarrassed the mainstream activists and delighted the drug warriors, who seized upon them as evidence that medical marijuana really was "a cruel hoax." Yet Peron's understanding of *medical* is consistent with the sweeping agenda of the American Psychiatric Association. True, the APA does not endorse pot smoking for stress relief (or any other purpose). But it does view excessive anxiety, shyness, irritability, restlessness, and sadness as medical problems that doctors may appropriately treat with drugs. It is hard to see a principled distinction between using marijuana to relieve stress and using Xanax or Valium for the same purpose. And if marijuana can make depressed people happier, how is it morally different from Prozac or Wellbutrin?[20]

To decide whether there's an important distinction here, it is not necessary to know which (if any) of the "mental disorders" described by the APA are actually "brain diseases." No one denies that some physical illnesses (Alzheimer's, for example) affect cognition, emotion, and behavior. But as Thomas Szasz has pointed out, such conditions are treated by neurologists, not psychiatrists. If chronic depression is in fact a brain disease, then it is not a "mental illness." Either way, depressed people may feel better after taking certain drugs. That fact does raise serious moral questions, and resolving them may depend partly on whether depression is viewed as a neurological defect unconnected to experience or as a learned response that can be changed without chemicals (an option that may be preferable in some situations). But these questions do not hinge on the drug's current legal status.

Chemical Shortcuts

We tend to assume that pharmaceuticals are morally unproblematic because they are approved by the government and prescribed by doctors. Conversely, we tend to assume that illegal drugs, unsanctioned by authority, are inherently immoral. This pretense breaks down when similar substances—say, methamphetamine and Ritalin—are used for different purposes, or when different substances—say, heroin and Prozac—are used for similar purposes. Then we are forced to think about what makes one kind of drug use life-enhancing and another kind self-destructive.

In *Listening to Prozac,* the psychiatrist Peter D. Kramer describes "fairly healthy people who show dramatic good responses to Prozac, people who are not so much cured of illness as transformed." These individuals, though troubled, did not have problems that rose to the level of what the APA would consider clinical depression. They generally functioned well enough but felt melancholy, shy, lonely, or dissatisfied. Kramer concedes that their use of Prozac to tweak their personalities is hard to distinguish from the way many people use illegal drugs such as cocaine and heroin.[21] Based on the same observation, the psychologist and addiction specialist Jeffrey Schaler disapproves of Prozac. "I oppose the use of heroin for the same reason I oppose the use of Prozac," he writes. "I think relying on these is an existential cop-out—a way of avoiding coping with life." People who like Prozac, such as those described in Kramer's book, would say that it helps them get on with their lives by relieving anxiety and brightening their outlook. But Schaler argues that using drugs this way is counterproductive because it eliminates the discomfort that spurs people to make the changes that would ultimately lead to better, more satisfying lives.[22] Surely there is truth to both positions; the trick is recognizing which more accurately describes a particular person's situation.

A 2001 letter in a psychiatry journal cited two cases in which antidepressants may have had the effect that worries Schaler. One case involved a depressed woman who said she wanted to leave her abusive boyfriend but lost her resolve after taking Paxil for several weeks. The other involved a depressed man accustomed to going through a twelve-pack of beer each day who lost interest in changing his drinking habits after six weeks on Prozac. "These patients continued to lead dysfunctional lives, and their motivation for major lifestyle changes seemed to decrease as depressive symptoms improved," the letter said. "Would the two patients have been better off and made definitive changes in their lives if treatment with antidepressants had been postponed?" In reply, another psychiatrist conceded that antidepressants might be counterproductive in some cases but argued that "drug treatment can also increase confidence and initiative in ways that allow some individuals to get out of bad situations."[23]

In some ways the issues raised by chemically assisted living are similar to those raised by debates between different schools of psychotherapy. Is it necessary (or preferable) to get at the root causes of one's unhappiness, delving into a long history of psychological wounds? What if a shallower approach, such as cognitive exercises that help reduce or eliminate persistent negative thoughts, is just as effective?[24] What if taking a pill can achieve the same result?

Consider the use of Paxil to treat "social anxiety disorder." The drug's manufacturer has an obvious stake in promoting the idea that extreme shyness is an illness that can be overcome with the help of a pharmaceutical. Some critics have argued that the marketing campaign for Paxil exaggerates the extent of the problem, said to be "America's third most common mental disorder," with "10 million sufferers." Others insist that it's simply wrong to think of shyness as a disease. "In my opinion," one psychologist told the *Washington Post,* "social anxiety is not a chemical problem in the brain. I see it as a problem with normal thinking and behaviors that have gone awry." The psychologist's preferred solution was fourteen weeks of cognitive-behavioral therapy. "It's like learning to ride a bike," he said. "You are practicing these skills over and over. No one can take them away from you for the rest of your life. The long-term benefits of cognitive therapy [are] better than [those of] medicine because with medicine, when you stop the symptoms come back."[25] This argument is not without force, but a Paxil booster might retort that cognitive therapy does not work for everyone, while a Freudian might insist that years of analysis would be more appropriate than either sort of quick fix.

It is easy to imagine situations where extra effort is worthwhile, perhaps because it leads to concrete changes (such as dumping a boyfriend or laying off the booze) or because it fosters greater self-insight, leaving one better prepared for future challenges. The sense of having conquered one's problems without drugs may also be an important ingredient in one's ultimate happiness. But it would be presumptuous to declare that shortcuts, whether or not they involve drugs, are never an acceptable choice.

The use of drugs as psychotherapeutic catalysts is a kind of shortcut, intended to help people get past psychological obstacles that might otherwise take months or years to overcome. But taking the drug is only the beginning: Once the barriers to communication or introspection are removed, there is still work involved in self-exploration and in applying the insights gained from it. While Prozac and MDMA both work mainly by raising serotonin levels (Prozac by blocking the neurotransmitter's reuptake, MDMA by causing more of it to be released), they are used quite differently by people looking for a way to be happier. Prozac is taken every day as a sort of ongoing supplement, while MDMA is taken occasionally as a temporary aid to self-improvement. LSD and other psychedelics serve a similar function; not many users think the key to happiness is to drop acid every day.

Some advocates of drug-assisted psychotherapy seek to take advantage of the prevailing medical paradigm by turning catalysts such as MDMA into prescription medicines. Rick Doblin's Multidisciplinary Association for Psychedelic Studies, which in 2001 received permission from the Food and Drug Administration to study MDMA as a treatment for posttraumatic stress disorder, is dedicated to jumping through whatever bureaucratic hoops are necessary to win regulatory approval for drugs that have been unreasonably neglected. Toward that end, MAPS has sponsored research on a variety of agents that are not generally recognized as medicines, including LSD, mescaline, psilocybin, ayahuasca, ibogaine, and ketamine. (A proposed application for several of these substances is the treatment of drug addiction, suggesting that one psychoactive substance can cure the "disease" caused by another.) Although such attempts to work within the system may enable some people to benefit from currently illegal substances without fear of arrest, this approach tends to reinforce the assumption that "medical" use of drugs is the only sort that should be allowed.

The argument for medical exceptions is strongest in life-or-death cases: AIDS or cancer patients who are in danger of wasting away unless they can stop vomiting and retain nourishment. It likewise seems cruel to deny people in pain access to a drug that can bring relief simply because other people use it to get high. But when the concept of medicine is expanded to include the treatment of unpleasant emotions or counterproductive thoughts, it becomes impossible to say definitively when drug use is "merely" recreational. At the same time, the problems addressed by physicians begin to resemble the problems addressed by priests, ministers, and rabbis.

Ritual Reality

Modern medicine shares certain conspicuous features with shaman-centered religions. Both offer physical healing and spiritual guidance aided by drugs. Doctors and witch doctors, medical men and medicine men, serve the same basic needs and to some extent depend on the same mechanisms, although they use different language to describe them. Physicians do not believe that disease is caused by disturbances in the spirit world, but they do recognize that a patient's state of mind can have a profound effect on his prognosis. There are various ways of understanding the remarkable rebound (described in Chapter 5) that Sue Stevens witnessed in her husband after they both took MDMA and talked about the emotional issues raised by his kidney cancer. But surely it is not out of the question that, in the right circumstances, a psychoactive drug could help mitigate the impact of an illness or even extend someone's life by changing his outlook.

Michael Buchanan, a retired professor in his seventies, began using ayahuasca, a psychedelic drink made from the bark of a South American vine, after he was diagnosed with liver cancer. "I was given a very grim prognosis," he said. "In my reading of the drug literature, I had come across references to ayahuasca's curative powers, so I sought it out." He learned how to use ayahuasca from followers of the Brazil-based Santo Daime movement, which, like the Native American Church, combines Christianity with ritual psychedelic use. Taking the drug about once a month, Buchanan experienced fantastic visions of plants and animals, intimations of death, and a deep sense of reassurance. Five years later, he was still alive. "It restores my sense of well-being," he said. " I credit my being alive to taking ayahuasca, and it also opened up my self to explore more fully who I am as a person and how I relate to nature and the cosmos."[26] Perhaps ayahuasca had nothing to do with Buchanan's survival, despite his vivid sense that it helped him keep the cancer at bay. But since the mind can affect the body, it is no more absurd to suppose that ayahuasca visions could help fight disease than to believe that prayer, biofeedback, guided imagery, or emotional support might have an impact on a patient's health.

Although the Santo Daime rituals Buchanan imitated seem bizarre to most Westerners, drugs and religion have been mixing for thousands of years. In addition to the wine used by Christians and Jews, drugs taken for religious purposes have included ayahuasca and other psychoactive plants of the rainforest (by Amazon tribes), coca (by the Incas), psychedelic mushrooms (by the Aztecs), tobacco and mescaline-containing cacti (by natives of North and South America), iboga root (by Africans), the Soma of the ancient Hindus (believed to be the fly-agaric mushroom), and the intoxicant at the center of the Eleusinian Mysteries practiced in ancient Greece (speculatively identified as LSD-like alkaloids in fungus-infested grain).[27] Despite these venerable precedents, Americans tend to view religious practices involving drugs with suspicion, considering them primitive and perhaps bogus.

Although the First Amendment's guarantee of religious freedom seems to promise tolerance of nonmainstream rites, the U.S. Supreme Court has concluded that the Constitution does not require religious exemptions from drug laws. In a 1990 case involving peyote use by members of the Native American Church, the Court held that "neutral rules of general applicability" do not violate the First Amendment even when they ban a practice central to a religion. In previous cases the Court had said that a law imposing a substantial burden on the free exercise of religion is valid only if the government shows that it is the least restrictive means of serving a compelling state interest.[28] Congress responded to the Court's reversal by passing the Religious Freedom Restoration Act of 1993, which sought to restore the "compelling interest" test. The Supreme Court later ruled that Congress did not have the authority to impose this requirement on the states.[29] But in 2002 the U.S. Court of Appeals for the 9th Circuit found that the statute did apply in "the federal realm," including U.S. territories (and, presumably, national parks and the District of Columbia). The court also implied that the law might shield Rastafarians from federal prosecution for marijuana possession.[30]

In general, however, legislators have a free hand in deciding which drug rituals should be permitted. Except for sacramental wine (which was exempted from Prohibition), peyote is the only ritual drug that has gained widespread statutory recognition in the United States. By contrast, it's unlikely that legislatures will ever recognize marijuana as a sacrament. The difference probably is not that Rastafarians are viewed as less sincere. It's that marijuana, unlike peyote, is popular as a recreational intoxicant, and its use (even by believers) is not limited to strictly circumscribed ritual occasions. Notwithstanding the example set by alcohol, the mixture of religion and recreation, like the mixture of medicine and recreation, makes most Americans uncomfortable. If a religious exemption were permitted for marijuana, enforcing its limits would mean inquiring into each user's motives to discover whether he was smoking "the sacred herb" for spiritual reasons or just for fun. Making such distinctions would be even harder than imposing restrictions on medical use.

Drug-Free and Proud

Seeking a medical or religious exemption from a drug prohibition amounts to asserting that *my* use of this substance is important, that it deserves respect in a way that more frivolous uses do not. But it immediately raises the question of what counts as medicine or religion. The malleability of these concepts invites users to be creative in justifying their behavior. If stress and anxiety are medical issues, isn't marijuana a medicine when it's used to relieve them? If an LSD trip can be a moving spiritual experience, isn't dropping acid a religious practice? The urge to offer such excuses is based on the sense that drug use is morally suspect without an elaborate and serious-sounding defense. That assumption, in turn, is based on the belief that certain psychoactive substances are so dangerous that they should be used only in special circumstances. Voodoo pharmacology, which warns that drugs control people rather than the other way around, reinforces that fear. But if it turns out that the physical and psychological hazards of a drug have been greatly exaggerated, that in fact it is no more dangerous than alcohol (and perhaps less so), its users should be able to dispense with the excuses. Wine drinkers generally do not feel compelled to proclaim that their beverage was endorsed by God, that it relieves their anxiety or reduces their risk of heart disease. They can simply say, "I like a nice glass of wine."

Not all objections to drug use rest on spurious distinctions between alcohol and other intoxicants. In addition to religious abstainers such as those discussed in Chapter 1, some people eschew psychoactive substances on secular grounds. James Randi, the magician famous for debunking paranormal claims, was taken aback to learn after Carl Sagan's death that the astronomer, whom Randi considered one of his heroes, had been a frequent marijuana smoker. "I find it repugnant that anyone can choose to unbalance their mind voluntarily, and to thereby surrender to chaos," Randi wrote. "I'm very much 'down' on drug use, to the point that I never use even pain killers unless it's absolutely necessary. I want to be 'here and now' all the time, if I can manage it. That's my choice. I don't drink, I don't smoke. . . . I'll never smoke pot. It might, as Carl seemed to think, enlarge my ability to think, and give me great ideas. Maybe. But I also want control, and I think that I would lose that."[31]

It's worth noting that Randi, who described himself as "the most ardent believer in freedom of choice and action," emphasized that "I have no right to saddle other persons with my mores." Yet it's not clear that Randi's objections to drug use constitute a moral judgment, as opposed to a statement of taste. For him, taking drugs means unbalancing the mind, surrendering to chaos, losing control. Assuming he is not talking about a permanent change (the fear of insanity represented by LSD), he is saying that he would not like the way drugs might affect his thinking and perceptions over the short term. For someone who prides himself on his rationality and empiricism, this is an understandable aversion. Interpreted as a moral principle, however, Randi's repugnance would seem to demand a constant focus on the "here and now," with no room for daydreaming, zoning out in front of the TV or while exercising, getting absorbed in a novel, or losing oneself in a piece of music. Presumably, Randi would have to permit the surrender to chaos that occurs in our dreams, since humans cannot survive without sleep. But it's not clear that they can survive—or, at least, be happy—without deliberately letting go of the here and now from time to time, whether through drugs or other means.

In his 1972 book *The Natural Mind,* Andrew Weil (who, before he became famous as an advocate of alternative medicine, did much to promote a calmer discussion of drug issues) argued that people are born with a desire to achieve altered states of consciousness. He noted that it's common to see little children spin themselves dizzy so they can experience the change in perception it causes, and later in life people discover that drugs are another way to achieve interesting sensations. But Weil maintained that drugs merely point the way to altered states that people can learn to achieve without chemicals.[32] Is it better, then, to develop the sort of discipline it would take to adjust one's mood and perspective at will? Perhaps meditation should replace that drink after a hard day's work. The idea fits certain visions of naturalness and self-sufficiency, but so does learning to do without diversions such as television—or dispensing with any technology. One can think of reasons to throw away anything that can be characterized as a crutch, but sometimes crutches are handy. While expert training and conscientious practice may enable people to do on their own some of the things that drugs help them do, most will find better uses for their time.

Noting the ubiquity of drug use across cultures, times, and even species, the psychopharmacologist Ronald Siegel calls the desire for intoxication "the fourth drive," as basic to human nature as the pursuit of food, water, and sex.[33] If Siegel is right, and the evidence suggests he is, the poverty of "Just Say No" as an approach to drugs is obvious. But moving beyond abstinence does not mean plunging headlong into excess. Without abstaining from food, it is possible to condemn gluttony as sinful, self-destructive, or both. Without abstaining from sex, it is possible to condemn promiscuity (not to mention rape, pederasty, bestiality, incest, adultery, homosexuality, and sex before marriage). Viewing intoxication as a basic human impulse is the beginning of moral judgment, not the end. It brings us into the territory of temperance.

MANAGING MODERATION

Discipline must come through liberty. . . . We do not consider an individual
disciplined only when he has been rendered as artificially silent as a mute or
as immovable as a paralytic. He is an individual annihilated, not disciplined.
We call an individual disciplined when he is master of himself, and can, therefore,
regulate his own conduct when it shall be necessary to follow some rule of life.
—MARIA MONTESSORI, *THE MONTESSORI METHOD* (1912)

Tolerance and Temperance

Living under drug prohibition, with no memory of life before it,
people find it difficult to imagine how the ethic of temperance can be
extended to other substances. They worry that self-control is a weak
substitute for the force of law. It's worth emphasizing, then, that the
law would still have a role to play. In particular:

- Drug sales to minors would be prohibited, since children
  are not mature enough to make decisions about intoxicants on their own.
- Driving a car (or operating other kinds of dangerous equip-

ment) while intoxicated would be prohibited, since it poses a threat to other people's lives and property. The legal standard for both alcohol and other drugs should be based on a reliable indicator of impairment, and penalties should vary with the level of intoxication.

- Neither intoxication nor addiction would be a defense for drug users who committed crimes. (The law should no longer recognize intoxication as a mitigating factor for drinkers either.)

In other words, the government would step in to protect people's rights, including the right of parents to shield their children from drugs. At least as important as the law, the same social and economic forces that encourage moderation in drinking—the need to earn a living, a sense of obligation to family and friends, the desire to see oneself and be perceived by others as responsible and productive—would encourage moderation in the use of other drugs. Many employers would continue to prohibit drug use in the workplace, especially in safety-sensitive positions, but few would care about drug use off the clock unless it affected job performance. Likewise, people generally would be concerned about the drug use of relatives or friends only if they saw evidence that it was excessive.

Although such influences do not always keep drug consumption under control, the data on current patterns of use indicate that they usually do. But perhaps these numbers are misleading. If drug laws are an important barrier preventing experimenters from becoming addicts, a larger percentage of users would develop destructive habits once the currently proscribed intoxicants were legal. On the other hand, it could be that the sort of people who use drugs when they're illegal are more likely to become addicted, in which case the percentage of users with drug-related problems might drop if prohibition were repealed. Either way, unless we assume that every potential addict is already using drugs, the total number of heavy consumers would rise. The question is how big a problem they would represent.

On this score, historical estimates are reassuring even when they're supposed to be alarming. In her history of drug use, the journalist Jill Jonnes, defending the war on drugs, estimates that there were 350,000 cocaine and opiate addicts in the United States at the beginning of the twentieth century, when the population was about 76 million.[1] In other words, at a time when these drugs were legal, inexpensive, and readily available over the counter or through the mail, less than 0.5 percent of the population became addicted. Even this figure may be an exaggeration. Jonnes seems to get her estimate of 250,000 opiate addicts in 1900 from Yale psychiatrist David F. Musto, author of *The American Disease: Origins of Narcotics Control*, an influential history originally published in 1973.[2] Musto's estimate, in turn, is based on contemporaneous reports, which were often impressionistic and contradictory, and extrapolations by other researchers, which depend on questionable assumptions. Drug policy scholar Arnold Trebach warns that "estimates of addiction rates then and now varied so widely that no responsible scholar could rely upon them, except in very general terms."[3] Jonnes also uses an estimate of 200,000 "cocaine addicts" in 1902 (which she cuts in half to account for "some overlap in these two groups of addicts"). She attributes the figure to the American Pharmaceutical Association.[4] Yet according to Trebach, the association's number referred to "users" (not just addicts) of various "habit-forming drugs" (not just cocaine).[5]

Furthermore, the "addicts" to which Jonnes refers were not the social menaces that people nowadays tend to imagine when they hear the term. She notes that "the bulk of them were genteel, middle-class women."[6] This profile again raises the issue of whether addiction per se is a problem. Whatever its psychological impact, regular opiate use did not dramatically disrupt these women's lives, destroy their health, or turn them into criminals. To judge whether any increase in addiction that followed the repeal of drug prohibition would be tolerable, we have to recognize the extent to which prohibition makes addiction more harmful to both users and innocent bystanders.

In thinking about a world without drug prohibition, it's also important to recognize that the range of products would be wider than it is today. During alcohol prohibition, beer and wine drinking fell relative to liquor consumption, because traffickers and customers preferred products that were more compact and delivered more bang for the buck.[7] After repeal, liquor's artificial advantage was removed, and since the late 1970s, as overall consumption has declined, the trend has been away from distilled spirits and toward beer and wine.[8] If they were so inclined, people could have 150-proof rum every time they drank, but they overwhelmingly prefer weaker products.

Something similar would happen in the market for the currently illegal drugs if they were no longer banned. Most people who used coca products would not choose to smoke crack or even snort cocaine. If the experience prior to the Harrison Narcotics Act of 1914 is any indication, they would prefer milder preparations, such as coca tea (still available in Peru and Bolivia) or coca chewing gum. The latter would be modeled after coca leaf chewing, the traditional method of ingestion in South America, which delivers a steady but low dose of the drug that is unlikely to interfere with work or lead to a pernicious habit. Likewise, heroin injection would represent a small segment of the market for opium products; far more people would drink opium tea or smoke opium.[9]

The idea of bringing back opium smoking may seem absurd, scary, or both, but there is reason to believe that most users could responsibly incorporate the drug into their lives. The extent of the harm caused by widespread opium use in China during the nineteenth and early twentieth centuries was a matter of much dispute and still is. One side, allied with the British government, which profited from the opium trade, declared that the drug was no worse than alcohol. The other side, consisting largely of missionaries who tended to view opium smoking as sinful, denounced the trade as the moral equivalent of slavery.[10] Martin Booth, who favors the latter view, nevertheless quotes a Chinese merchant who condemned opium smoking yet conceded: "Many use it occasionally, but are not addicted to the habit; they can use it or not, as they choose. Most Chinese who use opium do so for pleasure, just as other people smoke cigars or cigarettes."[11] Similarly, a British physician who worked in China for twenty-five years reported: "A Chinese takes a smoke of opium somewhat as an Englishman takes a glass of sherry. Some Englishmen must have two or three drinks of whiskey; in the same way, one Chinese may be contented with one-half a [gram] of opium, while another must have two or three [grams]. They think it is a great mistake to go to excess."[12] Based on a variety of sources, the psychiatrist John C. Kramer estimated that opium smokers in China typically consumed less than six grams a day, far below the average for addicts in treatment. "Most evidence suggests that moderation in the consumption of opium was the rule both in China and elsewhere," he wrote. "It appears likely that most opium smokers were not disabled by their practice."[13]

Just as there were positive aspects to the saloons that anti-alcohol campaigners saw as a locus of evil, the opium dens that were the targets of the first anti-drug laws in the United States provided Chinese immigrants with companionship and a refuge from an often hostile world. A tamed version of the saloon—the neighborhood bar—became a means of promoting civilized drinking. Under responsible management, it prevented isolation, maintained order, and discouraged excess. So, too, a new version of the opium den could be a clean, orderly, respectable retreat where people could go to forget their cares for a while. Something similar has already happened on a limited scale with marijuana. Visit a coffeehouse in Amsterdam where a variety of cannabis products are openly sold, and you will find a calm, convivial environment, with no hint of the distrust and danger that characterizes the black market. Dutch authorities, who have long tolerated the retail sale of marijuana to adults (which is still technically illegal), like to brag that they have made the drug boring. There may be some truth to that claim, since pot smoking among teenagers in the Netherlands actually declined during the decade after the Dutch adopted their relatively tolerant approach in 1976.[14] Marijuana use by teenagers later rose again, but in 1997 it was still considerably less common than in the United States. A Dutch survey found that 8 percent of sixteen- to nineteen-year-olds had smoked marijuana in the previous month, compared to about 16 percent for this age group in the United States.[15]

What About the Children?

Any discussion of repealing drug prohibition inevitably leads to questions about the message it would send to children. The usual assumption is that allowing adults to use drugs would make it harder to justify and enforce restrictions on minors. But even limited success at blocking underage access would be preferable to the situation that prevails in the current black market, where sellers have little incentive to distinguish between adults and minors. At the same time, ending the war on drugs would help parents impart a more honest message about drugs to their children.

When my daughter was not quite five, she asked me, "Daddy, do I do drugs?" The question was prompted by an ad that ABC Video had slapped onto the beginning of her Schoolhouse Rock tape. The spot cited the achievements of basketball player David Robinson, adding, "There's one thing David hasn't done. David doesn't do drugs." This message was not meant to be taken literally. After all, it was sponsored by the Partnership for a Drug-Free America, which has been supported by manufacturers of cigarettes, beer, coffee, and tranquilizers.[16] A drug-free America is the last thing these companies want to see. But the partnership's backers understand that legal, socially approved drugs are not *really* drugs. If David Robinson consumed any of their products, he would still be eligible to proclaim the advantages of a drug-free existence.

So I wasn't quite sure how to deal with my daughter's question. She took drugs when she was sick, and occasionally she drank Diet Coke. (If you don't think these are mind-altering substances, you have never seen a four-year-old loopy from Dimetapp or wired on caffeine.) Five years later, she still prefers grape juice at Sabbath meals, but someday she will probably switch to wine. When she is older, if she is like most adolescents, she will drink beer and coffee. She may even try marijuana or tobacco. If I took my cue from David Robinson and the Partnership for a Drug-Free America, I would tell Francine that only bad people who never amount to anything do drugs. But the truth is that almost everyone does drugs of one kind or another, and the vast majority suffer no lasting harm as a result. In light of this fact, inculcating habits of moderation and responsibility serves kids better than empty slogans.

Drug Abuse Resistance Education (DARE), the most popular drug education program in America, got a free ride for more than a decade before mainstream news outlets began reporting that it had no lasting effect on drug use.[17] In 2001 DARE America implicitly acknowledged the program's failure when it announced plans to overhaul its curriculum.[18] But DARE is worse than useless. By relying on scare tactics that depict a puff of marijuana as the first step on the road to ruin, it encourages teenagers to disregard all warnings about drugs. By insisting on abstinence instead of responsibility, it leaves kids ill-prepared to distinguish between use and abuse.

At a school where my wife once taught, the fifth-graders who graduated from DARE had to write "personal statements" summing up what they had learned. One girl said she wanted to go to college and raise a family, so she would never drink beer or smoke marijuana—activities that she had been led to believe would foreclose the possibility of a decent and productive life. What happens when this kid gets a little older and savvier, and recognizes that her DARE officer misled her? Will she figure out for herself the difference between smoking a joint on the weekend and going to school or work stoned, between drinking a beer at the end of the day and tossing back a six-pack before getting behind the wheel of a car? If she does, it will be no thanks to DARE.

Many of the people I interviewed for this book recalled that what passed for drug education in their schools actually made them more inclined to use drugs. Either it was obviously absurd, leading them to wonder what grown-ups were trying to hide, or they eventually realized, by observing friends and acquaintances, that much of what they'd been told was not true, at which point they began to dismiss anything authority figures said about drugs. They said they tried to be more honest with their own children, although several noted that the law could make that difficult. "Our kids saw us smoking pot when they were young," said a writer in his fifties. "I can only remember one time when I had to caution my older daughter about the unwisdom of saying too much about things like this to people outside the family. This was about '75, when the movement toward [marijuana legalization] was beginning to collapse."[19] Nowadays, things are trickier. "At this point in our culture," said Bob Wallace, "you really have to hide your interest in [drugs], because they'll go to school and talk about it, and that can be a problem."[20]

But both parents and people who planned to have kids generally agreed that it's appropriate to be more open once children are old enough to understand the need for discretion. "We did not flaunt drug use in front of them at all," said Rick Root, who has two stepchildren, now grown. "But they were aware that we used marijuana probably in their early teens. . . . We'd always tell them that basically it's no different from alcohol—there's a time and a place for everything."[21] Parents emphasized that discussions about drugs, like discussions about sex, should be calibrated to the child's level of maturity, but the information should always be accurate. "I see no reason to lie to them about drugs," said a high school teacher with three children. "The government is doing enough of that as it is."[22]

The message these parents said they were giving their children was that responsible drug use requires understanding the hazards of a given substance as well as its potential benefits; using it only when one is mature enough; refraining from use in dangerous situations;

and being careful not to use drugs for the wrong reasons, such as suppressing emotions or avoiding problems. "My kids hear from me that drugs are like scissors—they have their positive as well as negative effects," said a father of two. "I don't hide anything from them, and I believe they feel free to ask whatever questions they want."[23] William Gazecki, who has three young children, emphasized that adults can use drugs without sanctioning drug use by kids. "The choice to use any substance . . . is a choice that needs to be taken responsibly," he said. "I want to be able to give my sons a clear idea that this is not appropriate for you to even decide until you get to a certain place in your life." He noted that South Americans have openly chewed coca leaf for centuries, but the habit is understood as "something that adults do. You don't do that until you are a certain age."[24]

At the same time, as with alcohol, parents ought to have some leeway in letting older children try some of the milder drug products so they can become familiar with their effects. Responsible parents might allow a teenager to try, say, coca tea or marijuana under supervision. Since different people mature at different rates, this is the sort of decision that should be left to parents, who are closest to the situation and have their children's best interests at heart. Even parents who insist that their children abstain from all psychoactive substances (presumably including alcohol, caffeine, and nicotine) should try to demystify drugs by supplying accurate information about their effects, both good and bad.[25]

Whatever parents choose to tell their kids, it's clear that happy, well-adjusted people are less likely to get into trouble with drugs. Alison Witt has no children yet, but her take on the issue is borne out by research on drug use. "I think the best way to combat the drug problem," she said, "is being a good parent: saying be a good person, take care of yourself, learn to be successful, and learn to be happy. Drugs are sort of a nonissue then. If you bring children up to care about themselves and care about other people and want to do good, sure, experimentation may occur, but I don't think it would take over their lives."[26]

Paternalism's Price

The fact that drug use is usually not the end of the world, or even a cause for regret, has important implications for the drug policy debate. To be sure, it does not change everything. Even if the vast majority of people who use drugs do so in moderation, it is possible to argue that the war on drugs is still justified because of the harm that would otherwise be caused by the minority who don't. Empirically, this is a shaky proposition. It's not clear, first of all, that prohibition is very effective at preventing people from developing drug problems. The barriers it creates—cost, inconvenience, risk of arrest—are more likely to deter casual users, and potential addicts who are deterred may instead become alcoholics, thereby exposing themselves to more serious health risks than if they had taken up, say, heroin. Assuming that at least some people manage to avoid addiction only because of the obstacles erected by the drug laws, any harm thereby prevented has to be weighed against the enormous costs of the war on drugs, which include not only the explicit expenditures ($40 billion or so annually) but violence, official corruption, disrespect for the law, diversion of law-enforcement resources, years wasted in prison by drug offenders who are not predatory criminals, thefts that would not occur if drugs were more affordable, erosion of privacy rights and other civil liberties, and deaths from tainted drugs, unexpectedly high doses, and unsanitary injection practices encouraged by anti-paraphernalia policies. These costs, which bear a striking resemblance to the side effects of alcohol prohibition, are hard to measure, and some of them cannot be expressed in financial terms, but that does not make them any less real. It's doubtful that they can be justified even on purely utilitarian grounds.[27]

That question will continue to be debated. But in the absence of a persuasive explanation for why intoxication per se is wrong, self-righteous condemnations of drug use should give way to dispassionate evaluations of prohibition's costs and benefits. Honest supporters of the drug laws have to acknowledge that the case for prohibition rests on a morally questionable premise: that it's acceptable to punish one group of people for the sins of another—in this case, that the majority of drug users, who do not harm others or even themselves, should suffer because of a minority's failure to exercise self-control. The drug laws can be defended, but only in the way that alcohol prohibition might have been defended by someone who acknowledged that the typical drinker was not an alcoholic: by claiming that the burden imposed on the innocent majority is justified by the harm that a minority would otherwise cause to themselves and others. As the political scientist J. Donald Moon observes, "this justification for criminalizing the use of drugs amounts to using some people as mere instruments for the well-being of others. . . . The people who are benefited are, to a large extent, the same individuals who are discouraged from using drugs because of the threat of punishment. My punishment serves to stop you from doing something that would harm you."[28]

Such a policy will strike many people as fundamentally unjust. Certainly it seemed that way to Clarence Darrow. The renowned attorney remarked that "prohibition is an outrageous and senseless invasion of the personal liberty of millions of intelligent and temperate persons who see nothing dangerous or immoral in the moderate consumption of alcoholic beverages."[29] Temperate users of other drugs have at least as much cause to be outraged.

Larry Seguin, a truck driver in his fifties from upstate New York, became a drug policy activist after he was arrested on marijuana charges in 1998. Beginning when he served in Vietnam ("It was almost like marijuana was legal there," he recalled), Seguin smoked pot just about every day for thirty years. In 1980 he started growing marijuana for himself and his friends. He was busted while delivering an ounce to a Vietnam buddy in Rochester who had become a police informant. A search of Seguin's house turned up five pounds of marijuana. Facing the possibility of an eleven-year sentence, he pleaded guilty to possession and got three years' conditional discharge. "They were nice to me because I work two jobs and have a family," said Seguin, who has been married for three decades and is the father of two teenaged children and two grown stepchildren.[30] Although he didn't have to serve time, the conviction meant that if he was ever found guilty of a similar offense he'd face a mandatory minimum sentence of seven years.

Seguin's arrest was publicized locally, but he wasn't embarrassed. He was mad. "I've never done anything in my life I'm ashamed of," he said. "I take care of my family and work hard. . . . I've got top-notch recommendations from every place I've worked." Although marijuana was not interfering with his life (he smoked it after work, not on the job), "they wanted me to say I had a drug problem. . . . I almost had to say it at my drug evaluation at work, because the law says they can't fire you if you have a drug problem, but if you say you don't have a drug problem they consider that to mean they can't help you, and you can be terminated."[31] Despite his outstanding employment record, his trucking company insisted that he submit to regular drug tests, so he had to stop smoking pot.

Local authorities "were portraying me as a dangerous person with a drug problem, and my kids didn't see it," Seguin said. "To them I was Dad and worked hard and took care of them and paid the bills. That was probably the hardest thing—for the kids to see what I had to go through."[32] He became involved with several reform groups, including DrugSense, the Drug Reform Coordination Network, and the National Organization for the Reform of Marijuana Laws, and began sending letters criticizing the war on drugs to newspapers around the country. He volunteered to appear at local forums on "the drug problem" to refute the idea that drug users are irresponsible and unproductive. No one took him up on his offer, perhaps because the organizers were worried that his example would challenge their audiences' preconceptions.

If so, they were right to be worried. Once the silent majority of illegal drug users begins to speak out, the stereotypes that drive the war on drugs will be impossible to sustain.

NOTES

Author's Note

1. See, e.g., U.S. General Accounting Office, *Drug Use Measurement: Strengths, Limitations, and Recommendations for Improvement* (GAO, June 1993), 38–39, 48–49.

2. Mark A.R. Kleiman, *Marijuana: Costs of Abuse, Costs of Control* (New York: Greenwood Press, 1989), 36.

3. Substance Abuse and Mental Health Services Administration, *Summary of Findings From the 2000 National Household Survey on Drug Abuse* (U.S. Department of Health and Human Services, September 2001), 69.

4. Compare, for example, the findings of the National Comorbidity Survey (reported in J. C. Anthony et al., "Comparative Epidemiology of Dependence on Tobacco, Alcohol, Controlled Substances and Inhalants: Basic Findings From the National Comorbidity Survey," *Experimental and Clinical Psychopharmacology* 2 [1994]: 244–68) to results from the National Household Survey on Drug Abuse and the Monitoring the Future Study. For data on "drug-related" medical problems, see Substance Abuse and Mental Health Services Administration, *Drug Abuse Warning Network Annual Medical Examiner Data 1999* (U.S. Department of Health and Human Services, De-

cember 2000), and SAMHSA, *Year-End 2000 Emergency Department Data From the Drug Abuse Warning Network* (HHS, July 2001).

Introduction: The Silent Majority

1. Carol J. Loomis, "Sex. Reefer? And Auto Insurance!," *Fortune* (August 7, 1995), 76; "Breaking Away," *Rough Notes* (June 2000), 38–48; and Marcia Stepanek, "Rewriting the Rules of the Road," *Business Week* (September 18, 2000), 86.
2. Loomis.
3. Kevin Harter, "Drug Count Against CEO at Progressive 'Discharged,'" Cleveland *Plain Dealer* (January 8, 2000), A1; and David Bank, "Soros, Two Rich Allies Fund a Growing War on the War on Drugs," *Wall Street Journal* (May 30, 2001), A1.
4. Interview with Peter Collins (pseud.), March 12, 2000.
5. Nick Gillespie, "The 13th Step," *Reason* (March 2001), 5–7.
6. "Best of the Web," *OpinionJournal.com,* April 26, 2001.
7. Interview with Alan Mattus (pseud.), April 13, 2000.
8. Statement on drugs from the Forbes campaign's website, forbes2000.com.
9. Craig MacAndrew and Robert B. Edgerton, *Drunken Comportment: A Social Explanation* (Chicago: Aldine, 1969), 14–15.
10. Ibid. 88, 165.
11. See, e.g., Norman E. Zinberg, *Drug, Set, and Setting: The Basis for Controlled Intoxicant Use* (New Haven, Conn.: Yale University Press, 1984).
12. Frank Zappa, with Peter Occhiogrosso, *The Real Frank Zappa Book* (New York: Poseidon Press, 1989), 325.
13. See, e.g., "Barr Praises President for Leadership on Drug War," press release, February 12, 2002.
14. Alan Travis, "Police Chief: Cocaine OK at Weekends," *The Guardian* (November 21, 2001).
15. Jonathan Shedler and Jack Block, "Adolescent Drug Use and Psychological Health," *American Psychologist* 45:5 (May 1990): 612–30.
16. Ibid.
17. John Diaz, "Furor Over Report on Teenage Drug Use," *San Francisco Chronicle* (May 14, 1990), A10.
18. Neil Swan, "Researchers Probe Which Comes First: Drug Abuse or Antisocial Behavior?," *NIDA Notes* (May/June 1993): 6–7.
19. Thomas B. Roberts, *Harper's* (August 1999), 6.
20. Thomas Nicholson et al., "Drugnet: A Pilot Study of Adult Recreational Drug

Use via the WWW," *Substance Abuse* 19:3 (1998): 109–21, and "A Survey of Adult Recreational Drug Use Via the World Wide Web: The DRUGNET Study," *Journal of Psychoactive Drugs* 31:4 (December 1999): 415–22.

21. Nicholson et al. (1998).

22. Jack Dunphy, "More Drug Warring," *National Review Online* (March 2, 2001).

23. Substance Abuse and Mental Health Services Administration, 2001 National Household Survey on Drug Abuse, table H.2.

24. Michael Specter and James R. Dickenson, "Politicians Line Up to Admit or Deny Past Marijuana Use," *Washington Post* (November 8, 1987), A1.

25. Adam J. Smith, interview with John C. Warnecke, *The Week Online With DRCNet* (January 20, 2000).

26. Hendrik Hertzberg, "Gore's Greatest Bong Hits," *The New Yorker* (February 7, 2000), 31–32.

27. Tara Meyer, "Speaker, Democrats Trade Jabs Over Past Drug Use," Associated Press (July 20, 1996).

28. Specter and Dickenson.

29. *Meet the Press*, NBC, December 4, 1994.

30. Robin Toner, "Incoming Speaker Sharply Scolded," *New York Times* (December 6, 1994), A1.

31. National Institute on Drug Abuse, *National Household Survey on Drug Abuse: Main Findings 1988* (U.S. Department of Health and Human Services, 1990), 33.

32. Drug Enforcement Administration, *How to Hold Your Own in a Drug Legalization Debate* (U.S. Department of Justice, 1994), 11.

33. William J. Bennett, introduction to *National Drug Control Strategy* (Office of National Drug Control Policy, September 1989), 11.

34. Ronald J. Ostrow, "Casual Drug Users Should Be Shot, Gates Says," *Los Angeles Times* (September 6, 1990), A1.

35. Frank Bruni, "Shrugging Off Pressure, Bush Regains His Form," *New York Times* (August 26, 1999), A12.

36. Howard Fineman, "The Bush Brothers," *Newsweek* (November 2, 1998), 30.

37. John Affleck, "Bush Offers Parents Drug Advice," Associated Press (August 20, 1999).

38. Adam Clymer, "Bush, in Ohio, Says Questions About Drug Use Prove the Need to Elevate Politics," *New York Times* (August 21, 1999), A8.

39. Toby Rogers, "American Stoner," *High Times* (August 1999), 64–68.

40. See, e.g., Mark A.R. Kleiman, *Against Excess: Drug Policy for Results* (New York: Basic Books, 1992), 192–93.

41. See, e.g., "The War on Drugs Is Lost," *National Review* (February 12, 1996).
42. See, e.g., Thomas Szasz, *Our Right to Drugs: The Case for a Free Market* (New York: Praeger, 1992).
43. Gary Johnson, speech at the Cato Institute, Washington, D.C., October 5, 1999, and "Johnson Defends Most Drug Users," *Albuquerque Journal* (October 5, 1999), C3.

Chapter One: Chemical Reactions

1. *The Doctrine and the Covenants,* 89:5–9.
2. "The Wisdom of the Word of Wisdom" (Lesson 26), *Preparing for Exaltation: Teacher's Manual* (Salt Lake City: Intellectual Reserve, 1998), 147.
3. Spencer W. Kimball, "Guidelines to Carry Forth the Work of God in Cleanliness," *Ensign* (May 1974), 4.
4. Theodore M. Burton, "The Word of Wisdom," *Ensign* (May 1976), 28.
5. 1 Corinthians 3:16–17. All New Testament quotations are based on the King James Version.
6. "The Word of Wisdom: A Principle With Promise" (Lesson 22), *Doctrine and Covenants and Church History: Gospel Doctrine Teacher's Manual* (Salt Lake City: Intellectual Reserve, 1999), 121.
7. Burton, 28.
8. Boyd K. Packer, "Prayers and Answers," *Ensign* (November 1979), 19.
9. Gordon B. Hinckley, "Four B's for Boys," *Ensign* (November 1981), 40.
10. Boyd K. Packer, "Revelation in a Changing World," *Ensign* (November 1989), 14.
11. *Doctrine and Covenants and Church History,* 121. "The Lord's Law of Health" (Chapter 29), *Gospel Principles* (Salt Lake City: Intellectual Reserve, 1997), 192.
12. N. Eldon Tanner, "Success Is Gauged by Self-Mastery," *Ensign* (May 1975), 74.
13. "Drug Abuse" (Chapter 39), *Young Women Manual I* (Salt Lake City: Church of Jesus Christ of Latter-Day Saints, 1992), 171.
14. Ibid.
15. See, e.g., Barry Stimmel, *The Facts About Drug Use* (Yonkers, N.Y.: Consumer Reports Books, 1991), 183–88, or Cynthia Kuhn et al., *Buzzed* (New York: W.W. Norton, 1998), 55–69.
16. "Policies and Procedures," *New Era* (May 1972), 50.
17. "Q&A: Questions and Answers," *New Era* (October 1975), 34.
18. Clifford J. Stratton, "Caffeine—The Subtle Addiction," *Ensign* (June 1988), 60.

19. See, e.g., Helen Felix Izatt, "Ice Cream: A Summer Treat," *Ensign* (August 1972), 85; "Christmas Cooking Fun," *Friend* (December 1974), 11; and Jill Johnson Hymas, "Kitchen Krafts," *Friend* (September 1992), 47.

20. Monte J. Brough, "The Chocolate Bar," *New Era* (October 1990), 4.

21. John L. Esposito, ed., *The Oxford Encyclopedia of the Modern Islamic World* vol. 1 (New York: Oxford University Press, 1995), 375.

22. Marmaduke Pickthall, trans., *The Glorious Koran, Bi-Lingual Edition* (London: George Allen & Unwin, 1976), 2:219.

23. Ibid., 4:43.

24. Ibid., 5:90–91.

25. Ralph S. Hattox, *Coffee and Coffeehouses: The Origins of a Social Beverage in the Medieval Near East* (Seattle: University of Washington Press, 1985), 52.

26. Ibid., 54.

27. Ibid., 53–57.

28. Franz Rosenthal, *The Herb: Hashish Versus Medieval Muslim Society* (Leiden: E.J. Brill, 1971), 108–9.

29. Ibid., 117.

30. Hattox, 60.

31. Christopher Cooper, "In Yemen, Some Try This Antidrug Message: Just Say No—to Qat," *Wall Street Journal* (December 28, 2000), A1.

32. Daniel M. Varisco, "Stimulants sans Sin: A Social History of Qat, Coffee and Tobacco in Yemen," lecture at Rutgers University, April 26, 2000.

33. Gadul Haq Ali Gadul Haq et al., *Islamic Ruling on Smoking* (World Health Organization, 1996).

34. Walter H. Dixon, "Narcotics Legislation and Islam in Egypt," *Bulletin on Narcotics* (1972), issue 4: 11–18.

35. Ibid.

36. *Congressional Record* (February 25, 1999), S2030.

37. William Saletan, "Reagan Redux," *Mother Jones* (November 1998), 27.

38. "Sex, Drugs & Consenting Adults," ABC Special Report, May 26, 1998.

39. Oval Office Tapes, June 2, 1971, 3:16–4:15 P.M., Oval Office Conversation 510–3.

40. Edwin Meese III, "Drugs, Change, and Realism: A Critical Evaluation of Proposed Legalization," in Melvyn B. Krauss and Edward P. Lazear, eds., *Searching for Alternatives: Drug Control Policy in the United States* (Stanford, Calif.: Hoover Institution Press, 1991), 283–91.

41. Jill Jonnes, *Hep-Cats, Narcs, and Pipe Dreams: A History of America's Romance With Illegal Drugs* (New York: Scribner, 1996), 425–26.

42. William J. Bennett, "Should Drugs Be Legalized?," in Jeffrey A. Schaler, ed., *Drugs: Should We Legalize, Decriminalize or Deregulate?* (Amherst, N.Y.: Prometheus Books, 1998), 63–67.

43. William J. Bennett, *The De-Valuing of America: The Fight for Our Culture and Our Children* (New York: Simon & Schuster, 1992), 121.

44. Ibid.

45. Bennett (1998), 63.

46. William J. Bennett, introduction to *National Drug Control Strategy* (Office of National Drug Control Policy, September 1989), 11.

47. Bennett (1992), 118.

48. Quoted in Bennett (1992), 120.

49. James Q. Wilson, *On Character* (Washington, D.C.: AEI Press, 1995), 160.

50. James Q. Wilson, *The Moral Sense* (New York: Simon & Schuster, 1993), 94, 97.

51. Bennett (1989), 10.

52. Wilson (1993), 93–94.

53. Bennett (1989), 11.

54. Substance Abuse and Mental Health Services Administration, 2001 National Household Survey on Drug Abuse, table H.2.

55. "Portrait of America," Rasmussen Research, July 19, 2000.

56. Subscription advertisement, *Healthy Drinking* (March/April 1995).

57. Gene Ford, "The Dilemma and a Strategy," *Healthy Drinking* (March/April 1995), 64.

Chapter Two: Strong Drink

1. Genesis 27:28. All quotations from the Hebrew Bible are based on *Tanakh: A New Translation of the Holy Scriptures According to the Traditional Hebrew Text* (Philadelphia: Jewish Publication Society, 1985).

2. Genesis 49:11–12.

3. Deuteronomy 11:14.

4. Deuteronomy 28:39.

5. Amos 5:11.

6. Isaiah 24:7–11.

7. On the meaning of *shechar,* see Marcus Jastrow, *Dictionary of the Targumim, the Talmud Babli and Yerushalmi, and the Midrashic Literature* (New York: Judaica Press, 1992), 1576; D. Miall Edwards, "Drink, Strong," in James Orr, ed., *International Standard Bible Encyclopedia,* electronic edition (Cedar

Rapids, Iowa: Parsons Technology, 1998); and Antonio Escohotado, *A Brief History of Drugs* (Rochester, Vt.: Park Street Press, 1999), 10–11.

8. Wine offerings are mentioned, e.g., in Exodus 29:40, Leviticus 23:13, and Numbers 15:7. The composition of the Temple incense is described in the Babylonian Talmud, Tractate Kritut, 6a. Wine is listed as a Temple provision in 1 Chronicles 9:29 and as part of the tithe for the Priests and Levites in 2 Chronicles 31:4–5.

9. Deuteronomy 14:23–26.

10. Judges 9:13.

11. Psalms 104:14.

12. Proverbs 31:6.

13. Song of Songs 1:2, 1:4, 4:10.

14. Genesis 9:20–27.

15. Genesis 19:31–38.

16. 2 Samuel 13:28–29.

17. Proverbs 20:1, 24:29–35.

18. Isaiah 5:1, 28:7–8.

19. Hosea 7:14, 3:1.

20. The Wisdom of Sirach, 31: 27–29, from *The Apocrypha,* translated by Edgar J. Goodspeed (New York: Random House, 1959).

21. Jerusalem Talmud, Tractate Nedarim, 41b.

22. Jerusalem Talmud, Tractate Kiddushin, 66d.

23. Babylonian Talmud, Tractate Eruvin, 65a.

24. Babylonian Talmud, Tractate Bava Batra, 58b; Tractate Berachot, 35b.

25. Babylonian Talmud, Tractate Bava Batra, 58b.

26. Midrash Tanchuma, Warsaw Edition, on Parshat Noach, chapter 13.

27. The unit prescribed in the *Shulchan Aruch* is a *revi'it,* a quarter of a *log,* which is 137 milliliters, or about 4.6 U.S. fluid ounces. See "Arba Kosot," *Encyclopedia Judaica* (Jerusalem: Keter Publishing, 1997).

28. Babylonian Talmud, Tractate Megilla, 7b.

29. John L. Mitchell, "All Out Against Alcohol: Beverly Hills Doctor Is Relentless in Her Crusade Against Liquor Consumption," *Los Angeles Times* (September 3, 1989), part 9, 1.

30. See, e.g., Stanton Peele, *The Diseasing of America: Addiction Treatment Out of Control* (Lexington, Mass.: Lexington Books, 1989), 69, 71–73.

31. Elli Fenner, "Parshat Noach: Dvar Torah on the Sidra," Bnei Akiva of Great Britain and Ireland, 2000.

32. 1 Timothy 4:4. All quotations from the New Testament are based on the King James Version.

33. E. A. Wasson, *Religion and Drink* (New York: Burr Printing House, 1914), 137.

34. John 2:1–11.

35. Matthew 26:27–29.

36. 1 Timothy 5:23.

37. 1 Timothy 3:8, Titus 1:7.

38. 1 Peter 4:3.

39. Luke 21:34.

40. Ephesians 5:18.

41. Quoted in Andrew Barr, *Drink: A Social History of America* (New York: Carroll & Graf, 1999), 360–61.

42. Ibid., 361.

43. Samuele Bacchiocchi, *Wine in the Bible: A Biblical Study on the Use of Alcoholic Beverages* (Berrien Springs, Mich.: Biblical Perspectives, 1989).

44. "Family Temperance Pledge," undated original document.

45. Barrett Duke, "Abstinence: The Biblical Choice," and Robert L. Mounts, "Strong Drink Is Raging," Ethics and Religious Liberty Commission of the Southern Baptist Convention, 1997.

46. Quoted in Wasson, 151–52.

47. Ibid., 152.

48. Ibid., 165.

49. William J. Bouwsma, *John Calvin: A Sixteenth Century Portrait* (New York: Oxford University Press, 1988), 136.

50. Wasson, 172–75.

51. Escohotado, 16.

52. Plato, *Laws,* translated by Benjamin Jowett (Amherst, N.Y.: Prometheus Books, 2000), 45, 51.

53. Aristotle, *Ethics,* translated by J.A.K. Thomson (New York: Viking Penguin, 1976), 139, 141.

54. Bruce C. Daniels, *Puritans at Play: Leisure and Recreation in Colonial New England* (New York: St. Martin's, 1995), 3–24.

55. Ibid., 221.

56. Increase Mather, *Wo to Drunkards: Two Sermons Testifying Against the Sin of Drunkenness,* second edition (Boston: Timothy Green, 1712; originally published in 1673), 5–6, 7.

57. Ibid., 5–6.

58. Ibid., 16, 34.

59. Mark Edward Lender and James Kirby Martin, *Drinking in America: A History,* revised edition (New York: The Free Press, 1987), 205. Thomas M. Nephew et al., *Apparent Per Capita Alcohol Consumption: National, State, and Regional Trends, 1977–99* (National Institute on Alcohol Abuse and Alcoholism, September 2002), table 1.

60. Lender and Martin, 205.

61. Benjamin Rush, *An Inquiry Into the Effects of Ardent Spirits Upon the Human Body and Mind,* eighth edition (Brookfield: E. Merriam & Co., 1814; originally published in 1784), reprinted as an appendix to Yandell Henderson, *A New Deal in Liquor: A Plea for Dilution* (Garden City, N.Y.: Doubleday, Doran & Co., 1934), 189.

62. Ibid., 193–97.

63. Ibid., 198–99, 209, 211.

64. Ibid., 192, 212–14.

65. Quoted in Harry G. Levine, "The Discovery of Addiction," *Journal of Studies on Alcohol* 39:1 (1978): 152.

66. Ibid., 150.

67. Rush, 221.

68. Levine, 144.

69. Lyman Beecher, *Six Sermons on the Nature, Occasions, Signs, Evils, and Remedy of Intemperance* (New York: American Tract Society, 1862; originally published in 1826), 38.

70. Ibid., 5, 38–39

71. Ibid., 8, 9–10, 10–11, 38.

72. Ibid., 8–9, 39.

73. Ibid., 63, 65.

74. Lender and Martin, 205–6. Nephew et al., table 1.

75. Undated original document.

76. Thomas R. Pegram, *Battling Demon Rum: The Struggle for a Dry America, 1800–1933* (Chicago: Ivan R. Dee, 1998), 78.

77. Jeffrey A. Miron and Jeffrey Zwiebel, "Alcohol Consumption During Prohibition," *AEA Papers and Proceedings* 81:2 (May 1991): 242–47.

78. Jeffrey A. Miron, "The Effect of Alcohol Prohibition on Alcohol Consumption," National Bureau of Economic Research working paper (April 30, 1997).

79. Quoted in Barr, 241.

80. Quoted in Kenneth D. Rose, *American Women and the Repeal of Prohibition* (New York: New York University Press, 1996), 53.

81. Deets Picket, *Alcohol and the New Age* (New York: The Methodist Book Concern, 1926), 19, 24, 119.

82. For critiques of the disease model, see Herbert Fingarette, *Heavy Drinking: The Myth of Alcoholism As a Disease* (Berkeley: University of California Press, 1988); Stanton Peele, *Diseasing of America: Addiction Treatment Out of Control* (Lexington, Mass.: Lexington Books, 1989); and Jeffrey A. Schaler, *Addiction Is a Choice* (Chicago: Open Court, 2000).

83. Among Americans eighteen and older, the National Institute on Alcohol Abuse and Alcoholism estimates, 11 million were alcoholics and 7 million were "alcohol abusers" in 1995. (See NIAAA, "Projected Numbers of Alcohol Abusers, Alcoholics, and Alcohol Abusers and Alcoholics Combined, 1985, 1990, 1995," September 1987.) According to the National Household Survey on Drug Abuse, the total number of drinkers eighteen and older in 1995 was about 119 million. (See Substance Abuse and Mental Health Services Administration, *National Household Survey on Drug Abuse: Main Findings 1995,* U.S. Department of Health and Human Services, March 1997, 23, 96.)

84. See, e.g., David J. Pittman, *Primary Prevention of Alcohol Abuse and Alcoholism: An Evaluation of the Control of Consumption Model* (St. Louis: Social Science Institute, Washington University, 1980), and Stanton Peele, "The Limitations of Control-of-Supply Models for Explaining and Preventing Alcoholism and Drug Addiction," *Journal of Studies on Alcohol* 48 (1987): 61–77.

85. Arthur L. Klatsky, "Is Drinking Healthy?," and Carlos A. Camargo Jr., "Gender Differences in the Health Effects of Moderate Alcohol Consumption," in Stanton Peele and Marcus Grant, eds., *Alcohol and Pleasure: A Health Perspective* (Philadelphia: Brunner/Mazel, 1999), 141–70.

86. *Nutrition and Your Health: Dietary Guidelines for Americans,* fifth edition (U.S. Department of Agriculture and U.S. Department of Health and Human Services, 2000), 36–37.

87. Ibid., 36.

88. Marian Burros, "In an About-Face, U.S. Says Alcohol Has Health Benefits," *New York Times* (January 3, 1996), A1.

89. David Stout, "Government Allows Labels About Wine's Benefits," *New York Times* (February 6, 1999), A13. Ted Appel, "Thurmond Blocking Wine Labels," *Santa Rosa Press Democrat* (March 21, 1998), A1.

90. Morris E. Chafetz, *The Tyranny of Experts* (Lanham, Md.: Madison Books, 1996), 67.

91. For discussions of drinking during pregnancy, see Camargo, 162; Andrew Barr, *Drink: A Social History of America* (New York: Carroll & Graf, 1999), 156–61; and Thomas Stuttaford, *To Your Good Health!: The Wise Drinker's Guide* (Boston: Faber & Faber, 1997), 71–76.

92. Chafetz, 67.

93. Donald A. Redelmeier and Robert J. Tibshirani, "Association Between Cellular Telephone Calls and Motor Vehicle Collisions," *New England Journal of Medicine* 336:7 (February 13, 1997): 453–58.

94. National Highway Traffic Safety Administration, "Wake Up and Get Some Sleep," www.nhtsa.dot.gov/people/injury/drows_driving/index.html.

95. William C. Dement, "The Perils of Drowsy Driving," *New England Journal of Medicine* 337:11 (September 11, 1997): 783–84.

96. John M. Weiler et al., "Effects of Fexofenadine, Diphenhydramine, and Alcohol on Driving Performance," *Annals of Internal Medicine* 132:5 (March 7, 2000): 354–63.

97. Kate Zernike, "New Tactic on College Drinking: Play It Down," *New York Times* (October 3, 2000), A1.

98. Drug Strategies, *Millenium Hangover: Keeping Score on Alcohol* (Washington, D.C., 1999), 3, 34.

99. In the 2002 Monitoring the Future Study, 72 percent of twelfth-graders reported drinking during the previous year; 49 percent reported drinking during the previous month.

100. Drug Strategies, 4.

101. Pennsylvania Liquor Control Board, "Parental Roles," www.lcb.state.pa.us/edu/adult-parents.htm.

102. Aristotle, *Ethics,* translated by J.A.K. Thomson (New York: Viking Penguin, 1976), 141.

103. Nephew et al., table 1.

104. Young-He Yoon et al., *Liver Cirrhosis Mortality in the United States, 1970–98* (National Institute on Alcohol Abuse and Alcoholism, December 2001), 1.

105. Hsiao-ye Yi et al., *Trends in Alcohol-Related Fatal Traffic Crashes, United States, 1977–99* (National Institute on Alcohol Abuse and Alcoholism, December 2001), 19–20.

Chapter Three: Going Nowhere

1. Ronald J. Troyer and Gerald E. Markle, *Cigarettes: The Battle Over Smoking* (New Brunswick, N.J.: Rutgers University Press, 1983), 34.

2. Albert F. Blaisdell, *Our Bodies and How We Live* (New York: Ginn and Company, 1910), 239, 241.

3. Charles B. Towns, "The Injury of Tobacco and Its Relation to Other Drug Habits," *The Century Magazine* (March 1912), 766–72.

4. Charles Bulkley Hubbell, "The Cigaret Habit—A New Peril," *The Independent* (February 18, 1904), 375–78.

5. Henry Ford, ed., *The Case Against the Little White Slaver* (Detroit, 1914), 3.

6. Towns, 768.

7. Ford, 5.

8. Ibid., 21.

9. Gordon L. Dillow, "Thank You for Not Smoking: The Hundred-Year War Against the Cigarette," *American Heritage* (February/March 1981), 94–107.

10. Cassandra Tate, *Cigarette Wars: The Triumph of "The Little White Slaver"* (New York: Oxford University Press, 1999), 159–60.

11. Jerome L. Himmelstein, *The Strange Career of Marihuana: Politics and Ideology of Drug Control in America* (Westport, Conn.: Greenwood Press, 1983), 4.

12. Richard J. Bonnie and Charles H. Whitebread, *The Marijuana Conviction: A History of Marijuana Prohibition in the United States* (New York: Lindesmith Center, 1999; originally published in 1974), 228.

13. N. B. Eddy et al., "Drug Dependence: Its Significance and Characteristics," *Bulletin of the World Health Organization* (1965): 729.

14. Himmelstein, 127–28.

15. "More Controversy Over Pot," *Time* (May 31, 1971), 65.

16. "Marijuana: Is It Time for a Change in Our Laws?," *Newsweek* (September 7, 1970), 20–32.

17. Himmelstein, 128–29.

18. Ibid., 129–30.

19. Gabriel G. Nahas, *Keep Off the Grass,* revised edition (New York: Pergamon Press, 1979), 4, 15.

20. Peggy Mann, *Marijuana Alert* (New York: McGraw-Hill, 1985), 31.

21. Ibid., 34, 45, 47.

22. Donna Shalala, "Say 'No' to Legalization of Marijuana," *Wall Street Journal* (August 18, 1995), A10.

23. National Institute on Drug Abuse, *Marijuana: Facts Parents Need to Know* (U.S. Department of Health and Human Services, November 1998).

24. S. K. Overbeck, "Problems of Pot," *National Review* (June 1, 1971), 597–600.

25. David Madison, "High on Debate," *Salt Lake City Weekly* (February 16, 1998).

26. Lynn Zimmer and John P. Morgan, *Marijuana Myths, Marijuana Facts* (New York: Lindesmith Center, 1997), 120.

27. Janet E. Joy et al., eds., *Marijuana and Medicine: Assessing the Science Base* (Washington, D.C.: National Academy Press, 1999), 3.30, and Zimmer and Morgan, 73–79.

28. Harrison G. Pope et al., "Neuropsychological Performance in Long-Term Cannabis Users," *Archives of General Psychiatry* 58:10 (October 2001): 909–15.

29. Pierre Claude Nolin et al, *Cannabis: Our Position for a Canadian Public Policy,* report of the Canadian Senate's Special Committee on Illegal Drugs (September 2002), 16.

30. Joy et al., 3.31.

31. Harrison G. Pope et al., "Drug Use and Life-Style Among College Undergraduates: Nine Years Later," *Archives of General Psychiatry* 38 (1981): 588–91.

32. Lambros Comitas, "Cannabis and Work in Jamaica: A Refutation of the Amotivational Syndrome," *Annals of the New York Academy of Sciences* 282 (1976): 24–32.

33. Zimmer and Morgan, 65–68.

34. Substance Abuse and Mental Health Services Administration, *An Analysis of Worker Drug Use and Workplace Policies and Programs* (U.S. Department of Health and Human Services, July 1997), 1.

35. Michael T. French et al., "Illicit Drug Use, Employment, and Labor Force Participation," *Southern Economic Journal* 68:2 (October 2001): 349–68.

36. "U.S. Corporations Reduce Levels of Medical, Drug and Psychological Testing of Employees," American Management Association (June 14, 2000). Lewis L. Maltby, *Drug Testing: A Bad Investment* (New York: American Civil Liberties Union, 1999), 4.

37. Substance Abuse and Mental Health Services Administration, *Worker Drug Use and Workplace Policies and Programs: Results From the 1994 and 1997 NHSDA* (U.S. Department of Health and Human Services, September 1999), 3.

38. Interview with Joseph P. Franklin, March 21, 2000.

39. Interview, March 14, 2000.

40. Jacques Normand et al., eds., *Under the Influence?: Drugs and the American Work Force* (Washington, D.C.: National Academy Press, 1994), 7.

41. Ibid., 158–60.

42. Craig Zwerling et al., "The Efficacy of Preemployment Drug Screening for

Marijuana and Cocaine in Predicting Employment Outcome," *Journal of the American Medical Association* 264:20 (November 28, 1990): 2639–643.

43. John Horgan, "Postal Mortem," *Scientific American* (February 1991), 22–23.

44. Jacques Normand et al., "An Evaluation of Preemployment Drug Testing, *Journal of Applied Psychology* 75:6 (1990): 629–39.

45. Normand et al. (1994), 235.

46. "Employees Using Drugs," www.dfaf.org/factory/f101.htm, and "Reduce Drug Use/Reduce Costs," www.dfaf.org/factory/f106.htm.

47. Edward Shepard and Thomas Clifton, "Drug Testing and Labor Productivity: Estimates Applying a Production Function Model," *Working USA* (November–December 1998).

48. Kent Holdorf, *Ur-ine Trouble* (Scottsdale, Ariz.: Vandalay Press, 1994), 23–25. Maltby, 5–6.

49. National Commission on Marihuana and Drug Abuse, *Marihuana: A Signal of Misunderstanding* (Washington, D.C., 1972), 88.

50. Substance Abuse and Mental Health Services Administration, 2001 National Household Survey on Drug Abuse (September 2002), tables H.1 and H.2, figure 2.15.

51. Substance Abuse and Mental Health Services Administration, *National Household Survey on Drug Abuse: Main Findings 1998* (U.S. Department of Health and Human Services, March 2000), 164.

52. Drug and Alcohol Services Information System (SAMHSA), "How Men and Women Enter Substance Abuse Treatment," *The DASIS Report* (September 7, 2001). "Coerced Treatment Among Youths: 1993 to 1998," *The DASIS Report* (September 21, 2001).

53. J. C. Anthony et al., "Comparative Epidemiology of Dependence on Tobacco, Alcohol, Controlled Substances and Inhalants: Basic Findings From the National Comorbidity Survey," *Experimental and Clinical Psychopharmacology* 2:3 (1994): 244–68.

54. Nolin et al., 18.

55. Zimmer and Morgan, 125–29.

56. B. F. Sexton et al., *The Influence of Cannabis on Driving* (London: TRL Limited, 2000), 4.

57. K. W. Terhune et al., *The Incidence and Role of Drugs in Fatally Injured Drivers* (National Highway Traffic Safety Administration, 1992), 100.

58. "Deglamorising Cannabis," *The Lancet* 346:8985 (November 11, 1995): 1241.

59. Mark Kleiman, *Against Excess: Drug Policy for Results* (New York: Basic Books, 1992), 253.

60. Joy et al., 3.32–3.48.
61. "Senate Committee Recommends Legalization of Cannabis," press release from the Canadian Senate's Special Committee on Illegal Drugs, September 4, 2002.
62. Joy et al., 3.36–3.38.
63. Dale Gieringer, "Cannabis Vaporization: A Promising Strategy for Smoke Harm Reduction," *Journal of Cannabis Therapeutics* 1:3–4 (2001): 153–70.
64. Zimmer and Morgan, 134–41. Kleiman, 256–58.
65. Mahmoud ElSohly and Samir A. Ross, *Quarterly Report, Potency Monitoring Project, Report #61* (University, Miss.: Research Institute of Pharmaceutical Sciences, 1997), figure 1.
66. Lester Grinspoon, *Marihuana Reconsidered,* revised edition (Cambridge, Mass.: Harvard University Press, 1977), 227.
67. Donna Shalala, "Say 'No' to Legalization of Marijuana," *Wall Street Journal* (August 18, 1995), A10.
68. "The Drug Message," *Washington Times* (January 6, 1997), A2.
69. Ernie Freda, "Washington in Brief," *Atlanta Journal and Constitution* (December 18, 1992), B2.
70. Benjamin Rush, *Essays, Literary, Moral, & Philosophical* (Philadelphia: Thomas & Samuel F. Bradford, 1798), 270.
71. See, e.g., J. Smyth Rogers, *An Essay on Tobacco* (New York: How & Bates, 1836), 66–67.
72. Towns, 770.
73. Bonnie and Whitebread, 213.
74. "CASA Releases Report: Non-Medical Marijuana—Rite of Passage or Russian Roulette?," press release from the Center on Addiction and Substance Abuse (July 13, 1999).
75. Joy et al., 3.22.
76. Nolin et al., 15.
77. Quoted in Dan Baum, *Smoke and Mirrors: The War on Drugs and the Politics of Failure* (Boston: Little, Brown, 1996), 57–58.
78. SAMHSA (September 2002), table H.1.
79. Ibid.
80. *Non-Medical Marijuana: Rite of Passage or Russian Roulette?* (New York: Center on Addiction and Substance Abuse, 1999).
81. Dan Reed, "Group's Latest Campaign Is to Fight for the Right to Get Stoned," *San Jose Mercury News* (August 16, 1999), A1.
82. Interview with Bob Wallace, April 11, 2000.

83. Interview with William Gazecki, March 16, 2000.

84. Ibid.

85. Lester Grinspoon has collected some of these accounts at www.marijuana-uses.com.

86. Interview with Alan Mattus (pseud.), April 13, 2000.

87. Interview with Elizabeth Carr (pseud.), March 14, 2000.

88. SAMHSA (September 2002), table H.1.

89. Interview with Walter Stevenson (pseud.), January 24, 2000.

Chapter Four: Crazy, Man

1. Ann Landers, "LSD Still Dangerous As It Was in the '60s," *Los Angeles Times* (June 8, 1993), E2.

2. Lester Grinspoon and James B. Bakalar, *Psychedelic Drugs Reconsidered* (New York: Lindesmith Center, 1997; originally published in 1979), 9.

3. National Institute on Drug Abuse, "Hallucinogens and Dissociative Drugs," NIDA Research Report Series, www.nida.nih.gov/ResearchReports/Hallucinogens/halluc3html.

4. Deets Picket, *Alcohol and the New Age* (New York: The Methodist Book Concern, 1926), 50.

5. Richard J. Bonnie and Charles H. Whitebread, *The Marijuana Conviction: A History of Marijuana Prohibition in the United States* (New York: Lindesmith Center, 1999; originally published in 1974), 57.

6. Ibid., 72.

7. M. A. Hayes and L. A. Bowery, "Marihuana," *Journal of Criminal Law and Criminology* 23 (1932): 1086–94.

8. Bonnie and Whitebread, 112.

9. For a thorough account of the CIA experiments, see Martin A. Lee and Bruce Shlain, *Acid Dreams: The Complete Social History of LSD* (New York: Grove Weidenfeld, 1985).

10. Grinspoon and Bakalar, 198.

11. Ibid., 192–237.

12. Timothy Leary, *The Politics of Ecstasy* (Berkeley: Ronin Publishing, 1998), 9.

13. Ibid., 44, 123, 127.

14. Grinspoon and Bakalar, 66.

15. Leary, 78.

16. Ibid., 66, 67.

17. Lee and Shlain, 148.

18. Jay Stevens, *Storming Heaven: LSD and the American Dream* (New York: Harper & Row, 1987), 274.

19. Edward M. Brecher, *Licit and Illicit Drugs* (Boston: Little, Brown, 1972), 369.

20. Albert Rosenfeld, "The Vital Facts About the Drug," *Life* (March 25, 1966), 30–31.

21. "An Epidemic of 'Acid Heads,'" *Time* (March 11, 1966).

22. Leigh A. Henderson and William J. Glass, eds., *LSD: Still With Us After All These Years* (New York: Lexington Books, 1994), 55.

23. Ibid., 67–70.

24. Ibid., 62–66.

25. Grinspoon and Bakalar, 227.

26. Henderson and Glass, 60–62.

27. Interview with Elizabeth Carr (pseud.), March 14, 2000.

28. Interview with Bruce Rogers (pseud.), March 17, 2000.

29. Ibid.

30. Brecher, 375.

31. Henderson and Glass, 43.

32. Richard Bunce, "Social and Political Sources of Drug Effects: The Case of Bad Trips on Psychedelics," in Norman E. Zinberg and Wayne M. Harding, eds., *Control Over Intoxicant Use* (New York: Human Sciences Press, 1982), 105–25.

33. Howard S. Becker, "History, Culture, and Subjective Experience: An Exploration of the Social Bases of Drug-Induced Experiences," *Journal of Health and Social Behavior* 8 (September 1967): 163–76.

34. Brecher, 367.

35. Substance Abuse and Mental Health Services Administration, *Summary of Findings From the 2000 National Household Survey on Drug Abuse* (U.S. Department of Health and Human Services, September 2001), 187.

36. Monitoring the Future Study, University of Michigan, 2002, table 6.

37. Substance Abuse and Mental Health Services Administration, 2001 National Household Survey on Drug Abuse (September 2002), tables H.1 and H.2.

38. SAMHSA (September 2001), 187.

39. Monitoring the Future Study, tables 5 and 7.

40. Henderson and Glass, 70–75.

41. Interview with Walter Stevenson (pseud.), January 24, 2000.

42. Interview with William Gazecki, March 16, 2000.

43. Interview with Rogers.

44. Interview with Stevenson.

45. Interview with Carr.

46. Interview with Bill Santini (pseud.), March 14, 2000.

47. Henderson and Glass, 12, 18.

48. Interview with Bob Wallace, April 11, 2000.

49. Anthony Luversidge, interview with Kary Mullis, *Omni* (April 1992).

50. "Psychedelics and the Creation of Virtual Reality," *MAPS Bulletin* 10:3 (2000): 4.

51. "Robbins Rants," *MAPS Bulletin* 10:3 (2000): 27.

52. Grinspoon and Bakalar, 193.

53. Interview with Kenneth Donaldson (pseud.), December 17, 1999.

54. Interview with Collins.

55. Interview with Katrina Lubovic (pseud.), July 5, 2000.

56. Interview with Stevenson.

57. Interview with Carr.

58. Interviews with Stevenson, Carr, and Collins.

59. William James, *The Varieties of Religious Experience* (New York: Simon & Schuster, 1997; originally published in 1902), 33–34.

60. Matthew 7:15–20.

61. Deuteronomy 13:1–4, 18:22.

62. Rick Doblin, "Pahnke's 'Good Friday Experiment': A Long-Term Follow-Up and Methodological Critique," *Journal of Transpersonal Psychology,* 23:1 (1991): 1–28.

63. Ibid.

64. Ibid.

65. Ibid.

66. Huston Smith, *Cleansing the Doors of Perception: The Religious Significance of Entheogenic Plants and Chemicals* (New York: Tarcher/Putnam, 2000), 117, 129.

67. James, 304.

68. Ibid.

Chapter Five: Random Sex Acts

1. Ray Long and Rick Pearson, "City, State Target Instigators of Raves With Stiff Penalties," *Chicago Tribune* (May 3, 2001), B1.

2. Alexander Shulgin and Ann Shulgin, *PIHKAL: A Chemical Love Story* (Berkeley: Transform Press, 2000), 69, 72.

3. In *The Secret Chief* (Charlotte, N.C.: Multidisciplinary Association for Psy-

chedelic Studies, 1997), Myron J. Stolaroff presents excerpts from conversations with this therapist, now dead, whom he calls Jacob.

4. Interview, March 14, 2000.

5. Michael C. Mithoefer and Mark T. Wagner, *A Human Phase II Study: Safety and Efficacy of 3,4–Methylenedioxymethamphetamine (MDMA): Assisted Psychotherapy in the Treatment of Chronic Posttraumatic Stress Disorder (PTSD)*, FDA-approved protocol, November 2, 2001, www.maps.org/research/mdma/protocol/mdmaptsdvol1–sm.pdf.

6. Shulgin and Shulgin, 74.

7. Ibid., 72.

8. Jerry Adler, "Getting High on 'Ecstasy,'" *Newsweek* (April 15, 1985), 96.

9. Bruce Eisner, *Ecstasy: The MDMA Story* (Berkeley: Ronin Press, 1989), 6.

10. David Smith, "Questions and Answers: The Ecstasy Epidemic," *Newsweek* (August 4, 2000).

11. K. Krummen et al., "SEX on the Streets of Cincinnati," *Journal of Toxicology: Clinical Toxicology* 5:37 (August 1, 1999): 647.

12. Chong Seck Chim, "Shaking Heads Over Next Generation Methamphetamines," *New Straits Times* (August 16, 2000), 12.

13. John Downing, "Raves in the City: No Safe Place?," *Toronto Sun* (June 7, 2000), 17.

14. Jerome Beck and Marsha Rosenbaum, *Pursuit of Ecstasy: The MDMA Experience* (Albany: State University of New York Press, 1994), 74.

15. Interview with Michael Buchanan (pseud.), March 8, 2000.

16. Jerry Adler, "Getting High on 'Ecstasy,'" *Newsweek* (April 15, 1985), 96. Paul Berton, "An Attempt to Outlaw Ecstasy," *Maclean's* (May 20, 1985), 56.

17. Claudia Glenn Dowling, "The Trouble With Ecstasy," *Life* (August 1985), 88.

18. John Cloud and Nisid Hajari, "Happiness Is . . . a Pill?," *Time,* international edition (November 13, 2000), 40.

19. Joyce Brothers, "Getting Personal," *Good Housekeeping* (January 1, 2001), 38.

20. Mary Ann Marshall, "The Scary Truth About Ecstasy," *Cosmopolitan* (August 1, 2000), 154.

21. Richard Cole, "Study Finds Little Evidence of 'Date Rape Drug,'" Associated Press, Feburary 13, 1998. Also see Philip Jenkins, *Synthetic Panics* (New York: New York University Press, 1999), 160–82.

22. Knight Ridder, "Allure of Club Drugs Grows Across Country," *The Orlando Sentinel* (April 23, 2000), A20.

23. Annemarie Mannion, "Club Drugs' Popularity Trips Alarms," *Chicago Tribune* (October 20, 2000), 4.

24. Peter D. Rogers, "Ecstasy Brings Much Agony to Central Ohio," *Columbus Dispatch* (July 9, 2000), B3.

25. *Macbeth,* Act II, Scene 3, Line 34.

26. Emily Morison Beck, ed., *Familiar Quotations,* fifteenth edition (Boston: Little, Brown, 1980), 855.

27. Joann E. Rodgers, "The Enduring Myth of Aphrodisiacs," *Los Angeles Times* (December 14, 1987), B4.

28. James I, *Counterblaste to Tobacco* (London: English Reprints, 1870; originally published in 1604), 100.

29. Alexander D. Von Gernet, *The Transculturation of the Amerindian Pipe/ Tobacco/Smoking Complex and Its Impact on the Intellectual Boundaries Between "Savagery" and "Civilization," 1535–1935,* doctoral dissertation (McGill University, 1988), 332–33.

30. Quoted in Jordan Goodman, *Tobacco in History: The Cultures of Dependence* (New York: Routledge, 1993), 78.

31. Quoted in Jerome E. Brooks, *Tobacco: The Mighty Leaf* (Boston: Little, Brown, 1952), 220.

32. Quoted in David T. Courtwright, *Dark Paradise: Opiate Addiction in America Before 1940* (Cambridge, Mass.: Harvard University Press, 1982), 78.

33. Quoted in Richard Lawrence Miller, *The Case for Legalizing Drugs* (New York: Praeger, 1991), 88.

34. Quoted in David F. Musto, *The American Disease: Origins of Narcotics Control,* expanded edition (New York: Oxford University Press, 1987), 43.

35. Quoted in Miller, 90.

36. Quoted in Musto, 293. Italics added.

37. Quoted in Joseph F. Spillane, *Cocaine: From Medical Marvel to Modern Menace in the United States, 1884–1920* (Baltimore: Johns Hopkins University Press, 2000), 119.

38. M. A. Hayes and L. A. Bowery, "Marihuana," *Journal of Criminal Law and Criminology* 23 (1932): 1086–98.

39. Quoted in Larry Sloman, *Reefer Madness: A History of Marijuana* (New York: St. Martin's Griffin, 1979), 58–59.

40. Jonathan Keane, "Wake Up to the Chemical World," *New Statesman* (January 24, 1997), 12.

41. E-mail correspondence with Jasmine Menendez (pseud.), December 20, 1999.

42. Interview with Tom Cowan (pseud.), April 12, 2000.

43. Interview with Alison Witt (pseud.), March 13, 2000.

44. Interview with Walter Stevenson (pseud.), January 24, 2000.

45. Interview with Adam Newman (pseud.), March 13, 2000.

46. Interview with Bruce Rogers (pseud.), March 17, 2000.

47. Remarks at "Drug Policies for the New Millennium," conference sponsored by the Lindesmith Center–Drug Policy Foundation in Albuquerque, New Mexico, June 1, 2001.

48. Ibid.

49. Ibid.

50. For results of tests on two sets of samples, see Rick Doblin, "MAPS MDMA Analysis Project," *Newsletter of the Multidisciplinary Association for Psychedelic Studies* 6:3 (September 1996): 11–13, and Matthew Baggott et al., "Chemical Analysis of Ecstasy Pills," *Journal of the American Medical Association* 284:17 (November 1, 2000): 2190.

51. Interview with Buchanan.

52. E-mail correspondence with Menendez.

53. Interview with Stevenson.

54. E-mail correspondence with Menendez.

55. E-mail correspondence with Menendez, September 14, 2001.

56. Substance Abuse and Mental Health Services Administration, 2001 National Household Survey on Drug Abuse (September 2002), table H.2.

57. Monitoring the Future Study, University of Michigan, 2002, tables 4–7.

58. Substance Abuse and Mental Health Services Administration, *The DAWN Report: Club Drugs* (U.S. Department of Health and Human Services, December 2000), 4.

59. Doblin and Baggott et al.

60. Drug Enforcement Administration, "The Hallucinogen PMA: Dancing With Death," U.S. Department of Justice, October 2000.

61. Charles S. Grob, "Deconstructing Ecstasy: The Politics of MDMA Research," *Addiction Research*, 8:6 (2000), 549–88.

62. Ibid., 560–79.

63. Ibid., 580. Also see Alex Gamma, "Does Ecstasy Cause Memory Deficits?," January 7, 2001, www.maps.org/research/mdma/gamma2000.pdf.

64. Liesbeth Reneman et al., "Cortical Serotonin Transporter Density and Verbal Memory in Individuals Who Stopped Using 3,4–Methylenedioxymethamphetamine (MDMA or 'Ecstasy')," *Archives of General Psychiatry* 58:10 (October 2001): 901–6.

65. Grob, 569–71.

Chapter Six: Killer Drugs

1. Peter Bowles, "Life Term in Crack Slayings of 3 Kin," *Newsday* (December 28, 1989), A28.

2. Tom Morganthau, "Crack and Crime," *Newsweek* (June 16, 1986), 16.

3. Richard M. Smith, "The Plague Among Us: The Drug Crisis," *Newsweek* (June 16, 1986), 15.

4. John J. Goldman, "New York City Being Swamped by 'Crack,'" *Los Angeles Times* (August 1, 1986), A1.

5. Michael Isikoff, "Users of Crack Cocaine Link Violence to Drug's Influence," *The Washington Post* (March 24, 1989), A11.

6. Ron Rosenblum, "Crack Murder: A Detective Story," *The New York Times Magazine* (February 15, 1987), 24, and Ron Rosenblum, "Breaking the Crack Murders," *The New York Times Magazine* (November 15, 1987), 44.

7. Tom Morganthau, "Murder Wave in the Capital," *Newsweek* (March 13, 1989), 16.

8. Paul J. Goldstein et al., "Crack and Homicide in New York City, 1988: A Conceptually Based Event Analysis," *Contemporary Drug Problems* 16:4 (Winter 1989): 651–87.

9. Craig Reinarman et al., "The Contingent Call of the Pipe: Bingeing and Addiction Among Heavy Cocaine Smokers," in Craig Reinarman and Harry G. Levine, eds., *Crack in America: Demon Drugs and Social Justice* (Berkeley: University of California Press, 1997), 77–97.

10. Lawrence A. Greenfeld, *Alcohol and Crime: An Analysis of National Data on the Prevalence of Alcohol Involvement in Crime* (Bureau of Justice Statistics, U.S. Department of Justice, April 1998), vi, 2.

11. Greenfield, v.

12. Quoted in Andrew Barr, *Drink: A Social History of America* (New York: Carroll & Graf, 1999), 25.

13. Jeffrey Fagan, "Intoxication and Aggression," in Michael Tonry and James Q. Wilson, eds., *Drugs and Crime* (Chicago: University of Chicago Press, 1990), 241–320.

14. John P. Morgan and Lynn Zimmer, "The Social Pharmacology of Smokeable Cocaine: Not All It's Cracked Up to Be," in Reinarman and Levine, 131–70.

15. Quoted in David F. Musto, *The American Disease: Origins of Narcotics Control,* expanded edition (New York: Oxford University Press, 1987), 282.

16. Quoted in Joseph F. Spillane, *Cocaine: From Medical Marvel to Modern Menace in the United States, 1884–1920* (Baltimore: Johns Hopkins University Press, 2000), 119–20.

17. Spillane, 121.

18. Quoted in Richard J. Bonnie and Charles H. Whitebread, *The Marijuana Conviction: A History of Marijuana Prohibition in the United States* (New York: Lindesmith Center, 1999; originally published in 1974), 34, 37.

19. Ibid., 40.

20. M. A. Hayes and L. A. Bowery, "Marihuana," *Journal of Criminal Law and Criminology* 23 (1932): 1086–98.

21. Bonnie and Whitebread, 71.

22. Quoted in Edward M. Brecher, *Licit & Illicit Drugs* (Boston: Little, Brown, 1972), 411.

23. Bonnie and Whitebread, 77.

24. Ibid., 109.

25. Ibid., 146.

26. Ibid., 148.

27. Statement of H. J. Anslinger, hearing before a subcommittee of the Committee on Finance, U.S. Senate, 75th Congress, First Session, on H.R. 6906, July 12, 1937.

28. Additional Statement of H. J. Anslinger, hearings before the Committee on Ways and Means, U.S. House of Representatives, 75th Congress, First Session, on H.R. 6385, April 27–30 and May 4, 1937.

29. Bonnie and Whitebread, 219–20.

30. *Congressional Record,* 81, 5575 (June 10, 1937).

31. Bonnie and Whitebread, 101.

32. Jerry Mandel, "Hashish, Assassins, and the Love of God," *Issues in Criminology* 2 (1966): 153.

33. "PCP: 'A Real Terror of a Drug,'" *Time* (December 19, 1977), 53.

34. Ed Bruske, "Police Puzzle: Subduing PCP Users," *Washington Post* (December 2, 1984), B1.

35. "Killer Convicted on Television's '60 Minutes' Admission," Associated Press, February 25, 1982.

36. Linda Deutsch, "Defense Tries to Put Rodney King on Trial, but Latest Witness Backfires," Associated Press, March 27, 1993.

37. Martin Brecher et al., "Phencyclidine and Violence: Clinical and Legal Issues," *Journal of Clinical Psychopharmacology* 8:6 (December 1988): 397–401.

38. Interview with Bruce Rogers (pseud.), March 17, 2000.

39. Interview with Bob Wallace, April 11, 2000.

40. Edward M. Brecher, 281.

41. David C. Beeder, "Drug Fight to Target Midwest," *Omaha World Herald* (September 26, 1996), A1.

42. Chris Dettro, "'Meth' Targeted by Officials in Midwest," Springfield, Ill., *State Journal* (Springfield, Ill.) (September 27, 1996), B8.

43. Christopher S. Wren, "Sharp Rise in Use of Methamphetamines Generates Concern," *New York Times* (February 14, 1996), A16.

44. John Branton, "Meth Epidemic Puts Drug-Fighting Detectives at Greater Risk," Vancouver, Wash., *Columbian* (June 3, 1996), A1.

45. Dan Raley, "Strange Chemical High Is Becoming a Vicious Epidemic," *Seattle Post-Intelligencer* (February 6, 1996), A1.

46. Randy Fitzgerald, "A Demon Stalks the Land," *Reader's Digest* (February 1994), 87–92.

47. Lisa Levitt Ryckman, "Soul Destroyer: 'Meth' Shows Its Face in Violence and Despair As Grand Junction Enters Grave New World," *Rocky Mountain News* (December 1, 1996), A26.

48. Ibid.

49. Daniel Vasquez, "The New 'Speed,'" *San Jose Mercury News* (December 28, 1996), A1.

50. See Wren and Jim Walsh, "Beheading Linked to Drug Use," *The Arizona Republic* (July 26, 1995), A1.

51. *People v. Ricky Lee Earp,* S025423, June 24, 1999.

52. Correspondence with Julio Moran, December 17, 2001.

53. "*Reader's Digest* Reports Alarming Upsurge in Illegal Drug Fad," *Reader's Digest* press release, January 25, 1994.

54. Jane Perlez, "Mogadishu, Once Graceful, Is Riven by Greed," *The New York Times* (December 7, 1992), A1.

55. Michael Hedges, "Drug Gives Young Gunmen Courage," *Washington Times* (December 9, 1992).

56. Interviewed by Frank Sesno, CNN, September 16, 1992.

57. Jonathan Stevenson, "Krazy Qat," *The New Republic* (November 23, 1992), 17–18.

58. Brecher et al. (1988), 399–400.

59. Substance Abuse and Mental Health Services Administration, *Summary of Findings From the 1999 National Household Survey on Drug Abuse* (U.S. Department of Health and Human Services, August 2000), G-4. SAMHSA, *Drug Abuse Warning Network Annual Medical Examiner Data 1999* (HHS, December 2000), 39, 47.

60. Morgan and Zimmer, 149–54. Garry A. Emmett, "What Happened to the

'Crack Babies'?," *Drug Policy Analysis Bulletin* (February 1998): 1–3. Barry M. Lester et al., "Cocaine Exposure and Children: The Meaning of Subtle Effects," *Science* 282 (October 23, 1998): 633–34.

61. Substance Abuse and Mental Health Services Administration, 2001 National Household Survey on Drug Abuse (September 2002), tables H.1 and H.2. National Institute on Drug Abuse, *National Survey Results From the Monitoring the Future Study, 1975–1994*, volume II (HHS, 1996), 84–85.

62. J. C. Anthony et al., "Comparative Epidemiology of Dependence on Tobacco, Alcohol, Controlled Substances and Inhalants: Basic Findings From the National Comorbidity Survey," *Experimental and Clinical Psychopharmacology* 2 (1994): 244–68.

63. Interview with Kenneth Donaldson (pseud.), December 17, 1999.

64. Interview with Alison Witt (pseud.), March 13, 2000.

65. Interview with Katrina Lubovic (pseud.), July 5, 2000.

66. Interview with Larry Seguin, April 13, 2000.

67. Interview with Rick Root, March 8, 2000.

68. Interview with Lubovic.

69. Interview with Seguin.

70. Interview with Alan Mattus (pseud.), April 13, 2000.

71. Dan Waldorf et al., *Cocaine Changes: The Experience of Using and Quitting* (Philadelphia: Temple University Press, 1991), 156, 246, 254.

72. Peter Cohen and Arjan Sas, *Ten Years of Cocaine: A Follow-Up Study of 64 Cocaine Users in Amsterdam* (Amsterdam: University of Amsterdam, 1993), 11–13.

73. Waldorf et al., 10.

Chapter Seven: Too Good

1. Lee Davidson, "Hatch Joins DEA in Call for Tougher 'Meth' Laws," *Deseret News* (February 13, 1996).

2. Stanton Peele, "Addiction As a Cultural Concept," *Annals of the New York Academy of Medicine* 602 (1990): 205–20.

3. Martin Booth, *Opium: A History* (New York: St. Martin's Press, 1996), 83, 85, 91.

4. See Thomas Szasz, *Ceremonial Chemistry* (Garden City, N.Y.: Anchor Press, 1974), and Stanton Peele, *The Meaning of Addiction* (Lexington, Mass.: Lexington Books, 1985).

5. See, e.g., Arthur B. Light and Edward G. Torrance, "Opium Addiction: The Effects of Abrupt Withdrawal Followed by Readministration of Morphine

in Human Addicts," *Archives of Internal Medicine* 44:1 (July 1929): 1–16, and Andrew Weil and Winifred Rosen, *From Chocolate to Morphine: Everything You Need to Know About Mind-Altering Drugs,* revised edition (Boston: Houghton Mifflin, 1993), 85.

6. See, e.g., Harold Alksne et al., "A Conceptual Model of the Life Cycle of Addiction," *International Journal of the Addictions* 2:2 (Fall 1967): 221–40.

7. Jane Porter and Hershel Jick, "Addiction Rare in Patients Treated With Narcotics," *New England Journal of Medicine* 302:2 (January 10, 1980): 123.

8. Samuel Perry and George Heidrich, "Management of Pain During Debridement: A Survey of U.S. Burn Units," *Pain* 13 (1982): 267–80.

9. Russell K. Portenoy and Kathleen M. Foley, "Chronic Use of Opioid Analgesics in Non-Malignant Pain: Report of 38 Cases," *Pain* 25 (1986): 171–86.

10. See, e.g., Richard M. Marks and Edward J. Sachar, "Undertreatment of Medical Inpatients With Narcotic Analgesics," *Annals of Internal Medicine* 78:2 (February 1973): 173–81; Marcia Angell, "The Quality of Mercy," *New England Journal of Medicine* 306:2 (January 14, 1982): 98–99; John P. Morgan, "American Opiophobia: Customary Underutilization of Opioid Analgesics," in Barry Stimmel, ed., *Controversies in Alcoholism and Substance Abuse* (Binghamton, N.Y.: Haworth Press, 1986). For a summary of the issue, see Jacob Sullum, "No Relief in Sight," *Reason* (January 1997), 22–28.

11. Charles R. Schuster, "Does Treatment of Cancer Pain With Narcotics Produce Junkies?," in C. S. Hess Jr. and W. S. Fields, eds., *Drug Treatment of Cancer Pain in a Drug-Oriented Society* (New York: Raven, 1989), 2.

12. American Psychiatric Association, *Diagnostic and Statistical Manual of Mental Disorders,* fourth edition (Washington, D.C.: APA, 1994), 176, 178, 181.

13. David E. Smith and Georg R. Gay, eds., *"It's So Good, Don't Even Try It Once": Heroin in Perspective* (Englewood Cliffs, N.J.: Prentice-Hall, 1972).

14. Substance Abuse and Mental Health Services Administration, 2001 National Household Survey on Drug Abuse (September 2002), tables H.1 and H.2.

15. Monitoring the Future Study University of Michigan (2002), tables 5 and 7.

16. Leon G. Hunt and Carl D. Chambers, *The Heroin Epidemics: A Study of Heroin Use in the United States, 1965–1975* (New York: Spectrum, 1976), 112, 117, 120.

17. James C. Anthony et al., "Comparative Epidemiology of Dependence on Tobacco, Alcohol, Controlled Substances and Inhalants: Basic Findings From the National Comorbidity Survey," *Experimental and Clinical Psychopharmacology* 2 (1994): 244–68.

18. Lynn T. Kozlowski et al., "Comparing Tobacco Cigarette Dependence With Other Drug Dependencies," *Journal of the American Medical Association* 261:6 (February 10, 1989): 898–901. In the first survey, the problem drug was not specified.

19. "Effectiveness of Smoking-Control Strategies—United States," *Morbidity and Mortality Weekly Report* 41:35 (September 4, 1992): 645–47.

20. Charles Winick, "The Life Cycle of the Narcotic Addict and Addiction," *Bulletin on Narcotics* 16:1 (January–March, 1964): 1–11.

21. See, e.g., M. Snow, "Maturing Out of Narcotic Addiction in New York City," *International Journal of the Addictions* 8:6 (1973): 921–38.

22. See Dan Waldorf and Patrick Biernacki, "Natural Recovery From Heroin Addiction: A Review of the Incidence Literature," in Zinberg and Wayne M. Harding, eds., *Control Over Intoxicant Use* (New York: Human Sciences Press, 1982), 173–81.

23. Lee N. Robins et al., "Vietnam Veterans Three Years After Vietnam: How Our Study Changed Our View of Heroin," *The Yearbook of Substance Use & Abuse,* 2 (1980): 213–30.

24. Tom Morganthau, "Crack and Crime," *Newsweek* (June 16, 1986), 16.

25. Richard M. Smith, "The Plague Among Us," *Newsweek* (June 16, 1986), 15.

26. Tom Morganthau, "Kids and Cocaine," *Newsweek* (March 17, 1986), 58.

27. National Institute on Drug Abuse, *National Survey Results From the Monitoring the Future Study, 1975–1994,* volume II (U.S. Department of Health and Human Services, 1996), 83–85.

28. John P. Morgan and Lynn Zimmer, "The Social Pharmacology of Smokeable Cocaine," in Craig Reinarman and Harry G. Levine, eds., *Crack in America: Demon Drugs and Social Justice* (Berkeley: University of California Press, 1997), 131–70. Emphasis in the original.

29. Craig Reinarman et al., "The Contingent Call of the Pipe: Bingeing and Addiction Among Heavy Cocaine Smokers," in Reinarman and Levine, 77–97.

30. Richard M. Smith.

31. Bruce K. Alexander, "The Myth of Drug-Induced Addiction," testimony before the Senate Special Committee on Illegal Drugs (Canada), April 23, 2001, and Bruce K. Alexander et al., "Adult, Infant, and Animal Addiction," in Peele (1985): 73–96. Also see Stanton Peele and Richard J. DeGrandpre, "Cocaine and the Concept of Addiction: Environmental Factors in Drug Compulsions," *Addiction Research,* 6 (1998): 235–63.

32. See, e.g., Peele (1985) and Stanton Peele and Archie Brodsky, *The Truth About Addiction and Recovery* (New York: Simon & Schuster, 1991.

33. Interview with Bob Wallace, April 11, 2000.

34. Interview with Bruce Rogers (pseud.), March 17, 2000.

35. "Clinton Unveils New Antidrug Plan," *Facts on File World News Digest* (May 9, 1996), 321.

36. Graham Rayman, " 'Video Crack' or Cash Cow?," *Newsday* (February 24, 1995), A7. Phyllis Brill, "Heroin Use Spreading to Suburbs," Baltimore *Sun* (August 13, 1995), C1.

37. Otto Kreisher, "McCaffrey Sees Meth Replacing Cocaine As Top Drug Threat," Copley News Service, February 11, 1998.

38. Dirk Johnson, "Good People Go Bad in Iowa, and a Drug Is Being Blamed," *New York Times* (February 22, 1996), A1.

39. Chris Dettro, " 'Meth' Targeted by Officials in Midwest," Springfield, Ill., *State Journal-Register* (September 27, 1996), B8.

40. Michael Kirkland, "Reno: Drug Plague Spreads to Midwest," United Press International, September 26, 1996.

41. Gordon Witkin, "A New Drug Gallops Through the West," *U.S. News & World Report* (November 13, 1995), 50.

42. See, e.g., Michelle Ortiz Ray, "Methamphetamine Use Picking Up Speed in West, Officers Say," *Los Angeles Times* (June 25, 1995), B3, and " 'Meth' Use in the '90s: A Growing 'Epidemic,'" *USA Today* (September 7, 1995), A7.

43. Edward M. Brecher, *Licit and Illicit Drugs* (Boston: Little, Brown, 1972), 281, 294–95.

44. John A. Newmeyer, "The Epidemiology of Amphetamine Use," in David E. Smith, ed., *Amphetamine Use, Misuse, and Abuse* (Boston: G.K. Hall, 1979), 55–72. SAMHSA (2002), tables H.1 and H.2. NIDA, 81–85. Monitoring the Future Study, tables 5 and 7.

45. See, e.g., David Margolick, "Antismoking Climate Inspires Suits by the Dying," *New York Times* (March 15, 1985), B1, and Sherri Williams, "Almost Half of State's Teens Use Tobacco, a Study Says," Associated Press, August 9, 1999.

46. Natalie Pompilio and Keith O'Brien, "Deadly Lure," New Orleans *Times-Picayune* (May 27, 2001), A1.

47. Norman E. Zinberg, *Drug, Set, and Setting: The Basis for Controlled Intoxicant Use* (New Haven, Conn.: Yale University Press, 1984).

48. See, e.g., Constance Holden, " 'Behavioral' Addictions: Do They Exist?," *Science* (November 2, 2001), 980–82.

49. Jordan M. Scher, "Group Structure and Narcotic Addiction," *International Journal of Group Psychotherapy* 11 (1961): 88–93.

50. Norman E. Zinberg and David C. Lewis, "Narcotic Usage," *New England Journal of Medicine* 270:9 (May 7, 1964): 989–93.

51. Ibid.

52. Zinberg, 48, 50–51, 57, 119, 135–71. Norman E. Zinberg and Richard C. Jacobson, "The Natural History of 'Chipping,'" *American Journal of Psychiatry* 133:1 (January 1976): 37–40.

53. Douglas H. Powell, "A Pilot Study of Occasional Heroin Users," *Archives of General Psychiatry* 28 (April 1973): 586–94. Judith Stephenson Blackwell, "Drifting, Controlling and Overcoming: Opiate Users Who Avoid Becoming Chronically Dependent," *Journal of Drug Issues* 13:2 (Spring 1983): 219–35.

54. Robins et al.

55. Interview with Walter Stevenson (pseud.), January 24, 2000.

56. Interview with Bruce Rogers (pseud.), March 17, 2000.

57. Interview with Evelyn Schwartz (pseud.), January 23, 2000.

58. Ibid.

59. Anthony Browne, "Heroin Is Safe and Fun, Users Tell BBC Show," London *Observer* (March 25, 2001), A5.

60. See, e.g., Brecher, 33–35.

61. Interview with Schwartz.

62. Ibid.

63. Joseph B. Treaster, "Executive's Secret Struggle With Heroin's Powerful Grip," *New York Times* (July 22, 1992), A1.

64. Ibid.

65. Ibid.

66. Robins et al.

67. Alksne et al. Also see Ann Marlowe, *How to Stop Time: Heroin From A to Z* (New York: Basic Books, 1999).

68. Zinberg and Lewis. Also see George R. Gay et al., "The Pseudo Junkie: Evolution of the Heroin Lifestyle in the Non-Addicted Individual," *Anesthesia and Analgesia,* 53:2 (March–April 1974): 241–47.

69. A comparison of licit heroin's price in Europe to its cost on the street can be found in Henner Hess, "The Other Prohibition: The Cigarette Crisis in Post-War Germany," paper presented at the 47th Annual Conference of the American Society of Criminology, November 1995, 10.

70. Substance Abuse and Mental Health Services Administration, *Drug Abuse Warning Network Annual Medical Examiner Data 1999* (U.S. Department of Health and Human Services, December 2000), 39, 47.

71. See, e.g., Charles P. O'Brien et al., "Long-Term Consequences of Opiate Dependence," *New England Journal of Medicine* 304:18 (April 30, 1981): 1098–99, and Weil and Rosen, 85.

72. See, e.g., Marlowe.

Chapter Eight: Body and Soul

1. Andrew Barr, *Drink: A Social History of America* (New York: Carroll & Graf, 1999), 199–213.

2. Ibid., 212–13.

3. R. A. Hatcher et al., *Epitome of the Pharmacopeia of the United States and the National Formulary, With Comments* (Chicago: American Medical Association, 1926), 20, 170.

4. Communication with Food and Drug Administration historian John Swann, December 12, 2001.

5. Arthur L. Klatsky, "Is Drinking Healthy?," in Stanton Peele and Marcus Grant, eds., *Alcohol and Pleasure: A Health Perspective* (Philadelphia: Brunner/ Mazel, 1999), 141–56. Also see Abigail Zuger, "The Case for Drinking (All Together Now: In Moderation!)," *New York Times* (December 31, 2002), F1.

6. For discussions of the prescription drug system as the foundation for the war on drugs, see Thomas Szasz's books *Ceremonial Chemistry,* revised edition (Holmes Beach, Fla.: Learning Publications, 1985), and *Our Right to Drugs* (New York: Praeger, 1992).

7. Interview with Jim Dahl, November 13, 2000.

8. Ibid.

9. David W. Sifton, ed., *The PDR Pocket Guide to Prescription Drugs* (New York: Pocket, 1996), 1194.

10. Interview with Dahl.

11. Ibid.

12. Correspondence with Dahl, March 14, 2001.

13. Lester Grinspoon and James B. Bakalar, *Marihuana, the Forbidden Medicine* (New Haven, Conn.: Yale University Press, 1993).

14. See, e.g., Janet E. Joy et al., eds., *Marijuana and Medicine: Assessing the Science Base* (Washington, D.C.: National Academy Press, 1999), 3.1–3.62.

15. Sabin Russell, "U.S. Drug Czar Visits Haight, Denounces Medical Use of Pot," *San Francisco Chronicle* (August 16, 1996), A8.

16. *CNN Today* December 30, 1996.

17. Janet E. Joy et al., 4.1–4.59.

18. Greg Winter, "U.S. Cracks Down on Medical Marijuana in California," *New York Times* (October 31, 2001), A12.

19. Christopher S. Wren, "Votes on Marijuana Are Stirring Debate," *New York Times* (November 17, 1996), A16.

20. For a discussion of marijuana's possible usefulness in treating "depression and other mood disorders," see Grinspoon and Bakalar, 115–26.

21. Peter D. Kramer, *Listening to Prozac: A Psychiatrist Explores Antidepressant Drugs and the Remaking of the Self* (New York: Viking, 1993), xix, 235, 263.

22. Jeffrey A. Schaler, *Addiction Is a Choice* (Chicago: Open Court, 2000), 116–17, 129.

23. Robert J. Gregory and Ripu D. Jindal, "Ethical Dilemmas in Prescribing Antidepressants," *Archives of General Psychiatry* 58:11 (October 2001).

24. See, e.g., Julian Simon, *Good Mood: The New Psychology of Overcoming Depression* (La Salle, Ill.: Open Court Publishing, 1993).

25. Shankar Vedantam, "Drug Ads Hyping Anxiety Make Some Uneasy," *Washington Post* (July 16, 2001), A1.

26. Interview with Michael Buchanan (pseud.), March 8, 2000.

27. See Lester Grinspoon and James B. Bakalar, *Psychedelic Drugs Reconsidered* (New York: Lindesmith Center, 1997; originally published in 1979); Huston Smith, *Cleansing the Doors of Perception: The Religious Significance of Entheogenic Plants and Chemicals* (New York: Tarcher/Putnam, 2000); and Peter Stafford, *Psychedelics Encyclopedia* (Berkeley, Calif.: Ronin Publishing, 1992).

28. *Employment Division v. Smith,* 494 U.S. 872 (1990).

29. *City of Boerne v. Flores,* 521 U.S. 507 (1997).

30. *People of Guam v. Benny Toves Guerrero,* 9th Circuit, No. 00-71247 (2002).

31. James Randi, " 'Twas Brillig . . . Observations on a Bizarre World," *Skeptic* 7:3 (1999): 6–7.

32. Andrew Weil, *The Natural Mind: An Investigation of Drugs and the Higher Consciousness,* revised edition (Boston: Houghton Mifflin, 1986).

33. Ronald K. Siegel, *Intoxication: Life in Pursuit of Artificial Paradise* (New York: E.P. Dutton, 1989).

Conclusion: Managing Moderation

1. Jill Jonnes, *Hep-Cats, Narcs, and Pipe Dreams: A History of America's Romance With Illegal Drugs* (New York: Scribner, 1996), 25.

2. David F. Musto, *The American Disease: Origins of Narcotics Control,* expanded edition (New York: Oxford University Press, 1987), 5.

3. Arnold S. Trebach and James A. Inciardi, *Legalize It?: Debating American Drug Policy* (Washington, D.C.: American University Press, 1993), 48–54.

4. Jonnes, 25.

5. Trebach and Inciardi, 51.

6. Jonnes, 25.

7. John P. Morgan, "Prohibition Is Perverse Policy," in Melvyn B. Krauss and Edward P. Lazear, eds., *Searching for Alternatives: Drug-Control Policy in the United States* (Stanford, Calif.: Hoover Institution Press, 1991), 398–404.

8. Thomas N. Nephew et al., *Apparent Per Capita Alcohol Consumption: National, State and Regional Trends, 1977–99* (National Institute on Alcohol Abuse and Alcoholism, September 2002), table 1.

9. See, e.g., Andrew T. Weil, "Observations on Consciousness Alteration: Why Coca Leaf Should Be Available As a Recreational Drug," *Journal of Psychedelic Drugs* 9:1 (January–March 1977): 75–78, and Richard B. Karel, "A Model Legalization Proposal," in James A. Inciardi, ed., *The Drug Legalization Debate* (Newbury Park, Calif.: Sage Publications, 1991), 80–102.

10. For a contemporaneous summary of the arguments about opium, see Mordecai Cooke, *Seven Sisters of Sleep* (Rochester, Vt.: Park Street Press, 1997; originally published in 1860), 101–49.

11. Martin Booth, *Opium: A History* (New York: St. Martin's Press, 1996), 169.

12. John C. Kramer, "Speculations on the Nature and Pattern of Opium Smoking," in Norman E. Zinberg and Wayne M. Harding, eds., *Control Over Intoxicant Use* (New York: Human Sciences Press, 1982), 139–47.

13. Ibid.

14. G. F. van de Wijngaart, "The Dutch Approach: Normalization of Drug Problems," *Journal of Drug Issues* 20:4 (1990): 667–78.

15. Manja D. Abraham et al., *Licit and Illicit Drug Use in the Netherlands, 1997* (Amsterdam: Center for Drug Research, 1999), 68. Substance Abuse and Mental Health Services Administration, *National Household Survey on Drug Abuse: Main Findings 1997* (U.S. Department of Health and Human Services, April 1999), 47.

16. Financial supporters of the Partnership for a Drug-Free America have included Philip Morris, R.J. Reynolds, American Brands (maker of Lucky Strike cigarettes and Jim Beam whiskey), and Anheuser-Busch, as well as several pharmaceutical companies. See Cynthia Cotts, "Hard Sell in the Drug War," *The Nation* (March 9, 1992), 300–302.

17. See, e.g., "Studies Question Effectiveness of DARE Program," *Today,* NBC News, March 23, 1998, and Jodi Upton, "DARE Doesn't Work" and "DARE's

Clout Smothers Other Programs," *Detroit News* (February 27–28, 2000). Earlier critiques include Jeff Elliott, "Drug Prevention Placebo," *Reason* (March 1995), 14–21. For a summary of the evidence, see Donald R. Lynam et al., "Project DARE: No Effects at 10–Year Follow-Up," *Journal of Consulting and Clinical Psychology,* 67:4 (August 1999): 590–93.

18. Kate Zernike, "Antidrug Program Says It Will Adopt a New Strategy," *New York Times* (February 15, 2001), A1.

19. Interview, April 12, 2000.

20. Interview with Bob Wallace, April 11, 2000.

21. Interview with Rick Root, March 8, 2000.

22. E-mail questionnaire, December 15, 1999.

23. E-mail questionnaire, December 20, 1999.

24. Interview with William Gazecki, March 16, 2000.

25. For one father's attempt at honest drug talk, see Marshall Lewis, "Talking to Kids (and the World) About Drugs," users.erols.com/mlewis43/drugkids. html. Also see Marsha Rosenbaum, *Safety First: A Reality-Based Approach to Teens, Drugs, and Drug Education* (New York: Lindesmith Center, 1999).

26. Interview with Alison Witt (pseud.), March 13, 2000.

27. The estimate for annual spending on drug law enforcement is from the Drug Policy Alliance. Useful accounts of the damage caused by the war on drugs include Steven B. Duke and Albert C. Gross, *America's Longest War: Rethinking Our Tragic Crusade Against Drugs* (New York: Tarcher/Putnam, 1993); Dan Baum, *Smoke and Mirrors: The War on Drugs and the Politics of Failure* (Boston: Little, Brown, 1996); and Mike Gray: *Drug Crazy: How We Got Into This Mess and How We Can Get Out of It* (New York: Random House, 1998).

28. J. Donald Moon, "Drugs and Democracy," in Pablo De Greiff, ed., *Drugs and the Limits of Liberalism* (Ithaca, N.Y.: Cornell University Press, 1999), 133–55.

29. Quoted in Mark Edward Lender and James Kirby Martin, *Drinking in America: A History,* revised edition (New York: The Free Press, 1987), 155.

30. Interview with Larry Seguin, April 13, 2000.

31. Ibid.

32. Ibid.

BIBLIOGRAPHY

Books & Monographs

Abraham, Manja D., et al. *Licit and Illicit Drug Use in the Netherlands, 1997.* Amsterdam: Center for Drug Research, 1999.

American Psychiatric Association. *Diagnostic and Statistical Manual of Mental Disorders,* fourth edition. Washington, D.C.: APA, 1994.

Aristotle. *Ethics.* Translated by J.A.K. Thomson. New York: Viking Penguin, 1976.

Arthur, Timothy Shay. *Ten Nights in a Bar-Room and What I Saw There!* Philadelphia: John E. Potter & Co., 1860.

Bakalar, James B., and Lester Grinspoon. *Drug Control in a Free Society.* New York: Cambridge University Press, 1984.

Barr, Andrew. *Drink: A Social History of America.* New York: Carroll & Graf, 1999.

Baum, Dan. *Smoke and Mirrors: The War on Drugs and the Politics of Failure.* Boston: Little, Brown, 1996.

Beck, Jerome, and Marsha Rosenbaum. *Pursuit of Ecstasy: The MDMA Experience.* Albany: State University of New York Press, 1994.

Beecher, Lyman. *Six Sermons on the Nature, Occasions, Signs, Evils, and Remedy of Intemperance.* New York: American Tract Society, 1862.

Behr, Edward. *Prohibition: Thirteen Years That Changed America.* New York: Arcade, 1996.

Bennett, William J. *The De-Valuing of America: The Fight for Our Culture and Our Children.* New York: Simon & Schuster, 1992.

Blaisdell, Albert F. *Our Bodies and How We Live.* Boston: Ginn, 1910.

Bonnie, Richard J., and Charles H. Whitebread. *The Marijuana Conviction: A History of Marijuana Prohibition in the United States.* (New York: Lindesmith Center, 1999 (reprint).

Booth, Martin. *Opium: A History.* New York: St. Martin's Press, 1996.

Bouwsma, William J. *John Calvin: A Sixteenth Century Portrait.* New York: Oxford University Press, 1988.

Brecher, Edward M. *Licit & Illicit Drugs.* Boston: Little, Brown, 1972.

Brooks, Jerome E. *Tobacco: The Mighty Leaf.* Boston: Little, Brown, 1952.

Center on Addiction and Substance Abuse. *Non-Medical Marijuana: Rite of Passage or Russian Roulette?* New York: CASA, 1999.

Chafetz, Morris E. *The Tyranny of Experts.* Lanham, Md.: Madison Books, 1996.

Church of Jesus Christ of Latter-day Saints. *Young Women Manual I.* Salt Lake City: Intellectual Reserve, 1992.

———. *Gospel Principles.* Salt Lake City: Intellectual Reserve, 1997.

———. *Preparing for Exaltation: Teacher's Manual.* Salt Lake City: Intellectual Reserve, 1998.

———. *Doctrine and Covenants and Church History: Gospel Doctrine Teacher's Manual.* Salt Lake City: Intellectual Reserve, 1999.

Cohen, Peter, and Arjan Sas. *Ten Years of Cocaine: A Follow-Up Study of 64 Cocaine Users in Amsterdam.* Amsterdam: University of Amsterdam, 1993.

Cooke, Mordecai. *Seven Sisters of Sleep.* Rochester, Vt.: Park Street Press, 1997 (reprint).

Courtwright, David T. *Dark Paradise: Opiate Addiction in America Before 1940.* Cambridge, Mass.: Harvard University Press, 1982.

Daniels, Bruce C. *Puritans at Play: Leisure and Recreation in Colonial New England.* New York: St. Martin's Press, 1995.

Dayagi-Mendels, Michal. *Drink and Be Merry: Wine and Beer in Ancient Times.* Jerusalem: The Israel Museum, 1999.

De Greiff, Pablo, ed. *Drugs and the Limits of Liberalism.* Ithaca, N.Y.: Cornell University Press, 1999.

De Quincey, Thomas. *Confessions of an English Opium Eater.* New York: Penguin, 1986 (reprint).

Distilled Spirits Council of the United States. *Summary of State Laws & Regulations Relating to Distilled Spirits,* thirty-first edition. Washington, D.C.: DISCUS, 2000.

Drug Enforcement Administration. *How to Hold Your Own in a Drug Legalization Debate.* U.S. Department of Justice, 1994.

Drug Strategies. *Millenium Hangover: Keeping Score on Alcohol.* Washington, D.C., 1999.

Duke, Steven B., and Albert C. Gross. *America's Longest War: Rethinking Our Tragic Crusade Against Drugs.* New York: G. P. Putnam's Sons, 1993.

Eisner, Bruce. *Ecstasy: The MDMA Story.* Berkeley: Ronin Press, 1989.

ElSohly, Mahmoud, and Samir A. Ross. *Quarterly Report, Potency Monitoring Project, Report #61.* University, Miss.: Research Institute of Pharmaceutical Sciences, 1997.

Encyclopedia Judaica. Jerusalem: Keter Publishing, 1997.

Escohotado, Antonio. *A Brief History of Drugs.* Rochester, Vt.: Park Street Press, 1999.

Esposito, John L., ed. *The Oxford Encyclopedia of the Modern Islamic World.* New York: Oxford University Press, 1995.

Fingarette, Herbert. *Heavy Drinking: The Myth of Alcoholism As a Disease.* Berkeley: University of California Press, 1988.

Ford, Gene. *The Benefits of Moderate Drinking.* San Francisco: Wine Appreciation Guild, 1988.

Ford, Henry, ed. *The Case Against the Little White Slaver.* Detroit, 1914.

Gadul Haq, Gadul Haq Ali, et al. *Islamic Ruling on Smoking.* World Health Organization, 1996.

Goodman, Jordan. *Tobacco in History: The Cultures of Dependence.* New York: Routledge, 1993.

Goodspeed, Edgar J., trans. *The Apocrypha.* New York: Random House, 1959.

Gray, Mike. *Drug Crazy: How We Got Into This Mess and How We Can Get Out of It.* New York: Random House, 1998.

Greenfield, Lawrence A. *Alcohol and Crime: An Analysis of National Data on the Prevalence of Alcohol Involvement in Crime.* Bureau of Justice Statistics, U.S. Department of Justice, 1998.

Grinspoon, Lester. *Marihuana Reconsidered,* revised edition. Cambridge, Mass.: Harvard University Press, 1977.

Grinspoon, Lester, and James B. Bakalar. *Cocaine: A Drug and Its Social Evolution.* New York: Basic Books, 1976.

———. *Marihuana: Forbidden Medicine.* New Haven: Yale University Press, 1993.

————. *Psychedelic Drugs Reconsidered.* New York: The Lindesmith Center, 1997 (reprint).

Hatcher, R. A. *Epitome of the Pharmacopeia of the United States and the National Formulary, With Comments,* third edition. Chicago: American Medical Association, 1926.

Hattox, Ralph S. *Coffee and Coffeehouses: The Origins of a Social Beverage in the Medieval Near East.* Seattle: University of Washington Press, 1985.

Henderson, Leigh A., and William J. Glass, eds. *LSD: Still With Us After All These Years.* New York: Lexington Books, 1994.

Hess, C. S. Jr., and W. S. Fields, eds. *Drug Treatment of Cancer Pain in a Drug-Oriented Society.* New York: Raven, 1989.

Himmelstein, Jerome L. *The Strange Career of Marihuana: Politics and Ideology of Drug Control in America.* Westport, Conn.: Greenwood Press, 1983.

Hogshire, Jim. *Opium for the Masses.* Port Townsend, Wash.: Loompanics, 1994.

Holdorf, Kent. *Ur-ine Trouble.* Scottsdale, Ariz.: Vandalay Press, 1998.

Hunt, Leon G., and Carl D. Chambers. *The Heroin Epidemics: A Study of Heroin Use in the United States, 1965–1975.* New York: Spectrum, 1976.

Husak, Douglas N. *Drugs and Rights.* New York: Cambridge University Press, 1992.

Huxley, Aldous. *The Doors of Perception.* New York: Harper & Row, 1954.

Inciardi, James A., ed. *The Drug Legalization Debate.* Newbury Park, Calif.: Sage Publications, 1991.

James I. *Counterblaste to Tobacco.* London: English Reprints, 1870.

James, William. *The Varieties of Religious Experience.* New York: Simon & Schuster, 1997 (reprint).

Jastrow, Marcus. *Dictionary of the Targumim, the Talmud Babli and Yerushalmi, and the Midrashic Literature.* New York: Judaica Press, 1992.

Jeffrey, Francis, and John C. Lilly. *John Lilly, So Far.* Los Angeles: Jeremy P. Tarcher, 1990.

Jenkins, Philip. *Synthetic Panics.* New York: New York University Press, 1999.

Jewish Publication Society. *Tanakh: A New Translation of the Holy Scriptures According to the Traditional Hebrew Text.* Philadelphia: JPS, 1985.

Johnston, Lloyd D., et al. *Monitoring the Future: National Results on Adolescent Drug Use: Overview of Key Findings, 1999.* National Institute on Drug Abuse, 2000.

————. Tables from the 2002 Monitoring the Future Study. University of Michigan, 2002, www.monitoringthefuture.org/data/02data.htm/#2002 data-drugs.

Jonnes, Jill. *Hep-Cats, Narcs, and Pipe Dreams: A History of America's Romance With Illegal Drugs.* New York: Scribner, 1996.

Joy, Janet E., et al., eds. *Marijuana and Medicine: Assessing the Science Base.* Washington, D.C.: National Academy Press, 1999.

Kleiman, Mark A.R. *Marijuana: Costs of Abuse, Costs of Control.* New York: Greenwood Press, 1989.

———. *Against Excess: Drug Policy for Results.* New York: Basic Books, 1992.

Kramer, Peter D. *Listening to Prozac: A Psychiatrist Explores Antidepressant Drugs and the Remaking of the Self.* New York: Viking, 1993.

Krauss, Melvyn B., and Edward P. Lazear, eds. *Searching for Alternatives: Drug-Control Policy in the United States.* Stanford, Calif.: Hoover Institution Press, 1991.

Kuhn, Cynthia, et al. *Buzzed: The Straight Facts About the Most Used and Abused Drugs.* New York: W.W. Norton, 1998.

Leary, Tomothy. *The Politics of Ecstasy.* Berkeley: Ronin Publishing, 1998 (reprint).

Lee, Martin A., and Bruce Shlain. *Acid Dreams: The Complete Social History of LSD.* New York: Grove Weidenfeld, 1985.

Lender, Mark Edward, and James Kirby Martin. *Drinking in America: A History,* revised edition. New York: Free Press, 1987.

Lewin, Louis. *Phantastica.* Rochester, Vt.: Park Street Press, 1998 (reprint).

Lichine, Alexis. *Alexis Lichine's New Encyclopedia of Wines and Spirits,* third edition. New York: Alfred A. Knopf, 1984.

Lilly, John C. *Center of the Cyclone.* New York: Julian Press, 1972.

MacAndrew, Craig, and Robert Edgerton. *Drunken Comportment: A Social Explanation.* Chicago: Aldine, 1969.

Maltby, Lewis L. *Drug Testing: A Bad Investment.* New York: American Civil Liberties Union, 1999.

Mann, Peggy. *Marijuana Alert.* New York: McGraw-Hill, 1985.

Marlowe, Ann. *How to Stop Time: Heroin From A to Z.* New York: Basic Books, 1999.

Mather, Increase. *Wo to Drunkards: Two Sermons Testifying Against the Sin of Drunkenness,* second edition. Boston: Timothy Green, 1712.

Metzger, Th. *The Birth of Heroin and the Demonization of the Dope Fiend.* Port Townsend, Wash.: Loompanics, 1998.

Miller, Richard Lawrence. *The Case for Legalizing Drugs.* New York: Praeger, 1991.

Montessori, Maria. *The Montessori Method.* New York: Schocken Books, 1964 (first English edition 1912).

Musto, David F. *The American Disease: Origins of Narcotics Control,* revised edition. New York: Oxford University Press, 1987.

Nahas, Gabriel G. *Marihuana—Deceptive Weed.* New York: Raven Press, 1973.

———. *Keep Off the Grass,* revised edition. New York: Pergamon Press, 1979.

National Commission on Marihuana and Drug Abuse. *Marihuana: A Signal of Misunderstanding*. Washington, D.C., 1972.

National Institute on Alcohol Abuse and Alcoholism. *State Trends in Alcohol Problems, 1979–92*. U.S. Department of Health and Human Services, 1996.

National Institute on Drug Abuse. *National Household Survey on Drug Abuse: Main Findings 1988*. U.S. Department of Health and Human Services, 1990.

———. *Marijuana: Facts Parents Need to Know*. U.S. Department of Health and Human Services, 1998.

Nephew, Thomas M., et al. *Apparent Per Capita Alcohol Consumption: National, State, and Regional Trends, 1977–99*. National Institute on Alcohol Abuse and Alcoholism, 2002.

Nolin, Pierre Claude, et al. *Cannabis: Our Position for a Canadian Public Policy*. Report of the Senate Special Committee on Illegal Drugs, Canadian Senate, 2002.

Normand, Jacques, et al., eds. *Under the Influence?: Drugs and the American Work Force*. Washington, D.C.: National Academy Press, 1994.

Office of National Drug Control Policy. *National Drug Control Strategy*. The White House, 1989.

Orr, James, ed. *International Standard Bible Encyclopedia*, electronic edition. Cedar Rapids, Iowa: Parsons Technology, 1998.

Parker, Howard, et al. *Illegal Leisure: The Normalization of Adolescent Recreational Drug Use*. New York: Routledge, 1998.

Peele, Stanton. *The Meaning of Addiction*. Lexington, Mass.: Lexington Books, 1985.

———. *Diseasing of America: Addiction Treatment Out of Control*. Lexington, Mass.: Lexington Books, 1989.

Peele, Stanton, and Archie Brodsky. *The Truth About Addiction and Recovery*. New York: Simon & Schuster, 1991.

Peele, Stanton, and Marcus Grant, eds. *Alcohol and Pleasure: A Health Perspective*. Philadelphia: Brunner/Mazel, 1999.

Pegram, Thomas R. *Battling Demon Rum: The Struggle for a Dry America, 1800–1933*. Chicago: Ivan R. Dee, 1998.

Pendergrast, Mark. *Uncommon Grounds: The History of Coffee and How It Transformed Our World*. New York: Basic Books, 1999.

Pernanen, Kai. *Alcohol in Human Violence*. New York: Guilford Press, 1991.

Picket, Deets. *Alcohol and the New Age*. New York: The Methodist Book Concern, 1926.

Pickthall, Marmaduke, trans. *The Glorious Koran, Bi-Lingual Edition*. London: George Allen & Unwin, 1976.

Pittman, David J. *Primary Prevention of Alcohol Abuse and Alcoholism: An Evaluation of the Control of Consumption Model.* St. Louis: Social Science Institute, Washington University, 1980.

Plato. *Laws.* Translated by Benjamin Jowett. Amherst, N.Y.: Prometheus Books, 2000.

Reinarman, Craig, and Harry G. Levine, eds. *Crack in America: Demon Drugs and Social Justice.* Berkeley: University of California Press, 1997.

Richards, David A.J. *Sex, Drugs, Death, and the Law.* Totowa, N.J.: Rowman and Littlefield, 1982.

Rogers, J. Smyth. *An Essay on Tobacco.* New York: How & Bates, 1836.

Rose, Kenneth D. *American Women and the Repeal of Prohibition.* New York: New York University Press, 1996.

Rosenbaum, Marsha. *Safety First: A Reality-Based Approach to Teens, Drugs, and Drug Education.* New York: Lindesmith Center, 1999.

Rosenthal, Franz. *The Herb: Hashish Versus Medieval Muslim Society.* Leiden: E. J. Brill, 1971.

Roth, J. A. *Psychoactive Substances and Violence.* National Institute of Justice, U.S. Department of Justice, 1994.

Rudgely, Richard. *Essential Substances: A Cultural History of Intoxicants in Society.* New York: Kodansha International, 1993.

———. *The Encyclopedia of Psychoactive Substances.* New York: St. Martin's Press, 1999.

Rush, Benjamin. *Essays, Literary, Moral, & Philosophical.* Philadelphia: Thomas & Samuel F. Bradford, 1798.

———. *An Inquiry Into the Effects of Ardent Spirits Upon the Human Body and Mind,* eighth edition. Brookfield: E. Merriam & Co., 1814. Reprinted as an appendix to Yandell Henerson, *A New Deal in Liquor: A Plea for Dilution.* Garden City, N.Y.: Doubleday, Doran & Co., 1934.

Schaler, Jeffrey A. *Addiction Is a Choice.* Chicago: Open Court, 2000.

Schaler, Jeffrey A., ed. *Drugs: Should We Legalize, Decriminalize or Deregulate?* Amherst, N.Y.: Prometheus Books, 1998.

Schivelbusch, Wolfgang. *Tastes of Paradise: A Social History of Spices, Stimulants, and Intoxicants.* New York: Random House, 1992.

Sexton, B.F., et al. *The Influence of Cannabis on Driving.* London: TRL Limited, 2000.

Shulgin, Alexander, and Ann Shulgin. *PIHKAL: A Chemical Love Story.* Berkeley: Transform Press, 2000.

Siegel, Ronald K. *Intoxication: Life in Pursuit of Artificial Paradise.* New York: E. P. Dutton, 1989.

Sifton, David W., ed. *The PDR Pocket Guide to Prescription Drugs.* New York: Pocket, 1996.

Simon, Julian. *Good Mood: The New Psychology of Overcoming Depression.* La Salle, Ill.: Open Court Publishing, 1993.

Sloman, Larry. *Reefer Madness: A History of Marijuana.* New York: St. Martin's Griffin, 1979.

Smith, David E., and Georg R. Gay, eds. *"It's So Good, Don't Even Try It Once": Heroin in Perspective.* Englewood Cliffs, N.J.: Prentice-Hall, 1972.

Smith, David E., et al., eds. *Amphetamine Use, Misuse, and Abuse.* Boston: G. K. Hall, 1979.

Smith, Huston. *Cleansing the Doors of Perception: The Religious Significance of Entheogenic Plants and Chemicals.* New York: Tarcher/Putnam, 2000.

Spillane, Joseph F. *Cocaine: From Medical Marvel to Modern Menace in the United States, 1884–1920.* Baltimore: Johns Hopkins University Press, 2000.

Stafford, Peter. *Psychedelics Encyclopedia.* Berkeley, Calif.: Ronin Publishing, 1992.

Stevens, Jay. *Storming Heaven: LSD and the American Dream.* New York: Harper & Row, 1987.

Stimmel, Barry. *The Facts about Drug Use.* Yonkers: Consumer Reports Books, 1991.

Stimmel, Barry, ed. *Controversies in Alcoholism and Substance Abuse.* Binghamton, N.Y.: Haworth Press, 1986.

Stolaroff, Myron J. *The Secret Chief.* Charlotte, N.C.: Multidisciplinary Association for Psychedelic Studies, 1997.

Stuttaford, Thomas. *To Your Good Health!: The Wise Drinker's Guide.* Boston: Faber & Faber, 1997.

Substance Abuse and Mental Health Services Administration. *An Analysis of Worker Drug Use and Workplace Policies and Programs.* U.S. Department of Health and Human Services (HHS), 1997.

———. The DAWN Report: Club Drugs, *HHS, 2000.*

———. *Drug Abuse Warning Network Annual Medical Examiner Data 1999.* HHS, 2000.

———. *National Household Survey on Drug Abuse: Main Findings 1995.* HHS, 1997.

———. *National Household Survey on Drug Abuse: Main Findings 1997.* HHS, 1999.

———. *National Household Survey on Drug Abuse: Main Findings 1998.* HHS, 2000.

———. *Summary of Findings from the 1999 National Household Survey on Drug Abuse.* HHS, 2000.

———. *Summary of Findings from the 2000 National Household Survey on Drug Abuse.* HHS, 2001.

———. *Tables from the 2001 National Household Survey on Drug Abuse.* HHS, 2002, www.samhsa.gov/oas/NHSDA/2k1NHSDA/vol2/appendixh_1.htm.

———. *Worker Drug Use and Workplace Policies and Programs: Results From the 1994 and 1997 NHSDA.* HHS, 1999.

———. *Year-End 2000 Emergency Department Data From the Drug Abuse Warning Network.* HHS, 2001.

Szasz, Thomas. *Ceremonial Chemistry,* revised edition. Holmes Beach, Fla.: Learning Publications, 1985.

———. *Our Right to Drugs: The Case for a Free Market.* New York: Praeger, 1992.

Tate, Cassandra. *Cigarette Wars: The Triumph of "The Little White Slaver."* New York: Oxford University Press, 1999.

Terhune, K. W., et al. *The Incidence and Role of Drugs in Fatally Injured Drivers.* National Highway Traffic Safety Administration, 1992.

Thornton, Mark. *The Economics of Prohibition.* Salt Lake City: University of Utah Press, 1991.

Tonry, Michael, and James Q. Wilson, eds. *Drugs and Crime.* Chicago: University of Chicago Press, 1990.

Trebach, Arnold S. *The Heroin Solution.* New Haven, Conn.: Yale University Press, 1982.

Trebach, Arnold S., and James A. Inciardi. *Legalize It?: Debating American Drug Policy.* Washington, D.C.: American University Press, 1993.

Troyer, Ronald J., and Gerald E. Markle. *Cigarettes: The Battle Over Smoking.* New Brunswick, N.J.: Rutgers University Press, 1983.

Von Gernet, Alexander D. *The Transculturation of the Amerindian Pipe/Tobacco/ Smoking Complex and Its Impact on the Intellectual Boundaries Between "Savagery" and "Civilization," 1535–1935.* Doctoral dissertation, McGill University, 1988.

Waldorf, Dan, et al. *Cocaine Changes: The Experience of Using and Quitting.* Philadelphia: Temple University Press, 1991.

Wasson, E. A. *Religion and Drink.* New York: Burr Printing House, 1914.

Weil, Andrew. *The Natural Mind: An Investigation of Drugs and the Higher Consciousness,* revised edition. Boston: Houghton Mifflin, 1986.

Weil, Andrew, and Winifred Rosen. *From Chocolate to Morphine: Everything You Need to Know About Mind-Altering Drugs,* revised edition. New York: Houghton Mifflin, 1993.

Wilson, James Q. *The Moral Sense.* New York: Simon & Schuster, 1993.

———. *On Character.* Washington, D.C.: AEI Press, 1995.

Yi, Hsiao-ye, et al. *Trends in Alcohol-Related Fatal Traffic Crashes, United States, 1977–99.* National Institute on Alcohol Abuse and Alcoholism, 2001.

Yoon, Young-He, et al. *Liver Cirrhosis Mortality in the United States, 1970–98.* National Institute on Alcohol Abuse and Alcoholism, 2001.

Zappa, Frank, with Peter Occhiogrosso. *The Real Frank Zappa Book.* New York: Poseidon Press, 1989.

Zimmer, Lynn, and John P. Morgan. *Marijuana Myths, Marijuana Facts.* New York: Lindesmith Center, 1997. ·

Zinberg, Norman E. *Drug, Set, and Setting: The Basis for Controlled Intoxicant Use.* New Haven, Conn.: Yale University Press, 1984.

Zinberg, Norman E., and Wayne M. Harding, eds. *Control Over Intoxicant Use.* New York: Human Sciences Press, 1982.

Articles

Alexander, Bruce K. "The Myth of Drug-Induced Addiction." Testimony before the Senate Special Committee on Illegal Drugs (Canada), April 23, 2001.

Alksne, Harold, et al. "A Conceptual Model of the Life Cycle of Addiction." *International Journal of the Addictions* 2:2 (Fall 1967): 221–40.

Angell, Marcia. "The Quality of Mercy." *New England Journal of Medicine* 306:2 (January 14, 1982): 98–99.

Anthony, J. C., et al. "Comparative Epidemiology of Dependence on Tobacco, Alcohol, Controlled Substances and Inhalants: Basic Findings From the National Comorbidity Survey." *Experimental and Clinical Psychopharmacology* 2:3 (1994): 244–68.

Baggott, Matthew, et al. "Chemical Analysis of Ecstasy Pills." *Journal of the American Medical Association* 284:17 (November 1, 2000): 2190.

Becker, Howard S. "History, Culture, and Subjective Experience: An Exploration of the Social Bases of Drug-Induced Experiences." *Journal of Health and Social Behavior* 8 (September 1967): 163–76.

Bischke, Paul M. "Pleasure Drugs and Classical Virtues." Unpublished paper, 1997.

Blackwell, Judith Stephenson. "Drifting, Controlling and Overcoming: Opiate Users Who Avoid Becoming Chronically Dependent." *Journal of Drug Issues* 13:2 (Spring 1983): 219–35.

Bozarth, Michael A., et al. "Influence of Housing Conditions on the Acquisition of Intravenous Heroin and Cocaine Self-Administration in Rats." *Pharmacology, Biochemistry, and Behavior* 33 (1989): 903–7.

Brecher, Martin, et al. "Phencyclidine and Violence: Clinical and Legal Issues." *Journal of Clinical Psychopharmacology* 8:6 (December 1988): 397–401.

Comitas, Lambros. "Cannabis and Work in Jamaica: A Refutation of the Amotivational Syndrome." *Annals of the New York Academy of Sciences* 282 (1976): 24–32.

Dement, William C. "The Perils of Drowsy Driving." *New England Journal of Medicine* 337:11 (September 11, 1997): 783–84.

Dixon, Walter H. "Narcotics Legislation and Islam in Egypt." *Bulletin on Narcotics* (1972), issue 4: 11–18.

Doblin, Rick. "Pahnke's 'Good Friday Experiment': A Long-Term Follow-Up and Methodological Critique." *Journal of Transpersonal Psychology* 23:1 (1991): 1–28.

———. "MAPS MDMA Analysis Project." *Newsletter of the Multidisciplinary Association for Psychedelic Studies* 6:3 (September 1996): 11–13.

Eddy, N. B., et al. "Drug Dependence: Its Significance and Characteristics." *Bulletin of the World Health Organization* (1965): 729.

Emmett, Garry A. "What Happened to the 'Crack Babies'?" *Drug Policy Analysis Bulletin* (February 1998): 1–3.

French, Michael T., et al. "Illicit Drug Use, Employment, and Labor Force Participation." *Southern Economic Journal* 68:2 (October 2001): 349–68.

Gamma, Alex. "Does Ecstasy Cause Memory Deficits?" Multidisciplinary Association for Psychedelic Studies, January 7, 2001, www.maps.org/research/mdma/gamma2000.pdf.

Gay, George R., et al. "The Pseudo Junkie: Evolution of the Heroin Lifestyle in the Non-Addicted Individual." *Anesthesia and Analgesia* 53:2 (March–April 1974): 241–47.

Gieringer, Dale. "Cannabis Vaporization: A Promising Strategy for Smoke Harm Reduction." *Journal of Cannabis Therapeutics* 1:3–4 (2001): 153–70.

Goldstein, Paul J., et al. "Crack and Homicide in New York City, 1988: A Conceptually Based Event Analysis." *Contemporary Drug Problems* 16:4 (Winter 1989): 651–87.

Gregory, Robert J., and Ripu D. Jindal. "Ethical Dilemmas in Prescribing Antidepressants." *Archives of General Psychiatry* 58:11 (October 2001).

Grob, Charles S. "Deconstructing Ecstasy: The Politics of MDMA Research." *Addiction Research* 8:6 (2000): 549–88.

Hayes, M. A., and L. A. Bowery. "Marihuana." *Journal of Criminal Law and Criminology* 23 (1932): 1086–94.

Hess, Henner. "The Other Prohibition: The Cigarette Crisis in Post-War Germany." Paper presented at the 47th Annual Conference of the American Society of Criminology, November 1995.

Kalix, Peter. "Khat: A Plant With Amphetamine Effects." *Journal of Substance Abuse Treatment* 5 (1988): 163–69.

————. "Pharmacological Properties of the Stimulant Khat." *Pharmacology & Therapeutics* 48 (1990): 397–416.

————. "Cathinone, a Natural Amphetamine." *Pharmacology & Toxicology* 70 (1992): 77–86.

Khajawall, Ali M., et al. "Chronic Phencyclidine Abuse and Physical Assault." *American Journal of Psychiatry* 139:12 (December 1982): 1604–6.

Kozlowski, Lynn T., et al. "Comparing Tobacco Cigarette Dependence With Other Drug Dependencies." *Journal of the American Medical Association* 261:6 (February 10, 1989): 898–901.

Krummen, K., et al. "SEX on the Streets of Cincinnati." *Journal of Toxicology: Clinical Toxicology* 5:37 (August 1, 1999): 647.

Lester, Barry M., et al. "Cocaine Exposure and Children: The Meaning of Subtle Effects." *Science* 282 (October 23, 1998): 633–34.

Levine, Harry Gene. "The Discovery of Addiction." *Journal of Studies on Alcohol* 39:1 (1978): 143–74.

Light, Arthur B., and Edward G. Torrance. "Opium Addiction: The Effects of Abrupt Withdrawal Followed by Readministration of Morphine in Human Addicts." *Archives of Internal Medicine* 44:1 (July 1929): 1–16.

Luik, John C. " 'I Can't Help Myself': Addiction As Ideology." *Human Psychopharmacology* 11 (1986): S21–S32.

Lynam, Donald R., et al. "Project DARE: No Effects at 10–Year Follow-Up." *Journal of Consulting and Clinical Psychology* 67:4 (August 1999): 590–93.

Mandel, Jerry. "Hashish, Assassins, and the Love of God." *Issues in Criminology* 2 (1966): 153.

Marks, Richard M., and Edward J. Sachar. "Undertreatment of Medical Inpatients With Narcotic Analgesics." *Annals of Internal Medicine* 78:2 (February 1973): 173–81.

Miron, Jeffrey A. "The Effect of Alcohol Prohibition on Alcohol Consumption." National Bureau of Economic Research working paper, April 30, 1997.

Miron, Jeffrey A., and Jeffrey Zwiebel. "Alcohol Consumption During Prohibition." *AEA Papers and Proceedings* 81:2 (May 1991): 242–47.

National Institute on Alcohol Abuse and Alcoholism. "Projected Numbers of Alcohol Abusers, Alcoholics, and Alcohol Abusers and Alcoholics Combined, 1985, 1990, 1995." September 1987.

Nencini, Paolo, and Abdullahi Ahmed. "Khat Consumption: A Pharmacological Review." *Drug and Alcohol Dependence* 23 (1989): 19–29.

Nicholson, Thomas, et al. "Drugnet: A Pilot Study of Adult Recreational Drug Use via the WWW." *Substance Abuse* 19:3 (1998): 109–21.

————. "A Survey of Adult Recreational Drug Use Via the World Wide Web: The DRUGNET Study." *Journal of Psychoactive Drugs* 31:4 (December 1999): 415–22.

Normand, Jacques, et al. "An Evaluation of Preemployment Drug Testing." *Journal of Applied Psychology* 75:6 (1990): 629–39.

O'Brien, Charles P., et al. "Long-Term Consequences of Opiate Dependence." *New England Journal of Medicine* 304:18 (April 30, 1981): 1098–99.

Pantelis, Christos, et al. "Use and Abuse of Khat." *Psychological Medicine* 19 (1989): 657–68.

Peele, Stanton. "The Limitations of Control-of-Supply Models for Explaining and Preventing Alcoholism and Drug Addiction." *Journal of Studies on Alcohol* 48 (1987): 61–77.

————. "Addiction As a Cultural Concept." *Annals of the New York Academy of Medicine* 602 (1990): 205–20.

Peele, Stanton, and Richard J. DeGrandpre. "Cocaine And the Concept of Addiction: Environmental Factors in Drug Compulsions." *Addiction Research* 6 (1998): 235–63.

Perry, Samuel, and George Heidrich. "Management of Pain During Debridement: A Survey of U.S. Burn Units." *Pain* 13 (1982): 267–80.

Pope, Harrison G., et al. "Drug Use and Life-Style Among College Undergraduates: Nine Years Later." *Archives of General Psychiatry* 38 (1981): 588–91.

————. "Neuropsychological Performance in Long-Term Cannabis Users." *Archives of General Psychiatry,* 58:10 (October 2001): 909–15.

Portenoy, Russell K., and Kathleen M. Foley. "Chronic Use of Opioid Analgesics in Non-Malignant Pain: Report of 38 Cases." *Pain* 25 (1986): 171–86.

Porter, Jane, and Hershel Jick. "Addiction Rare in Patients Treated With Narcotics," *New England Journal of Medicine* 302:2 (January 10, 1980): 123.

Powell, Douglas H. "A Pilot Study of Occasional Heroin Users." *Archives of General Psychiatry* 28 (April 1973): 586–94.

Redelmeier, Donald A., and Robert J. Tibshirani. "Association Between Cellular Telephone Calls and Motor Vehicle Collisions." *New England Journal of Medicine* 336:7 (February 13, 1997): 453–58.

Reneman, Liesbeth, et al. "Cortical Serotonin Transporter Density and Verbal Memory in Individuals Who Stopped Using 3,4–Methylenedioxymethamphetamine (MDMA or 'Ecstasy')." *Archives of General Psychiatry* 58:10 (October 2001): 901–906.

Robins, Lee N., et al. "Vietnam Veterans Three Years After Vietnam: How Our Study Changed Our View of Heroin." *Yearbook of Substance Use & Abuse* 2 (1980): 213–30.

Schenk, S., et al. "Isolation Housing Decreases the Effectiveness of Morphine in the Conditioned Taste Aversion Paradigm." *Psychopharmacology* 92 (1987): 48–51.

Scher, Jordan M. "Group Structure and Narcotic Addiction." *International Journal of Group Psychotherapy* 11 (1961): 88–93.

Shaham, Yavin, et al. "Effect of Stress on Oral Morphine and Fenatyl Self-Administration in Rats." *Pharmacology, Biochemistry, and Behavior* 41 (1992): 615–19.

Shedler, Jonathan, and Jack Block. "Adolescent Drug Use and Psychological Health." *American Psychologist* 45:5 (May 1990): 612–30.

Snow, M. "Maturing Out of Narcotic Addiction in New York City." *International Journal of the Addictions* 8:6 (1973): 921–38.

U.S. Centers for Disease Control and Prevention. "Effectiveness of Smoking-Control Strategies—United States." *Morbidity and Mortality Weekly Report* 41:35 (September 4, 1992): 645–47.

Van de Wijngaart, G. F. "The Dutch Approach: Normalization of Drug Problems." *Journal of Drug Issues* 20:4 (1990): 667–78.

Varisco, Daniel Martin. "Stimulants Sans Sin: A Social History of Qat, Coffee and Tobacco in Yemen." Lecture at Rutgers University, April 26, 2000.

Weil, Andrew T. "Observations on Consciousness Alteration: Why Coca Leaf Should Be Available As a Recreational Drug." *Journal of Psychedelic Drugs* 9:1 (January-March 1977): 75–78.

Weiler, John M., et al. "Effects of Fexofenadine, Diphenhydramine, and Alcohol on Driving Performance." *Annals of Internal Medicine* 132:5 (March 7, 2000): 354–63.

Winick, Charles. "The Life Cycle of the Narcotic Addict and Addiction." *Bulletin on Narcotics* 16:1 (January–March, 1964): 1–11.

Zinberg, Norman E., and Richard C. Jacobson. "The Natural History of 'Chipping.'" *American Journal of Psychiatry* 133:1 (January 1976): 37–40.

Zinberg, Norman E., and David C. Lewis. "Narcotic Usage." *New England Journal of Medicine* 270:9 (May 7, 1964): 989–93.

Zinberg, Norman E., et al. "What Is Drug Abuse?" *Journal of Drug Issues* 8:1 (Winter 1978): 9–35.

Zwerling, Craig, et al. "The Efficacy of Preemployment Drug Screening for Marijuana and Cocaine in Predicting Employment Outcome." *Journal of the American Medical Association* 264:20 (November 28, 1990): 2639–43.

INDEX

Ford, Henry, 104, 105
Fortune, 7
Frank, Barney, 19
Franklin, Joseph P., 116–117
Freedom of the Will, 74

Gates, Daryl, 20
Gazecki, William, 132–133, 154, 280
Gelles, Richard, 197
Germans, 81
GHB, 174
Gillespie, Nick, 9
Gin, 250. *See also* Alcohol
Gingrich, Newt, 19–20, 127
Ginsburg, Douglas, 19
Glaucoma, 256
Gomila, Frank, 201
God, 25, 32, 33, 36, 38, 48, 56, 57–58, 59, 60, 61, 63, 64, 66, 67, 69, 70, 77, 84, 268
Good Friday Experiment, 163–165
Gore, Al, 18–19, 127
Grant, Cary, 143
Greeks, 62, 67–68, 202, 266
Grinspoon, Lester, 137, 143–144, 149–150, 158
Grob, Charles S., 189–190

Hall, Phillip, 192–193, 194, 202
Harper's, 15
Harrelson, Woody, 22
Harrison Narcotics Act, 274
Hashish, 4, 39–40, 42, 109, 140, 205. *See also* Marijuana
Hashishin, 205
Hatch, Orrin, 222
Healthy Drinking, 52
Hebrew Bible, 25, 81, 162; and alcohol, 55–60
Henderson, Leigh A., 148–149, 153–154
Hensley, Albert, 165
Hepatitis, 245, 247
Heroin, 17, 27, 32, 35, 43, 44, 51, 128, 130, 171, 221–248, 260, 261, 274. *See also* Morphine; Opiates/Opiods; Opium; and addiction, 221–225, 227–231, 233, 237–238, 242–243; and crime, 244, 246–247; health hazards of, 245, 247, 281; and moderation, 239–246; popularity of, 18, 52, 227–228, 231; withdrawal from, 223–227
Hertzberg, Hendrik, 18–19
Himmelstein, Jerome L., 106, 108
Hinduism, 163, 266
Home Depot, 120
Hoover Institution, 45

Hosea, 59–60
How Parents Can Help Children Live Marijuana Free, 110
Hubbell, Charles B., 103–104

ibn Sabah, Hasan, 205
Iboga/ibogaine, 163, 263, 266. *See also* Psychedelics
Incas, 265
Ingersoll, John, 107
Inquiry Into the Effects of Ardent Spirits Upon the Human Body and Mind, An, 72
Isaiah, 56–57, 59, 60
Islam. *See* Muslims
Isolation tanks, 142–143
Italians, 62
It's So Good, Don't Even Try It Once, 227

Jaffe, Jerome, 129
James, William, 162, 165–166
Jesus, 33, 37, 63, 64, 162, 163, 164, 165
Jews, 60, 81; and alcohol, 61–63; and asceticism, 60–61
John the Baptist, 63
Johnson, Gary, 28–29
Jonnes, Jill, 46–47, 273–274
Jordan, David Starr, 105
Journal of Criminal Law and Criminology, 140, 179, 201
Journal of Toxicology, 171

Keane, Jonathan, 181
Ketamine, 207–208, 263
King James I, 177
King, Rodney, 206
Kleiman, Mark, 23, 125
Koch, Christopher, 178–179
Korsakoff's syndrome, 139
Kramer, John C., 275
Kramer, Peter D., 260–261
Krauthammer, Charles, 50

Lancet, The, 124
Landers, Ann, 136–137, 148, 153
Last Supper, 63
Laudanum, 251
Leary, Timothy, 144–146, 166, 180
Lee, Martin, 146
Lee, Philip, 88
Lender, Mark Edward, 71
Levine, Harry G., 75
Lewis, David C., 239–240
Lewis, Peter B., 7–8
Licata, Victor, 202–203
Life, 147–148, 173

Multidisciplinary Association for Psychedelic
Studies (MAPS), 263–264
Multiple sclerosis, 256
Murphy, Sheigla, 196, 218
Muslims, 24, 38–43; and alcohol, 38–39; and
coffee, 40; and hashish, 39–40, 42; and
intoxication, 39, 40, 45, 46–47; and qat,
40–41; and self-harm, 40, 41–42; and
tobacco, 41–42
Mustafa, Mahdi Abdul-Hamid, 41
Musto, David F., 273

Nahas, Gabriel, 108–109, 112
Narcotics. See Heroin; Morphine;
Opiates/opioids; Opium
Nash, Ogden, 175
Nashville Tennesseean, 18
National Academy of Sciences, 113, 118,
119–120, 125, 129, 258
National Commission on Marihuana and
Drug Abuse, 122
National Comorbidity Survey, 123
National Council on Alcoholism, 89
National Highway Traffic Safety
Administration (NHTSA), 90–92, 124
National Household Survey on Drug Abuse,
3, 20, 115, 116, 153, 187, 227–228
National Institute on Drug Abuse (NIDA), 15,
100, 109, 110, 136, 137–138, 141, 206,
225
National Organization for the Reform of
Marijuana Laws (NORML), 130–131, 284
National Review, 110
Native American Church, 165, 265, 266
Natural Mind, The, 269
Nelson, Willie, 22
Nestle, Marion, 88
New Jersey Narcotic Study Commission, 147
Newman, Adam, 183
New Republic, 212
New Statesman, 181
New Straits Times, 168, 172
Newsweek, 21, 171, 173, 193, 194, 231–232,
233
New Testament, 33, 81, 162, 165; and
alcohol, 63–64
New Yorker, The, 19
New York State Council on Drug Addiction,
107
New York Times, 211, 244–245
New York Times Magazine, The, 194
New York Tribune, 198
Nicotine, 13, 43, 50, 163, 225, 229–230,
280. See also Tobacco

Nitrous oxide, 165–166
Nixon, Richard, 45, 129

Office of National Drug Control Policy, 47,
110, 222, 257
Opiates/opioids, 6, 117, 221–225, 227–231,
239–248, 273. See also Heroin; Morphine;
Opium; as medicines, 76, 224–225,
251–252, 253–254
Opium, 75, 140, 180, 199, 205, 251, 252,
275–276. See also Heroin; Morphine;
Opiates/opioids; and addiction, 223, 275;
banned, 178; and sex, 26, 178, 179
Our Bodies and How We Live, 103

Paddick, Brian, 14
Pahnke, Walter, 163–165
Panetta, Leon, 19
Partnership for a Drug-Free America, 100,
110, 222, 277
Passover, 61–62
Paxil, 253, 261, 262
PCP (phencyclidine), 26, 53, 117; and
violence, 205–208
PDR Pocket Guide to Prescription Drugs, The,
254
Peele, Stanton, 223, 233
Pegram, Thomas R., 81
Pennsylvania Liquor Control Board, 95
Pennsylvania Pharmacy Board, 178–179
Pentecostal Christians, 44
Percocet, 255. See also Opiates/opioids
Peron, Dennis, 249, 259
Peru, 274
Pesce, Mark, 157
Peterson, H. Burke, 37
Peterson, Robert E., 192
Peyote, 137, 165, 267. See also Mescaline;
Psychedelics
Pharmacopeia of the United States, 250–251
Plato, 67–68
Playboy, 145, 180
PMA (paramethoxyamphetamine), 188
Politics of Ecstasy, The, 144
Polo, Marco, 205
posttraumatic stress disorder, 170, 263
Presbyterians, 65, 80
Progressive Insurance, 7–8
Protestants, 60, 81, 163
Prohibition, 25, 49, 52, 55, 62, 65, 81–84,
86, 250, 267, 274, 282–283
Prozac, 191, 248, 259, 260–261, 263
Psilocybin, 137, 150, 154, 163–165, 263. See
also Magic mushrooms; Psychedelics